REUSE METHODOLOGY MANUAL

FOR SYSTEM-ON-A-CHIP DESIGNS

SECOND EDITION

Trademark Information

Synopsys, COSSAP, and Logic Modeling are registered trademarks of Synopsys, Inc.

Cyclone, Formality, Floorplan Manager, Module Compiler, Power Compiler, SWIFT Interface, Test Compiler, VSS Expert, and VSS Professional are trademarks of Synopsys, Inc.

Mentor Graphics is a registered trademark of Mentor Graphics Corporation.

DFTAdvisor, FastScan, FISPbus, FlexTest, QuickPower, QuickSim II, and Seamless CVE are trademarks of Mentor Graphics Corporation.

All other trademarks are the exclusive property of their respective holders and should be treated as such.

REUSE METHODOLOGY MANUAL

FOR SYSTEM-ON-A-CHIP DESIGNS

SECOND EDITION

by

Michael Keating
Synopsys, Inc.

Pierre Bricaud
Mentor Graphics Corporation

KLUWER ACADEMIC PUBLISHERS
Boston / Dordrecht / London

Distributors for North, Central and South America:
Kluwer Academic Publishers
101 Philip Drive
Assinippi Park
Norwell, Massachusetts 02061 USA
Telephone (781) 871-6600
Fax (781) 871-6528
E-Mail <kluwer@wkap.com>

Distributors for all other countries:
Kluwer Academic Publishers Group
Distribution Centre
Post Office Box 322
3300 AH Dordrecht, THE NETHERLANDS
Telephone 31 78 6392 392
Fax 31 78 6546 474
E-Mail <orderdept@wkap.nl>

 Electronic Services <http://www.wkap.nl>

Library of Congress Cataloging-in-Publication Data

A C.I.P. Catalogue record for this book is available
from the Library of Congress.

Table of Contents

Foreword

The electronics industry has entered the era of multimillion-gate chips, and there's no turning back. By the year 2001, Sematech predicts that state-of-the-art ICs will exceed 12 million gates and operate at speeds surpassing 600 MHz. An engineer designing 100 gates/day would require a hypothetical 500 years to complete such a design, at a cost of $75 million in today's dollars. This will never happen, of course, because the time is too long and the cost is too high. But 12-million gate ICs will happen, and soon.

How will we get there? Whatever variables the solution involves, one thing is clear: the ability to leverage valuable intellectual property (IP) through design reuse will be the invariable cornerstone of any effective attack on the productivity issue. Reusable IP is essential to achieving the engineering quality and the timely completion of multimillion-gate ICs. Without reuse, the electronics industry will simply not be able to keep pace with the challenge of delivering the "better, faster, cheaper" devices consumers expect.

Synopsys and Mentor Graphics have joined forces to help make IP reuse a reality. One of the goals of our Design Reuse Partnership is to develop, demonstrate, and document a reuse-based design methodology that works. The *Reuse Methodology Manual* (RMM) is the result of this effort. It combines the experience and resources of Synopsys and Mentor Graphics. Synopsys' expertise in design reuse tools and Mentor Graphics' expertise in IP creation and sourcing resulted in the creation of this manual that documents the industry's first systematic reuse methodology. The RMM describes the design methodology that our teams have found works best for designing reusable blocks and for integrating reusable blocks into large chip designs.

It is our hope that this manual for advanced IC designers becomes the basis for an industry-wide solution that accelerates the adoption of reuse and facilitates the rapid development of tomorrow's large, complex ICs.

Aart J. de Geus   *Walden C. Rhines*
Chairman & CEO   *President & CEO*
Synopsys, Inc.   *Mentor Graphics Corporation*

Preface to the Second Edition

The first edition of the RMM has been very warmly received, much to the surprise and delight of the authors. But in considering what changes to make for the second edition, we thought it useful to try to determine why the book has been so popular. What is the key value that readers have found in the book, and how could we add to this value?

Certainly a great deal of the success of the book has been due to the fact that it is the first book on a subject of great importance to virtually all chip designers. But the particular comments on the book, both positive and critical, have been very interesting.

One common observation among readers is that the title may not be accurate; the book is really about good design practices in general, not just about reuse. Another observation is that the book does not serve as a stand-alone manual for reuse, but rather as a guide for readers to develop their own, more detailed design reuse methodologies. Finally, a number of readers have offered very insightful suggestions of areas in the book that need to be addressed in more detail.

This last issue we have attempted to address in the second edition. We have expanded virtually every chapter with additional information, based on suggestions from readers and on our own experience over the last year in doing reuse-based design. We have also added some new material on low-power design for reuse and the prerequisites for doing reuse-based design. We expect to continue updating the RMM, as we and the industry learn more about reuse and its role in SoC design.

But none of these updates will change the basic nature of the book. The RMM will never be a complete recipe for how to do reuse-based design. It will never contain all the design and coding guidelines that a design team should follow. It will never cover in complete detail how to create timing models for full-custom hard IP. These tasks are left for other books, and for the tutorials and user guides provided by tool vendors.

The reason for this insistence on brevity over completeness has to do with the fundamental role of the RMM. There are whole (and very large) books devoted to coding guidelines, such as Ben Cohen's *VHDL Coding Styles and Methodologies*, and whole (and very large) books devoted to ASIC design, such as Michael Smith's *Application-Specific Integrated Circuits*. But in these large, detailed studies, it is very easy to get consumed with the details and lose sight of the big picture. To be honest, an RMM on the same proportions as these books, with the equivalent level of detail, would be more than most readers would be willing to read from cover to cover.

In contrast, the RMM is about forests, rather than trees. It is about the real pitfalls of design, the key areas to watch out for. Most of all, it is about a paradigm shift required for large designs.

There is a common thread underlying all of the material in the RMM. It is the observation that we need to restrict the design space in order to do the kinds of designs that will make multimillion gate chips feasible. The size of chips today, and the time-to-market pressure put on their designers, requires a different set of tradeoffs, a different optimization function from previous generations of design. Many of the designer's tricks for saving a picosecond here or a gate there are counter-productive in today's designs. Designs need to be simple to be scalable, and they need to be regular in structure to take full advantage of today's design tools. To achieve this, designers need to employ a disciplined approach to design.

We hope that the RMM can help motivate this design discipline, give the key elements of the design style required, and provide sufficient detail that engineers and managers can implement the discipline in their own teams.

To support this goal, we have tried to stress in the second edition a fundamental theme of any good design discipline, the concept of locality. Local problems are easy to find and to fix. Global problems are inherently harder to deal with; as designs get larger, global problems can quickly become intractable, causing schedule delays and even project cancellations.

The three most basic rules that leverage this concept of locality to produce better, and more reusable, designs are:

- Use a fully synchronous design style, and most importantly register the inputs and outputs of macros. This makes timing optimization a local problem.
- Do rigorous, bottom up verification; make sure a block or module is completely verified before it is integrated into the next level of hierarchy. This helps to make verification as local as possible.

- Plan before doing; write a reasonable specification before design begins. This initial planning can help produce well-architected, well-partitioned designs that can employ locality effectively.

For teams not yet employing these rules, especially teams not yet registering their inputs and outputs, adoption of these three rules can have a dramatic effect in reducing design time. And these three rules are the first and most important steps toward making designs reusable. Throughout the RMM, we have tried to point out how to implement these rules, and the effect that they can have on the design cycle.

We believe that in the future, it simply will not be possible to design large chips without following these design guidelines, and without adopting a disciplined approach to design. Design tools will be able to assemble multimillion gate chips only if they can make certain simplifying assumptions about the locality of timing closure and verification problems. Otherwise, the global problems of meeting timing and verifying functionality will become totally overwhelming.

We hope that by stressing the underlying principles of good design and of design reuse, the RMM can provide designers a practical path toward the design practices that can ultimately tame Moore's law.

Mike Keating   *Pierre Bricaud*
Mountain View, California   *Sophia Antipolis, France*

Acknowledgements

We would like to thank the following people who made substantial contributions to the ideas and content of the *Reuse Methodology Manual*:

- Warren Savage, Ken Scott, and their engineering teams, including Shiv Chonnad, Guy Hutchison, Chris Kopetzky, Keith Rieken, Mark Noll, and Ralph Morgan
- Glenn Dukes and his engineering team
- John Coffin, Ashwini Mulgaonkar, Suzanne Hayek, Pierre Thomas, Alain Pirson, Fathy Yassa, John Swanson, Gil Herbeck, Saleem Haider, Martin Lampard, Larry Groves, Norm Kelley, Kevin Kranen, Angelina So, and Neel Desai

We would also like to thank the following individuals for their helpful suggestions on how to make the RMM a stronger document:

- Nick Ruddick, Sue Dyer, Jake Buurma, Bill Bell, Scott Eisenhart, Andy Betts, Bruce Mathewson

The following people were particularly helpful in preparing the second edition:

- David Flynn, Simon Bates, Ravi Tembhekar, Steve Peltan, Anwar Awad, Daniel Chapiro, Steve Carlson, John Perry, Dave Tokic, Francine Furgeson

We also thank Rhea Tolman and Bill Rogers for helping to prepare the manuscript.

Finally, we would like to thank Tim and Christina Campisi of Trayler-Parke Communications for the cover design.

To our wives,
Deborah Keating and Brigitte Bricaud,
for their patience and support

CHAPTER 1   *Introduction*

Silicon technology now allows us to build chips consisting of tens of millions of transistors. This technology promises new levels of system integration onto a single chip, but also presents significant challenges to the chip designer. As a result, many ASIC developers and silicon vendors are re-examining their design methodologies, searching for ways to make effective use of the huge numbers of gates now available.

These designers see current design tools and methodologies as inadequate for developing million gate ASICs from scratch. There is considerable pressure to keep design team size and design schedules constant even as design complexities grow. Tools are not providing the productivity gains required to keep pace with the increasing gate counts available from deep submicron technology. Design reuse — the use of pre-designed and pre-verified cores — is the most promising opportunity to bridge the gap between available gate-count and designer productivity.

This manual outlines an effective methodology for creating reusable designs for use in a System-on-a-Chip (SoC) design methodology. Silicon and tool technologies move so quickly that no single methodology can provide a permanent solution to this highly dynamic problem. Instead, this manual is an attempt to capture and incrementally improve on current best practices in the industry, and to give a coherent, integrated view of the design process. We expect to update this document on a regular basis as a result of changing technology and improved insight into the problems of design reuse and its role in producing high-quality SoC designs.

1.1   Goals of This Document

Development methodology necessarily differs between system designers and ASSP designers, as well as between DSP developers and chipset developers. However, there is a common set of problems facing everyone who is designing SoC-scale ASICs:

- Time-to-market pressures demand rapid development.
- Quality of results, in performance, area, and power, are key to market success.
- Increasing chip complexity makes verification more difficult.
- Deep submicron issues make timing closure more difficult.
- The development team has different levels and areas of expertise, and is often scattered throughout the world.
- Design team members may have worked on similar designs in the past, but cannot reuse these designs because the design flow, tools, and guidelines have changed.
- SoC designs include embedded processor cores, and thus a significant software component, which leads to additional methodology, process, and organizational challenges.

In response to these problems, many design teams are turning to a block-based design approach that emphasizes design reuse. Reusing macros (sometimes called "cores") that have already been designed and verified helps to address all of the above problems. However, ASIC design for reuse is a new paradigm in hardware design. Ironically, many researchers in software design reuse point to hardware design as the prime model for design reuse, in terms of reusing the same chips in different combinations to create many different board designs. However, most ASIC design teams do not code their RTL or design their testbenches with reuse in mind and, as a result, most designers find it faster to develop modules from scratch than to reverse engineer someone else's design.

Some innovative design teams are trying to change this pattern and are developing effective design reuse strategies. This document focuses on describing these techniques. In particular, it describes:

- How reusable macros fit into an SoC development methodology
- How to design reusable soft macros
- How to design reusable hard macros
- How to integrate soft and hard macros into an SoC design
- How to verify timing and functionality in large SoC designs

In doing so, this document addresses the concerns of two distinct audiences: the creators of reusable designs (macro authors) and chip designers who use these reusable blocks (macro integrators). For macro authors, the main sections of interest will be those on how to design reusable hard and soft macros, and the other sections will be primarily for reference. For integrators, the sections on designing hard and soft macros are intended primarily as a description of what to look for in reusable designs.

SoC designs are made possible by deep submicron technology. This technology presents a whole set of design challenges. Interconnect delays, clock and power distribution, and place and route of millions of gates are real challenges to physical design in the deep submicron technologies. These physical design problems can have a significant impact on the functional design of systems on a chip and on the design process itself. Interconnect issues, floorplanning, and timing design must be addressed early in the design process, at the same time as the development of the functional requirements. This document addresses issues and problems related to providing logically robust designs that can be fabricated on deep submicron technologies and that, when fabricated, will meet the requirements for clock speed, power, and area.

SoC designs have a significant software component in addition to the hardware itself. However, this manual focuses primarily on the creation and reuse of reusable hardware macros. This focus on hardware reuse should not be interpreted as an attempt to minimize the importance in the software aspects of system design. Software plays an essential role in the design, integration, and test of SoC systems, as well as in the final product itself.

1.1.1 Assumptions

This document assumes that the reader is familiar with standard high-level design methodology, including:

- HDL design and synthesis
- Design for test, including full scan techniques
- Floorplanning and place and route

1.1.2 Definitions

In this document, we will use the following terms interchangeably:

- Macro
- Core
- Block

All of these terms refer to a design unit that can reasonably be viewed as a stand-alone sub-component of a complete SoC design. Examples include a PCI interface macro, a microprocessor core, or an on-chip memory.

Other terms used throughout this document include:

- **Subblock** – A subblock is a sub-component of a macro, core, or block. It is too small or specific to be a stand-alone design component.
- **Hard macro** – A hard macro (or core or block) is one that is delivered to the integrator as a GDSII file. It is fully designed, placed, and routed by the supplier.
- **Soft macro** – A soft macro (or core or block) is one that is delivered to the integrator as synthesizable RTL code.

1.1.3   Virtual Socket Interface Alliance

The Virtual Socket Interface Alliance (VSIA) is an industry group working to facilitate the adoption of design reuse by setting standards for tool interfaces and design practices. VSIA has done an excellent job in raising industry awareness of the importance of reuse and of identifying key technical issues that must be addressed to support widespread and effective design reuse.

The working groups of the VSIA have developed a number of proposals for standards that are currently in review. To the extent that detailed proposals have been made, this document attempts to be compliant with them.

Some exceptions to this position are:

- Virtual component: VSIA has adopted the name "virtual component" to specify reusable macros. We have used the shorter term "macro" in most cases.
- Firm macro: VSIA has defined an intermediate form between hard and soft macros, with a fairly wide range of scope. Firm macros can be delivered in RTL or netlist form, with or without detailed placement, but with some form of physical design information to supplement the RTL itself. We do not address firm macros specifically in this document; we feel that it is more useful to focus on hard and soft macros. As technology evolves for more tightly coupling synthesis and physical design, we anticipate that the category of firm macros will be merged with that of soft macros.

1.2   Design for Reuse: The Challenge

An effective block-based design methodology requires an extensive library of reusable blocks, or macros. The developers of these macros must, in turn, employ a design methodology that consistently produces reusable macros. This design reuse methodology is based on the following principles:

- Creation of every stage of design, from specification to silicon, with the understanding that it will be modified and reused in other projects by other design teams

- The use of tools and processes that capture the design information in a consistent, easy-to-communicate form
- The use of tools and processes that make it easy to integrate modules into a design when the original designer is not available

1.2.1 Design for Use

Design for reuse presents significant new challenges to the design team. But before considering innovations, remember that to be *reusable*, a design must first be *usable*: a robust and correct design. Many of the techniques for design reuse are just good design techniques:

- Good documentation
- Good code
- Thorough commenting
- Well-designed verification environments and suites
- Robust scripts

Both hardware and software engineers learn these techniques in school, but in the pressures of a real design project, they often succumb to the temptation to take short-cuts. A shortcut may appear to shorten the design cycle for code that is used only once, but it often prevents the code from being effectively reused by other teams on other projects. Initially, complying with these design reuse practices might seem like an extra burden, but once the design team is fully trained, these techniques speed the design, verification, and debug processes of a project by reducing iterations throughout the code and verification loop.

1.2.2 Design for Reuse

In addition to the requirements above for a robust design, there are some additional requirements for a hardware macro to be fully reusable. The macro must be:

- **Designed to solve a general problem** – This often means the macro must be easily configurable to fit different applications.
- **Designed for use in multiple technologies** – For soft macros, this means that the synthesis scripts must produce satisfactory quality of results with a variety of libraries. For hard macros, this means having an effective porting strategy for mapping the macro onto new technologies.
- **Designed for simulation with a variety of simulators** – A macro or a veri-fication testbench that works with only a single simulator is not portable. Some new simulators support both Verilog and VHDL. However, good design reuse

practices dictate that both a Verilog and VHDL version of each model and verification testbench should be available, and they should work with all the major commercial simulators.

- **Verified independently of the chip in which it will be used** – Often, macros are designed and only partially tested before being integrated into a chip for verification, thus saving the effort of developing a full testbench for the design. Reusable designs must have full, stand-alone testbenches and verification suites that afford very high levels of test coverage.

- **Verified to a high level of confidence** – This usually means very rigorous verification as well as building a physical prototype that is tested in an actual system running real software.

- **Fully documented in terms of appropriate applications and restrictions** – In particular, valid configurations and parameter values must be documented. Any restrictions on configurations or parameter values must be clearly stated. Interfacing requirements and restrictions on how the macro can be used must be documented.

These requirements increase the time and effort needed for the development of a macro, but they provide the significant benefit of making that macro reusable.

1.2.3   Fundamental Problems

Teams attempting to reuse code today are frequently faced with code that wasn't designed for reuse. The guidelines and techniques described in this document are the result of our experience with problems, such as:

- The design representation is not appropriate. For example, the RTL is available in Verilog but the new chip design is in VHDL, or a gate-level netlist using a .5µ library is available, but an incompatible .35µ library is now being used.

- The design comes with incomplete design information, often with no functional specification and with unreadable, uncommented code.

- Supporting scripts are not available or are so obtuse as to be unusable.

- The full design was never properly archived, so pieces of the design are scattered over various disks on various machines, some of which no longer exist.

- The tools used to develop the design are no longer supported; vendors have gone out of business.

- The tools used to develop the design had poor inter-operability; scripts to patch the tools together have disappeared.

- A hard macro is available, but the simulation model is so slow that system-level simulation is not practical.

1.3 Design Reuse: A Business Model

All the software reuse books, and our own experiences, say that reuse is not just a technical issue. In fact, most of the barriers to the adoption of reuse are management and cultural in nature. In this document, except for the chapter Implementing a Reuse Process, we focus on the technical aspects of reuse. But it is useful to look at the business and organization context within which design and design reuse occur. The business models we touch on here are important for defining the cost-benefit equation that drives when and how reuse occurs in real organizations.

1.3.1 Changing Roles in SoC Design

First we look at a change that is occurring in the role of systems houses and semiconductor companies. Traditionally, systems houses (and systems groups within semiconductor companies) designed ASICs to the RTL level, through functional verification and synthesis. The team then handed the design off to ASIC houses for physical implementation. Large semiconductor companies had their system, ASIC, and full custom divisions. The systems groups designed to the RTL level and the ASIC group did physical implementation for internal and external customers. The only people who designed chips from start to finish were the groups that could differentiate their chips from those done with standard ASIC methodologies: namely, the full custom chip design groups.

SoC designs, and the IP they require, is driving a significant change in this model. System designers can no longer do complete RTL designs. Their chips require processors, memory, and other blocks that are provided by the ASIC vendor. The ASIC vendor must now do more of the chip integration, manage the IP, and provide simulation and synthesis models to the systems designers. As these chips become more complex and IP-dominated, systems houses look to ASIC vendors and semiconductor companies to do more and more of the design. In many cases, the systems houses provide specifications to their silicon vendor, and the vendor does the entire chip design. This frees the systems house to focus on software and applications aspects of the design.

1.3.2 Retooling Skills for New Roles

As silicon vendors start to do more of the design, they often find that their ASIC groups don't have the front-end design experience to do the design tasks that customers are demanding. So they turn to their chip designers — the full custom design groups — to design these new SoCs. The trouble is that these design teams have often spent their careers developing full custom chips, focusing on performance at the expense of time-to-market. These teams often have not developed the RTL-based design skills needed to create SoC designs; more importantly, they do not have the culture of balancing performance and time-to-market.

As a result, we see a significant retooling of design skills in the industry. Systems houses are focused on improving software and system architecture skills to differentiate their products. They depend on their silicon providers to provide not just silicon, but IP and integration services required to implement very complex chips. ASIC vendors and semiconductor houses are learning to develop and manage IP. And design teams within these silicon providing companies are developing skills and methodologies for integrating IP into large designs.

1.3.3   Sources of IP for SoC Designs

Let us examine this shift in design roles in more detail by considering two representative cases.

First, let us consider a system designer who is designing a large chip, perhaps a cell phone with some advanced features for supporting Internet access. This design will require a 32-bit processor, a DSP, large amounts of on-chip memory, numerous blocks from previous cell-phone designs, and some new designs for the Internet support blocks. Typically, the processor and DSP will come from the silicon vendor; perhaps an ARM core for the processor and a TI or DSP Group DSP core. The memory will typically be designed by using a memory generator from the silicon vendor. And the rest of the blocks will be from internal sources: reusing blocks from previous designs and developing new blocks.

Next, let us consider another scenario. Consider a large semiconductor company that is making automotive chips. These chips again use on-chip, 32-bit processors and large amounts of memory; in addition they use many blocks from previous generations of designs. Often the new design integrates multiple chips (of the previous generation) into one new chip. In this case, the processor may be a proprietary processor from another group in the company; perhaps half or more of the other blocks are from other internal groups, who designed the different chips that made up the previous generation chip set.

We note that in either case, most of the IP that is used to create an SoC design comes from internal sources. Only a small fraction comes from third-party IP providers; these may be key blocks, such as processors, but the actual number of third-party IP blocks in these designs is likely to be small. Developing and managing the internally sourced IP is probably the single greatest reuse challenge facing design teams today.

1.3.4   Cost Models Drive Reuse

For third-party IP providers, the investment in making a design fully reusable is clearly justified: if their IP fails to meet designers expectations in terms of quality or ease of use, they will not have a business.

But since most reuse is internal, we need to examine closely the business justification for investing in making designs reusable.

Our current estimate is that designing a typical block for reuse costs about 2-3x the cost of designing the same block for a single use. Some of this additional cost may not be real: the increase in robustness and ease of integration will earn back some of this effort on the very first chip design using the block.

Nonetheless, there is certainly an additional investment required to make a block reusable, not only in time and effort, but in discipline and methodology as well.

Re-designing an existing block to make it reusable (or more reusable) in future designs can also be costly, depending on the amount of rework required.

The benefits of design for reuse (and re-design for reuse) can be significant. Our current estimates are that integrating a highly reusable block requires one tenth or less the effort of developing that same block for a single use. Thus, reusing the block provides a 10x productivity benefit or higher for that part of the design. For blocks that are not fully designed for reuse, this benefit can drop to 2x. Thus, there can be more than a 5x productivity benefit in using a block that has been designed (or re-designed) for reuse, over reusing a block that was not designed for reuse.

1.3.5   How Much Reuse and When

One of the critical questions, then, is which blocks should be designed (or re-designed) for reuse. Clearly, any block that will be used without modification in ten or more designs justifies full design for reuse. The 10x productivity benefit over ten or more chip designs more than justifies the reuse effort. Domain independent IP such as processors, their peripherals, and standard interfaces such as PCI and USB clearly need to be designed for reuse.

Domain specific blocks, such as multi-media or data communication blocks, deserve full design-for-reuse if they can be used on several generations of product or on several different products in a short period of time. The challenge here is build the flexibility into these designs so that they can be modified for different applications through setting of parameters rather than through changing code. Studies show that white box reuse (reuse with code modification) significantly degrades the productivity advantage of reuse compared to black box reuse (reuse without modifying the code).

Application specific blocks — blocks intended for a single chip design — may well not justify the effort to make them reusable. For instance, a block that implements a standard that will be obsolete by the time the next generation chip is designed, does not justify a full design for reuse. These blocks, of course, should be designed for ease of integration, since that effort will always pay for itself.

For blocks that will only be used three or four times, the issue of design effort is more difficult. Such blocks probably do not warrant full design for reuse, but certainly justify some effort towards reusability. Designers of these blocks should follow the design and coding guidelines outlined in this book, since these benefit any design and required little additional effort. Packaging the IP for reuse, however, is probably not justified in these cases.

We need to issue one warning, though. Most chip designs are actually redesigns of existing chips, adding new features, fixing bugs, improving performance, or integrating several chips into one chip. Thus, functions that at first look as if they will only be used once end up being used many times. Blocks that implement these functions, if they are well designed and designed for reuse, can dramatically improve the time-to-market for these succeeding generations of chips.

In this document, we describe how to make blocks completely reusable. It is aimed primarily at internal reuse: for those design teams that design both blocks and chips, and who wish to reuse blocks on several generations of chips. In actual practice, individuals and teams need to assess how much they should invest in making an individual block reusable. This decision is driven by economics; how much investment to make in the short term to achieve benefits in the long term.

We cannot stress strongly enough, however, the critical need to develop most blocks so that they can be easily integrated into multiple designs without modifying the code. We are on the verge of being able to fit 7-10 million gates into a square centimeter of silicon. The only way to design chips this large is to employ widespread, blackbox reuse.

CHAPTER 2

The System-on-a-Chip Design Process

This chapter gives an overview of the System-on-a-Chip (SoC) design methodology. The topics include:

- Canonical SoC design
- System design flow
- The role of specifications throughout the life of a project
- System design process

2.1 A Canonical SoC Design

Consider the chip design in Figure 2-1. We claim that, in some sense, this design represents the canonical or generic form of SoC design. It consists of:

- A microprocessor and its memory subsystem
- A datapath that includes interfaces to the external system
- Blocks that perform transformations on data received from the external system
- Another I/O interface to the external system

This design is somewhat artificial, but it contains most of the structures and challenges found in real SoC designs. The processor could be anything from an 8-bit 8051 to a 64-bit RISC. The memory subsystem could be single or multi-leveled, and could include SRAM and/or DRAM. The communication interfaces could include PCI, Ethernet, USB, A-to-D, D-to-A, electro-mechanical, or electro-optical converters. The data transformation block could be a graphics processor or a network router. The design process required to specify such a system, to develop and verify the blocks, and to assemble them into a fabricated chip contains all the basic elements and challenges of an SoC design.

Real SoC designs are, of course, much more complex than this canonical example. A real design would typically include several sets of IP interfaces and data transformations. Many SoC designs today include multiple processors, and combinations of processors and DSPs. The memory structures of SoC designs are often very complex as well, with various levels of caching and shared memory, and specific data structures to support data transformation blocks, such as MPEG2. Thus, the canonical design is just a miniature version of an SoC design that allows us to discuss the challenges of developing these chips by utilizing reusable macros.

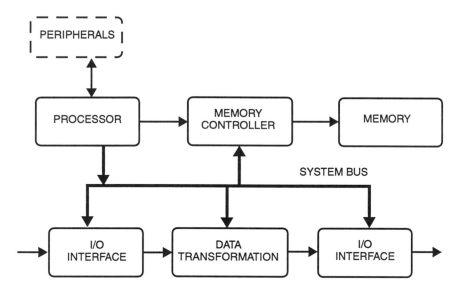

Figure 2-1   Canonical hardware view of SoC

2.2   System Design Flow

To meet the challenges of SoC, chip designers are changing their design flows in two major ways:

- From a waterfall model to a spiral model
- From a top-down methodology to a combination of top-down and bottom-up

2.2.1 Waterfall vs. Spiral

The traditional model for ASIC development, shown in Figure 2-2, is often called a *waterfall model*. In a waterfall model, the project transitions from phase to phase in a step function, never returning to the activities of the previous phase. In this model, the design is often tossed "over the wall" from one team to the next without much interaction between the teams.

This process starts with the development of a specification for the ASIC. For complex ASICs with high algorithmic content, such as graphics chips, the algorithm may be developed by a graphics expert; this algorithm is then given to a design team to develop the RTL for the ASIC.

After functional verification, either the design team or a separate team of synthesis experts synthesizes the ASIC into a gate-level netlist. Then timing verification is performed to verify that the ASIC meets timing. Once the design meets its timing goals, the netlist is given to the physical design team, which places and routes the design. Finally, a prototype chip is built and tested. This prototype is delivered to the software team for software debug.

In most projects, software development is started shortly after the hardware design is started. But without a model of the hardware to use for debug, the software team can make little real progress until the prototype is delivered. Thus, hardware and software development are essentially serialized.

This flow has worked well in designs of up to 100k gates and down to .5 μ. It has consistently produced chips that worked right the first time, although often the systems that were populated with them did not. But this flow has always had problems. The handoffs from one team to the next are rarely clean. The RTL design team may have to go back to the system designer and tell him that the algorithm cannot be implemented. The synthesis team may go back to the RTL team in and inform them that the RTL must be modified to meet timing.

For large, deep submicron designs, this waterfall methodology simply does not work. Large systems have sufficient software content that hardware and software must be developed concurrently to ensure correct system functionality. Physical design issues must be considered early in the design process to ensure that the design can meet its performance goals.

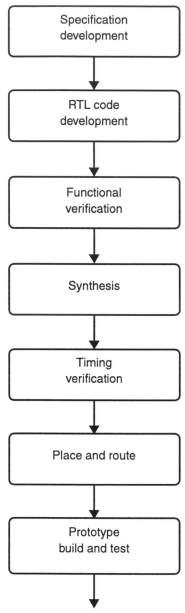

Deliver to system integration and software test

Figure 2-2   Traditional waterfall ASIC design flow

As complexity increases, geometry shrinks, and time-to-market pressures continue to escalate, chip designers are turning to a modified flow to produce today's larger SoC designs. Many teams are moving from the old waterfall model to the newer *spiral development model*. In the spiral model, the design team works on multiple aspects of the design simultaneously, incrementally improving in each area as the design converges on completion.

Figure 2-3 shows the spiral SoC design flow. This flow is characterized by:

- Parallel, concurrent development of hardware and software
- Parallel verification and synthesis of modules
- Floorplanning and place-and-route included in the synthesis process
- Modules developed only if a predesigned hard or soft macro is not available
- Planned iteration throughout

In the most aggressive projects, engineers simultaneously develop top-level system specifications, algorithms for critical subblocks, system-level verification suites, and timing budgets for the final chip integrations. That means that they are addressing all aspects of hardware and software design concurrently: functionality, timing, physical design, and verification.

2.2.2   Top-Down vs. Bottom-Up

The classic top-down design process can be viewed as a recursive routine that begins with specification and decomposition, and ends with integration and verification:

1. Write complete specifications for the system or subsystem being designed.
2. Refine its architecture and algorithms, including software design and hardware/software cosimulation if necessary.
3. Decompose the architecture into well-defined macros.
4. Design or select macros; this is where the recursion occurs.
5. Integrate macros into the top level; verify functionality and timing.
6. Deliver the subsystem/system to the next higher level of integration; at the top level, this is tapeout.
7. Verify all aspects of the design (functionality, timing, etc.).

With increasing time-to-market pressures, design teams have been looking at ways to accelerate this process. Increasingly powerful tools, such as synthesis and emulation tools, have made significant contributions. Developing libraries of reusable macros also aids in accelerating the design process.

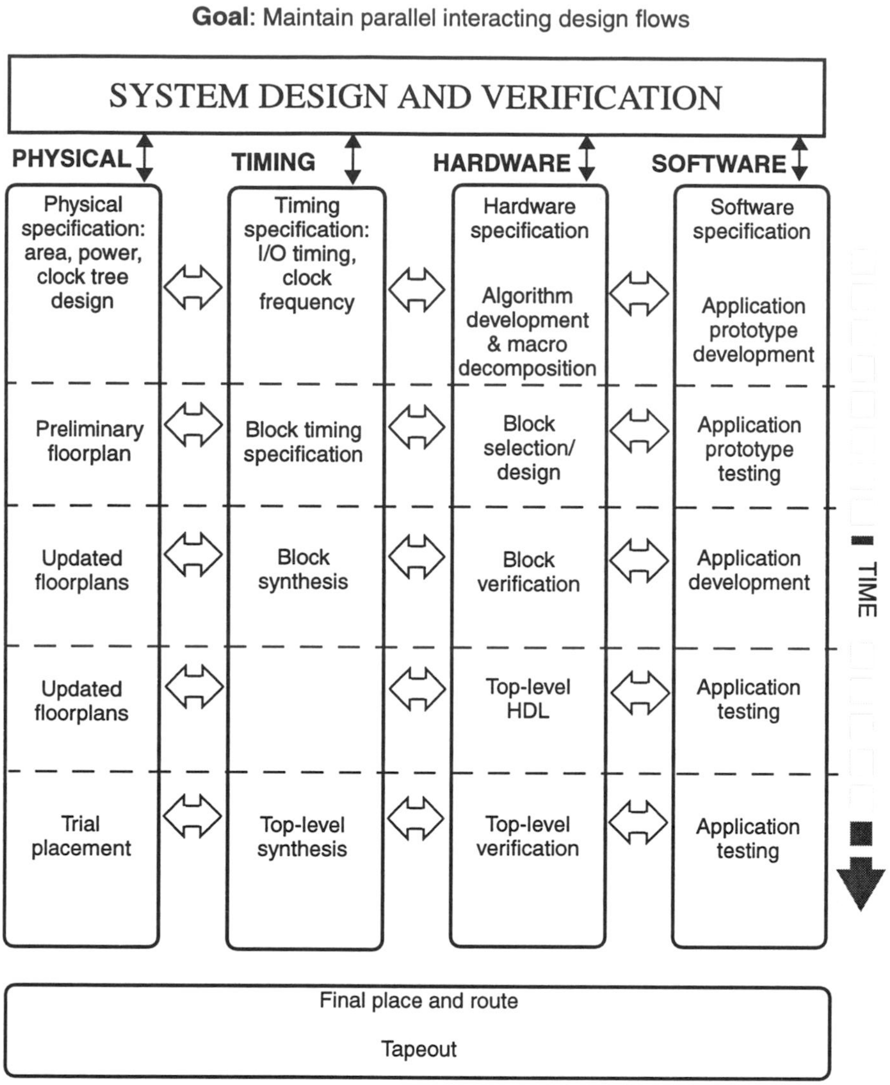

Goal: Maintain parallel interacting design flows

SYSTEM DESIGN AND VERIFICATION			
PHYSICAL	**TIMING**	**HARDWARE**	**SOFTWARE**
Physical specification: area, power, clock tree design	Timing specification: I/O timing, clock frequency	Hardware specification / Algorithm development & macro decomposition	Software specification / Application prototype development
Preliminary floorplan	Block timing specification	Block selection/ design	Application prototype testing
Updated floorplans	Block synthesis	Block verification	Application development
Updated floorplans		Top-level HDL	Application testing
Trial placement	Top-level synthesis	Top-level verification	Application testing

TIME

Final place and route

Tapeout

Figure 2-3   Spiral SoC design flow

However, like the waterfall model of system development, the top-down design methodology is an idealization of what can really be achieved. A top-down methodology assumes that the lowest level blocks specified can, in fact, be designed and built. If it turns out that a block is not feasible to design, the whole specification process has to be repeated. For this reason, real world design teams usually use a mixture of top-down and bottom-up methodologies, building critical low-level blocks while they refine the system and block specifications. Libraries of reusable hard and soft macros clearly facilitate this process by providing a source of preverified blocks, proving that at least some parts of the design can be designed and fabricated in the target technology and perform to specification.

2.2.3   Construct by Correction

The Sun Microsystems engineers that developed the UltraSPARC processor have described their design process as "construct by correction." In this project, a single team took the design from architectural definition through place and route. In this case, the engineers had to learn how to use the place and route tools, whereas, in the past, they had always relied on a separate team for physical design. By going through the entire flow, the team was able to see for themselves the impact that their architectural decisions had on the area, power, and performance of the final design.

The UltraSPARC team made the first pass through the design cycle — from architecture to layout — as fast as possible, allowing for multiple iterations through the entire process. By designing an organization and a development plan that allowed a single group of engineers to take the design through multiple complete iterations, the team was able to see their mistakes, correct them, and refine the design several times before the chip was finally released to fabrication. The team called this process of iteration and refinement "construct by correction".

This process is the opposite of "correct by construction" where the intent is to get the design completely right during the first pass. The UltraSPARC engineers believed that it was not possible at the architectural phase of the design to foresee all the implication their decisions would have on the final physical design.

The UltraSPARC development projects was one of the most successful in Sun Microsystems' history. The team attributes much of its success to the "construct by correction" development methodology.

2.2.4   Summary

Hardware and software teams have consistently found that iteration is an inevitable part of the design process. There is significant value in planning for iteration, and developing a methodology that minimizes the overall design time. This usually means minimizing the number of iterations, especially in major loops. Going back to the specification after an initial layout of a chip is expensive; we want to do it as few times as possible, and as early in the design cycle as possible.

We would prefer to iterate in tight, local loops, such as coding, verifying, and synthesizing small blocks. These loops can be very fast and productive. We can achieve this if we can plan and specify the blocks that we need with confidence that the blocks can be built to meet the needs of the overall design. A rich library of pre-designed blocks clearly helps here; parameterized blocks that allow us to make tradeoffs between function, area, and performance are particularly helpful.

In the following sections we describe design processes in flow diagrams because they are a convenient way of representing the process steps. Iterative loops are often not shown explicitly, in order to simplify the diagrams. However, we do not wish to imply a waterfall methodology. Often, it is necessary to investigate some implementation details before completing the specification. In the process flow diagrams, one stage can begin before the previous stage is completed, but no stage can be considered complete until the previous stage is completed.

A word of caution: the inevitability of iteration should never be used as an excuse to short-change the specification process. Taking the time to carefully specify a design is the best way to minimize the number of iterative loops and to minimize the amount of time spent in each loop.

2.3   The Specification Problem

The first part of the design process consists of recursively developing, verifying, and refining a set of specifications until they are detailed enough to allow RTL coding to begin. The rapid development of clear, complete, and consistent specifications is a difficult problem. In a successful design methodology, it is the most crucial, challenging, and lengthy phase of the project. If you know what you want to build, implementation mistakes are quickly spotted and fixed. If you don't know, you may not spot major errors until late in the design cycle or until fabrication.

Similarly, the cost of documenting a specification during the early phases of a design is much less than the cost of documenting it after the design is completed. The extra discipline of formalizing interface definitions, for instance, can occasionally reveal inconsistencies or errors in the interfaces. On the other hand, documenting the design after it is completed adds no real value for the designer and either delays the project or is skipped altogether.

2.3.1   Specification Requirements

In an SoC design, specifications are required for both the hardware and software portions of the design. The specifications must completely describe the behavior of the design as seen by the outside world, including:

Hardware

- Functionality
- Timing
- Performance
- External interface to other hardware
- Interface to SW
- Physical design issues such as area and power

Software

- Functionality
- Timing
- Performance
- Interface to HW
- SW structure, kernel

Traditionally, specifications have been written in a natural language, such as English, and have been plagued by ambiguities, incompleteness, and errors. Many companies, realizing the problems caused by natural language specifications, have started using executable specifications for some or all of the system.

2.3.2   Types of Specifications

There are two major techniques currently being used to help make hardware and software specifications more robust and useful: *formal specification* and *executable specification*.

- **Formal specification** – In formal specification, the desired characteristics of the design are defined independently of any implementation. This type of specification is considered promising in the long term. Once a formal specification is generated for a design, formal methods such as property checking can be used to prove that a specific implementation meets the requirements of the specification. A number of formal specification languages have been developed, including one for VHDL called VSPEC [1]. These languages typically provide a mechanism for describing not only functional behavior, but timing, power, and area requirements as well. To date, formal specification has not been used widely for commercial designs, but continues to be an important research topic.

- **Executable specifications** – Executable specifications are currently more useful for describing functional behavior in most design situations. An executable specification is typically an abstract model for the hardware and/or software being specified. For high level specifications, the executable specification is typically written in C, C++, SDL[1], Vera, or Specman. At the lower levels, hardware is usually described in Verilog or VHDL. Developing these software models early in the design process allows the design team to verify the basic functionality and interfaces of the hardware and software long before the detailed design begins.

  Most executable specifications address only the functional behavior of a system, so it may still be necessary to describe critical physical specifications — timing, clock frequency, area, and power requirements — in a written document. Efforts are under way to develop more robust ways to capture timing and physical design requirements.

2.4   The System Design Process

The system design process shown in Figure 2-4 employs both executable and written specifications. This process involves the following steps:

1. System specification

The process begins by identifying the *system requirements*: the required functions, performance, cost, and development time for the system. These are formulated into a *preliminary specification*, often written jointly by engineering and marketing. Then, a *high-level algorithmic model* for the overall system is developed, usually in C/C++. Tools such as COSSAP, SPW, and Matlab may be more useful for some algorithmic-intensive designs, and tools such as Bones, NuThena, SDT more useful for control dominated designs.

This high-level model provides an executable specification for the key functions of the system. It can then be used as the reference for future versions of the design. For instance, many microprocessor design teams start by developing a C/C++ behavioral model of the processor that is instruction accurate. As the design is realized in RTL, the behavior of the RTL design is compared to the behavior of the C model to verify its correctness.

The software team can use this high-level model of the hardware as a vehicle for developing and testing the system software. With the software content of SoC designs increasing rapidly, it is essential to start the software design as early as possible.

2. Model refinement and test

A verification environment for the high-level model is developed to *refine and test* the algorithm. This environment provides a mechanism for refining the high-level design, and verifying the functionality and performance of the algorithm. If properly designed, it can also be used later to verify models for the hardware and software, such as an RTL model verified using hardware/software cosimulation. For systems with very high algorithmic content, considerable model development, testing, and refinement occurs before the hardware/software partitioning.

For instance, a graphics or multimedia system may be initially coded in C/C++ with all floating point operations. This approach allows the system architect to code and debug the basic algorithm quickly. Once the algorithm is determined, a fixed-point version of the model is developed. This allows the architect to determine what accuracy is required in each operation to achieve performance goals while minimizing die area.

Finally, a cycle-accurate and bit-accurate model is developed, providing a very accurate model for implementation. In many system designs, this refinement of the model from floating point to fixed point to cycle accurate is one of the key design challenges.

These multiple models are very useful when the team is using hardware/software cosimulation to debug the software. The behavioral model can provide very fast simulation for most development and debugging. Later, the detailed, cycle-accurate model can be used for final software debug.

3. Hardware/software partitioning (decomposition)

As the high-level model is refined, the system architects determine the *hardware/software partition*; that is, the division of system functionality between hardware and software. This is largely a manual process requiring judgment and experience on the part of the system architects and a good understanding of the cost/performance trade-offs for various architectures. A rich library of preverified, characterized macros and a rich library of reusable software modules are essential for identifying the size and performance of various hardware and software functions. Tools, such as NuThena's Forsight can assist in the validation and performance estimates of a partition.

The final step in hardware/software partitioning is to define the interfaces between hardware and software, and specify the communication protocols between them.

4. Block specification

The output of the hardware/software partitioning phase is a *hardware specification* and a *software specification*. The hardware specification includes a description of the basic functions, the timing, area, and power requirements, and the physical and software interfaces, with detailed descriptions of the I/O pins and the register map.

5. **System behavioral model and cosimulation**

Once the hardware/software partition is determined, a behavioral model of the hardware is developed in parallel with a prototype version of the software. Often these can be derived from the system model and from behavioral models of hardware functions that already exist in a library of macros. Hardware/software cosimulation then allows the hardware model and prototype software to be refined to the point where a robust executable and written functional specifications for each are developed. This hardware/software cosimulation continues throughout the design process, verifying interoperability between the hardware and software at each stage of design.

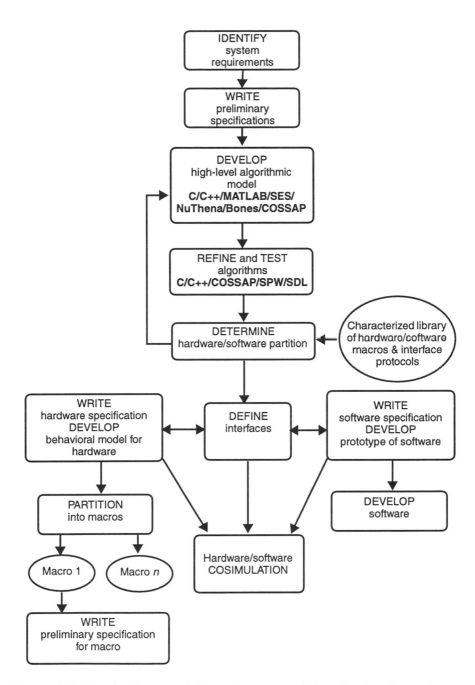

Figure 2-4   Top-level system design and recommended applications for each step

References

1. Ellsberger, Jan, et al. *SDL: Formal Object-Oriented Language for Communicating Systems.* Prentice Hall, 1997.

CHAPTER 3

System-Level Design Issues: Rules and Tools

This chapter discusses system-level issues such as layout, clocking, floorplanning, on-chip busing, and strategies for synthesis, verification, and testing. These elements must be agreed upon *before* the components of the chip are selected or designed.

Topics in this chapter include:

- The standard model
- Design for timing closure
- Design for verification
- System interconnect and on-chip buses
- Design for low power
- Design for test
- Prerequisites for reuse

3.1 The Standard Model

As more design teams use IP to do SoC designs, there is a consensus emerging about some of the key aspects of reuse-based design. We call this view the "standard model" for design reuse.

In this standard model, the fundamental proposition is this: well-designed IP is the key to successful SoC design. No matter how good our SoC integration flow, if the blocks we are using are not designed well, the road to tapeout is long and very, very painful. On the other hand, well designed IP can be integrated with virtually any (reasonably capable) SoC flow, and produce good results quickly.

In this chapter, we discuss the design guidelines for producing well-designed IP, as well as how to integrate well-designed IP into an SoC design. These guidelines are largely driven by the needs of the IP integrator and chip designer. In this sense, they are basically system-level design guidelines.

In the next chapter, we discuss detailed coding guidelines, many of which are intended to implement the design guidelines discussed here.

There are some basic premises underlying all the guidelines in this book:

- **Discipline** – Building large systems (on a chip or otherwise) requires restricting the design domain to practices that consistently produce scalable, supportable, and easy to integrate designs.

- **Simplicity** – The simpler the design, the easier it is to analyze, to process with various tools, to verify, and to reach timing closure. All designs have problems; the simpler the design, the easier it is to find and fix them.

- **Locality** – Problems are easiest to find and solve when you know where to look. Making timing and verification problems local rather than global has a huge payoff in reducing design time and improving the quality of a design. Careful block and interface design is essential for achieving this locality.

The authors, and many designers like us, learned these principles while designing large systems, and often learned them the hard way. For example (Mike speaking here), one of my first jobs was designing very large (hundreds of boards, each with hundreds of chips) ECL systems. When I arrived on the job, I was given a "green book" of how to do ECL system design. One of the rules was always to buffer inputs next to the edge connector, and always to buffer outputs next to the connector. This buffering essentially isolated the board, so that the backplane traces could be designed as transmission lines without knowing the details of how the daughter boards would load each signal. Essentially it made both backplane and board design local (and relatively simple) design problems. The global problem, of designing a transmission line backplane with arbitrary stubs on the daughter boards, is totally intractable.

Similarly, on large chip designs, we can make block design into a local problem by carefully designing the interfaces. Good interfaces decouple internal timing and function (as much as possible) from the external behavior of the block, and thus from the timing and functional behavior of the other blocks. Thus, each block can be designed and verified in isolation. If the interfaces are consistent, then the blocks should plug and play; any remaining problems should be real, system-level design problems and not bugs in the block designs themselves.

This concept of locality is also fundamental to object oriented programming. Here, classes are used to isolate internal data structures and functions from the outside world. Again, by carefully designing the interfaces between the class and the rest of the program, design and debug of key functionality can be isolated from the rest of the program. Software engineers have found that this approach greatly facilitates design and debug of huge software systems, and greatly improves the quality of these systems.

There are two problems that dominate the SoC design process: achieving timing closure (that is, getting the physical design to meet timing), and functional verification. Before we discuss design techniques for addressing these issues, we need to address the issue of hard vs. soft IP. This issue can affect how we approach the problems of timing closure and verification.

3.1.1   Soft IP vs. Hard IP

As the industry gets more experience in reuse-based SoC design, the distinction between hard and soft IP is beginning to blur. Until recently, there was a sharp distinction between which IP should be hard and which should be soft. If we look at the canonical design in Figure 3-5, this view held that the processor should be hard and the interface blocks and peripherals should be soft. The memory, of course, is generated and treated essentially as a hard block. Reasonable people would disagree as to whether the data transformation block should be hard or soft.

Today, the processor may well be available in soft form, and many of the other blocks may be available as hard macros. ARM and the DSP Group have both announced soft versions of their traditionally hard processor cores [1,2].

The emerging trend is that all IP starts out as soft IP, and the RTL is considered the golden reference. This approach is essential for rapid migration to new processes. If a piece of IP is taken to GDSII, then this hard representation should be stored in the IP repository along with the soft version. If another design is done in the same technology, and if it can use the same functionality and physical characteristics as the hard version, then the hard version can be used in the chip design.

On the other hand, if the process is new, or if the blockage from a piece of hard IP makes design of the overall chip difficult, then the soft version should be used. Thus, the soft and hard versions of the IP are just different views of the IP, each appropriate for different situations.

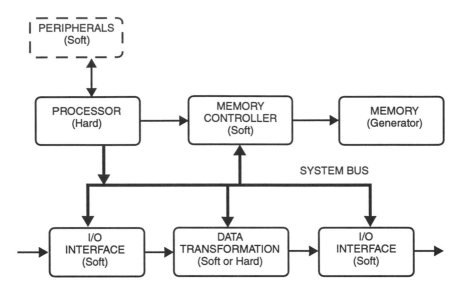

Figure 3-1   Sources of IP for the canonical design

3.1.2   The Role of Full Custom Design in Reuse

The standard model for reuse calls for standard cell design using RTL as the reference representation of the design. Designs are then synthesized to the target technology and physical design is performed. This approach does not use full custom design because full custom design results in non-synthesizable, and therefore, less portable designs.

Some design teams have traditionally relied on full custom techniques to differentiate their designs in terms of timing performance, area, or low power. Unfortunately, these teams have tended also to differentiate themselves in slow time-to-market. We see full custom design rapidly disappearing from the vast majority of designs. The small incremental benefits from full custom does not justify the time-to-market problem that these non-portable, hard to modify designs produce.

The performance penalty for semi-custom, standard cell-based design appears to be quite small. In one recent design, a full custom processor was redesigned using the design methodology described in this book. The results were:

- Maximum clock frequency was the same as for the full custom design.
- Power was within a few percent of the original full custom version after Power Compiler was used to insert clock gating. Clock gating was used in the full custom design, but not in the redesigned code. Consequently, power was at first about 2x

higher in the redesign than in the custom design. By using Power Compiler instead of hand-instantiated clock gating in the redesign, both low power and full reusability were achieved.

- Area was initially about 7% larger than the full custom design. However, all of this difference was found to be in a small, arithmetic operator. By replacing this operator with a full custom version, the area for the entire processor was the same as for the full custom version.

These results show why even processor designers are using full custom techniques only for small portions of their designs. Processor designers tend to use synthesis for control logic and full custom only for data paths. The above results indicate that selective use of full custom only on small parts of the data path may produce the same results.

These observations lead to an interesting model for IP designers and integrators. We expect non-processor designs to avoid full custom design completely. But for processor designs, integrators can use the RTL version of the processor as-is for rapid deployment in a new technology. For the most aggressive designs, they may selectively replace one or two key blocks with full custom versions. This approach allows the integrator to balance time-to-market against performance, without incurring the full cost of a full custom design.

3.2 Design for Timing Closure: Logic Design Issues

Timing and synthesis issues include interface design, synchronous or asynchronous design, clock and reset schemes, and selection of synthesis strategy.

3.2.1 Interfaces and Timing Closure

The proper design of block interfaces can make timing closure — both at the block level and system level — a local problem that can be (relatively) easily solved.

One of the major issues compounding the problem of timing closure for large chips is the uncertainty in wire delays. In deep-submicron technologies, the wire delay between gates can be much larger than the intrinsic delay of the gate. Wire load models provide estimates of these wire delays for synthesis, but these are only estimates. As blocks become larger, the variance between the average delay (well estimated by the wire load model) and the actual delay on worst case wires can become quite large. To meet timing constraints, it may be necessary to increase the drive strengths of cells driving long wires. For very long wires, additional buffers must be inserted at intermediate points between the gates to ensure acceptable rise and fall times as well as delays.

The problem is, of course, that the architect and designer do not know which wires will require additional buffering until physical design. If the designer has to wait until layout to learn that the design has to be modified to meet timing, then the project can easily suffer significant delays. If timing problems are severe enough to require architectural changes, such as increasing the pipeline depth, then other blocks, and even software, may be affected.

Timing driven place and route tools can help deal with some of these timing problems by attempting to place critical timing paths so as to minimize total wire length. But these tools cannot correct for fundamental architectural issues, such as an insufficient number of pipeline stages. And like most optimization tools, they work better on relatively small, local problems than on large, global ones.

Macro Interfaces

For macros, both inputs and outputs should be registered, as shown in Figure 3-2. This approach makes timing closure within each block completely local; internal timing has no effect on the timing of primary inputs and outputs of the block. Macro A and Macro B can be designed independently, and without consideration of their relative position on the chip. This design gives a full clock cycle to propagate outputs from one block to inputs of another. If necessary, buffers can to be inserted at the top level to drive long wires between blocks, without requiring redesign of Macros A and B.

This kind of defensive timing design is useful in all large chip designs, but is essential for reuse-based SoC design. The IP designer does not know the timing context in which the block will be used. Output wires may be short or they may be many millimeters. Defensive timing design is the only way to ensure that timing problems will not limit the use of the IP in multiple designs.

The major exception to this policy is the interface between a processor and cache memory. This interface is critical for high-performance designs, and usually requires special design. However, we prefer to think of the processor plus cache as being the true macro, and that the interface between this macro and the rest of the system should comply with the design guidelines mentioned above.

Subblock Interfaces

There is a corresponding design guideline for subblocks of macros, as shown in Figure 3-3. For these designs, registering the outputs of the subblocks is sufficient to provide locality in timing closure. Because Macro A is designed as a unit, and is relatively small, the designer has all the timing context information needed to develop reasonable timing budgets for the design.

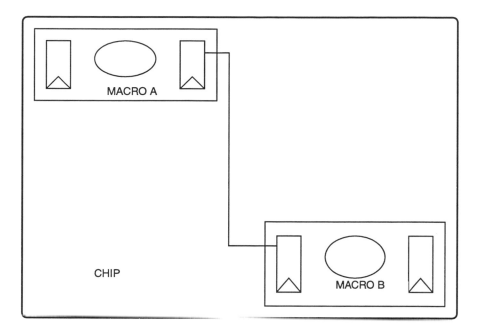

Figure 3-2   Registering inputs and outputs of major blocks

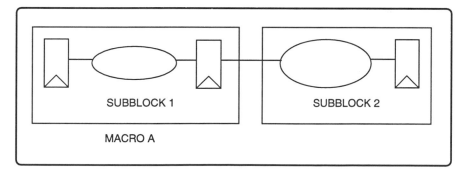

Figure 3-3   Registering outputs of subblocks

Because subblock 1 is relatively close to subblock 2, there is a very small chance that the output wires from subblock 1 to subblock 2 will be long enough to cause timing problems [3]. The wire load estimates, synthesis results, and the timing constraints that we provide to the physical design tools should all be accurate enough to achieve rapid timing closure in physical design.

There are several issues with this approach:

*   When is a block large enough that we must register outputs?
*   When is a block large enough that we must register both inputs and outputs?
*   When can we break these rules and how do we minimize timing risks when we do?

The first issue is reasonably straightforward: any block that is synthesized as a unit should have its outputs registered. Synthesis, and time budgeting for synthesis, is where we start striving for timing closure. This is where we want to start establishing locality in the timing of our designs.

The second issue has a similar answer: any block that is floorplanned as a unit should have its inputs and outputs registered. With blocks, especially reusable blocks, that are floorplanned as standalone units, we do not necessarily know how long the wires on its outputs and inputs will be. Registering all interfaces gives us the best chance of achieving timing closure for an arbitrary chip with an arbitrary floorplan. Consider our canonical design. In some designs, we can ensure that the system bus controller and the data transformation block will be close. However, we would like to design the data transformation block so that it can be used in a wide variety of chip designs, including those where the bus controller is ten or more millimeters away. For this reason, we want to register all the interfaces of the data transformation block.

We should violate these guidelines only when we absolutely need to, and only when we understand the timing and floorplanning implications of doing so. For example, the PCI specification requires several levels of logic between the PCI bus and the first flop in the PCI interface block, for several critical control signals. In this case we cannot register all the inputs of the PCI bus directly; but as a result we must floorplan the chip so that the PCI block is very close to the I/O pads for those critical control signals.

Registering the interfaces to the major blocks of a design is the single most powerful tool in ensuring timing closure. Localizing timing closure issues allows the synthesis, timing analysis, and timing-driven place and route tools to work effectively.

Once we have reduced timing closure to a series of local timing problems, there are several techniques for the internal design of blocks that we can use to facilitate rapid timing closure. These techniques are based on the same concept of locality as above. We want to make timing closure within blocks a series of local problems as well. They key to achieving this locality is to use a fully synchronous, flip-flop based design style.

3.2.2 Synchronous vs. Asynchronous Design Style

Rule – The system should be synchronous and register based. Latches should be used only to implement small memories or FIFOs. The FIFOs and memories should be designed so that they are synchronous to the external world and are edge triggered. Exceptions to this rule should be made with great care and must be fully documented.

In the past, latch-based designs have been popular, especially for some processor designs. Multi-phase, non-overlapping clocks were used to clock the various pipeline stages. Latches were viewed as offering greater density and higher performance than register (flop) based designs. These benefits were sufficient to justify the added complexity of design.

Today, the tradeoffs are quite different. Deep submicron technology has made a huge number of gates available to the chip designer and, in most processor-based designs, the size of on-chip memory is dwarfing the size of the processor pipeline. Also, with deep submicron design, delays are dominated by interconnect delay, so the difference in effective delay between latches and flip-flops is minimal.

On the other hand, the cost of the increased complexity of latch-based design has risen significantly with the increase in design size and the need for design reuse.

Latch timing is inherently ambiguous, as illustrated in Figure 3-4. The designer may intend data to be set up at the D input of the latch before the leading edge of the clock, in which case data is propagated to the output on the leading edge of clock. Or, the designer may intend data to be set up just before the trailing edge of the clock, in which case data is propagated to the output (effectively) on the trailing edge of the clock.

Designers may take advantage of this ambiguity to improve timing. "Time borrowing" is the practice of absorbing some delay by:

- Guaranteeing that the data is set up before the leading clock edge at one stage
- Allowing data to arrive as late as one setup time before the trailing clock edge at the next stage

The problem caused by the ambiguity of latch timing, and exacerbated by time borrowing, is that it is impossible by inspection of the circuit to determine whether the designer intended to borrow time or the circuit is just slow. Thus, timing analysis of each latch of the design is difficult. Over a large design, timing analysis becomes impossible. Only the original designer knows the full intent of the design. Thus, latch-based design is inherently not reusable.

For this reason, true latch-based designs are not appropriate for SoC designs. Some LSSD design styles are effectively register-based and are acceptable if used correctly.

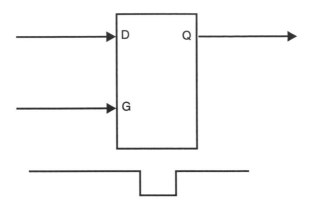

From which edge of the clock is
data propagated to the output?

Figure 3-4   Latch timing

3.2.3   Clocking

Rule – The number of clock domains and clock frequencies must be documented. It is especially important to document:

- Required clock frequencies and associated phase locked loops
- External timing requirements (setup/hold and output timing) needed to interface to the rest of the system

Guideline – Use the smallest possible number of clock domains. If two asynchronous clock domains interact, they should meet in a single module, which should be as small as possible. Ideally, this module should consist solely of the flops required to transfer the data from one clock domain to the other. The interface structure between the two clock domains should be designed to avoid metastability [4,5].

Guideline – If a phase locked loop (PLL) is used for on-chip clock generation, then some means of disabling or bypassing the PLL should be provided. This bypass makes chip testing and debug much easier, and facilitates using hardware modelers for system simulation.

3.2.4   Reset

Rule – The basic reset strategy for the chip must be documented. It is particularly important to address the following issues:

*   Is the reset synchronous or asynchronous?
*   Is there an internal or external power-on reset?
*   Is there more than one reset (hard vs. soft reset)?
*   Is each macro individually resettable for debug purposes?

There are advantages and disadvantages to both synchronous and asynchronous reset.

Synchronous reset:

*   Is easy to synthesize — reset is just another synchronous input to the design.
*   Requires a free-running clock, especially at power-up, for reset to occur.

Asynchronous reset:

*   Does not require a free-running clock.
*   Is harder to implement — reset is a special signal, like clock. Usually, a tree of buffers is inserted at place and route.
*   Must be synchronously de-asserted in order to ensure that all flops exit the reset condition on the same clock. Otherwise, state machines can reset into invalid states.
*   Makes static timing analysis, cycle-based simulation more difficult, and can make the automatic insertion of test structures more difficult.

The major danger with using synchronous reset is the problem of resetting tristate buses. Tristate buses must be reset immediately on power-up in order to prevent multiple drivers from driving the bus. Asynchronous power-up reset is the most straightforward way of addressing this. Our response to this issue is to recommend that users not employ tristate buses. Tristate buses require very careful physical design to ensure that only one driver is enabled at a time, and to ensure that the bus does not float between operations. (A floating bus could float to threshold voltage, causing a large amount of current to flow in the receivers.)

Because there is no guarantee that there will not be any tristate buses in the target chip environment, many IP providers are choosing to design their IP with asynchronous reset.

3.2.5   Timing Exceptions and Multicycle Paths

In general, the standard model of reuse is for a fully synchronous system. Asynchronous signals and other timing exceptions should be avoided; they make chip-level integration significantly more difficult. The optimization tools — synthesis and timing-driven place and route — work best with fully synchronous designs. Once the clock frequency is defined, these tools can work to ensure that every path from flop to flop meets this timing constraint. Any exception to this model — any asynchronous signals, multicycle paths, or test signals that do not need to meet this timing constraint — must be identified. Otherwise, the optimization tools will focus on optimizing these (false) long paths, and not properly optimize the real critical timing paths. Identifying these exceptions is a manual task, and prone to error. Our experience has shown that the fewer the exceptions, the better the results of synthesis and physical design.

3.3   Design for Timing Closure: Physical Design Issues

Once a design synthesizes and meets timing, timing closure becomes a physical design issue. Can we physically place and route the design so as to meet the timing constraints of the design? One of the keys to achieving rapid timing closure in physical design is to plan the physical design early.

3.3.1   Floorplanning

Rule – Floorplanning must begin early in the design process. The size of the chip is critical in determining whether the chip will meet its timing, performance, and cost goals. Some initial floorplan should be developed as part of the initial functional specification for the SoC design.

This initial floorplan can be critical in determining both the functional interfaces between macros and the clock distribution requirements for the chip. If macros that communicate with each other must be placed far apart, signal delays between the macros may exceed a clock cycle, forcing a lower-speed interface between the macros.

3.3.2   Synthesis Strategy and Timing Budgets

Rule – Overall design goals for timing, area, and power should be documented before macros are designed or selected. In particular, the overall chip synthesis methodology needs to be planned very early in the chip design process.

We recommend a bottom-up synthesis approach. Each macro should have its own synthesis script that ensures that the internal timing of the macro can be met in the target technology. This implies that the macro should be floorplanned as a single unit to ensure that the original wire load model still holds and is not subsumed into a larger floorplanning block.

Chip-level synthesis then consists solely of connecting the macros and resizing output drive buffers to meet actual wire load and fanout. To facilitate this, the macro should appear at the top level as two blocks: the internals of the macro (which are dont_touched) and the output buffers (which undergo incremental compile).

3.3.3   Hard Macros

Rule – A strategy for floorplanning, placing, and routing a combination of hard and soft macros must be developed *before* hard macros are selected or designed for the chip. Most SoC designs combine hard and soft macros, and hard macros are problematic because they can cause blockage in the placement and routing of the entire chip. Too many hard macros, or macros with the wrong aspect ratio, can make the chip unroutable or unacceptably big, or can create unacceptable delays on critical nets.

3.3.4   Clock Distribution

Rule – The design team must decide on the basic clock distribution architecture for the chip early in the design process. The size of the chip, the target clock frequency, and the target library are all critical in determining the clock distribution architecture.

To date, most design teams have used a balanced clock tree to distribute a single clock throughout the chip, with the goal of distributing the clock with a low enough skew to prevent hold-time violations for flip-flops that directly drive other flip-flops.

For large, high-speed chips, this approach can require extremely large, high-power clock buffers. These buffers can consume as much as half of the power in the chip and a significant percentage of the real estate.

Guideline – For chips attempting to achieve lower power consumption, design teams are turning to a clock distribution technique similar to that used on boards today. A lower-speed bus is used to connect the modules and all transactions between modules use this bus. The bus is fully synchronous and a clock is distributed as one of the bused signals. The clock distribution for this bus still requires relatively low skew, but the distribution points for the clock are much fewer. Each macro can then synchronize its own local clock to the bus clock, either by buffering the bus clock or by using a phase locked loop. This local clock can be a multiple of the bus clock, allowing higher frequency clocking locally.

3.4   Design for Verification: Verification Strategy

Design teams consistently list timing closure and verification as the major problems in chip design. For both of these problems, careful planning can help reduce the number of iterations through the design process. And for both problems, the principle of locality can help reduce both the number of iterations and the time each iteration takes, by making problems easier to find and to fix.

The objective of verification is to ensure that the block or chip being verified is 100% functionally correct. In practice, this objective is rarely, if ever, achieved. In software, several defects per thousand lines of code is typical for new code [6,7]. RTL code is unlikely to be dramatically better.

We have found that the best strategy for minimizing defects is to do bottom up verification; that is, to verify each module as thoroughly as possible before it is integrated into the next level module (or chip). Finding and fixing bugs is easier in small designs. Then, the major verification task in the next level module is to test the interaction between sub-modules.

The major difficulty in bottom-up verification is developing testbenches at every level of hierarchy. For this reason, designers often do cursory testing at the submodule level (where a submodule is typically designed by a single engineer) before integrating it into the large block (typically designed by five or six engineers). This approach may be more convenient, but it usually results in poorer verification.

With modern testbench creation languages, such as Vera and Specman, creating testbenches at the submodule level is considerably easier than before. For well-designed blocks with clean, well-defined interfaces, these tools plus code coverage tools allow the designer to do very thorough verification at the submodule level, as well as at the module and chip levels.

Rule – The system-level verification strategy must be developed and documented before macro selection or design begins. Selecting or designing a macro that does not provide the modeling capability required for system-level verification can prevent otherwise successful SoC designs from completing in a timely manner. See Chapter 11 for a detailed discussion of system-level verification strategies.

Rule – The macro-level verification strategy must be developed and documented before design begins. This strategy should be based on bottom-up verification. Clear goals, testbench creation methodology, and completion metrics should all be defined. See Chapter 7 for a detailed discussion of macro-level verification.

Guideline – The verification strategy determines which verification tools can be used. These tools could include event-driven simulation, cycle-based simulation, and/or emulation. Each of these tools could have very specific requirements in terms of coding style. If a required macro or testbench is not coded in the style required by the tool, the design team may have to spend a significant amount of effort to translate the code.

The verification strategy also determines the kinds of testbenches required for system-level verification. These testbenches must accurately reflect the environment in which the final chip will work, or else we are back in the familiar position of "the chip works, but the system doesn't." Testbench design at this level is non-trivial and must be started early in the design process.

3.5   System Interconnect and On-Chip Buses

The wide variety of buses used in SoC designs presents a major problem for reuse-based design. A number of companies and standards committees have attempted to standardize buses and interfaces, with mixed results. In this section, we discuss some of the issues facing designers attempting to design IP for multiple environments and SoC designers attempting to integrate IP from various (incompatible) sources.

3.5.1   Basic Interface Issues

The version of our canonical design shown in Figure 3-5 shows a common configuration for buses on an SoC design. A hierarchy of buses is used to deal with the different bandwidth requirements of the various blocks in the system. A high-speed processor bus provides a high-bandwidth channel between the processor and its primary peripherals. A lower-bandwidth system bus provides a channel between the processor and the other blocks in the system. In our case, the data transformation block only needs setup information from the processor; the high speed path is from the I/O block to the data transformation block.

The challenge to the SoC designer is determining which detailed bus architectures to use for the various buses.

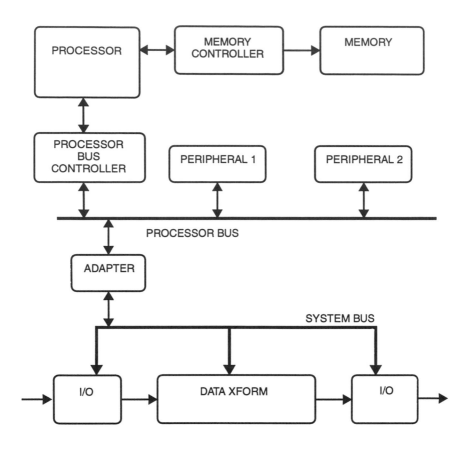

Figure 3-5   A hierarchical bus structure

3.5.2   Tristate vs. Mux Buses

The first consideration in designing any on-chip bus is whether to use a tristate bus or a multiplexer-based bus. Tristate buses are popular for board-level design, because they reduce the number of wires in the design. Tristate buses are problematic for on-chip interconnect, however. It is essential to ensure that only one driver is active on the bus at any one time; any bus contention, with multiple drivers active at the same time, can reduce the reliability of the chip significantly. For high-performance buses, where we want to be driving the bus on nearly every cycle, this requirement can produce very timing-critical, technology-dependent designs. Similarly, tristate buses must never be allowed to float; if they float to threshold voltage, they can cause high currents in the receiver, again reducing long-term chip reliability. Either some form of bus-keeper, or a guarantee that exactly one driver is driving the bus at all times, is required. This requirement is particularly difficult to meet during power-on.

Guideline – For these reasons, we recommend using multiplexer-based buses whenever possible. They are not nearly as technology-dependent as tristate buses, and thus result in much more portable designs. They are simpler and much less likely to affect long-term reliability of the chip. Thus, they are easier to implement, and in general lead to shorter development times.

3.5.3 Reuse Issues and On-Chip Buses

One major problem in reuse-based design is the large number of different bus architectures used in chip designs. Different processors, of course, all have different buses; but even different divisions within the same company, using the same processor, will use slightly different bus architectures. This fact makes interchange of IP even between different divisions of the same company very problematic.

To address this problem, some companies have attempted to standardize on a single bus. However, the requirements of different designs have prevented this approach from being successful. Some chip designs have very aggressive timing goals, and need very wide, high performance buses. Other designs are targeting low-power applications, and need a narrow, low-power bus. These differing requirement have prevented any effective standardization of buses within companies, much less across the industry.

VSIA, running into these problems when it tried to establish a standard bus, has proposed a different approach. Under their proposal, IP blocks would be designed with VSI standard interfaces. A series of bus adapters would then bolt on to the IP, allowing the IP to work with any on-chip bus. This approach is shown in Figure 3-6.

This bus adapter approach is elegant in concept, but poses some problems in practice. The IP now has several layers of interface between the core functionality and the bus: the IP side VSI interface, and the two interfaces in the adapter. These multiple layers may well degrade the performance of the IP, and will certainly add gates to the design.

A number of companies are examining this adapter approach carefully, and are developing internal projects for testing it. But it is too early to tell if this approach will become widely adopted [8]. Other companies have decided to standardize on a few buses, typically three or four, and to design IP to work with all of these standard buses. Usually this means that macros are designed so that the interface block is a separate subblock of the IP. Three or four different interface blocks are designed to allow the macro to interface to all of the standard buses.

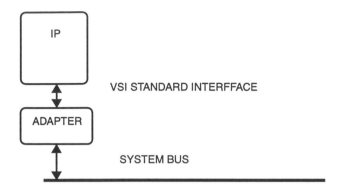

Figure 3-6   A bus-adapter approach to IP-bus interoperability

3.5.4   IP-to-IP Interfaces

Another challenge for reuse-based design is the interface between various IP blocks. For example, in our canonical design in Figure 3-5, if the I/O block and the data transformation block are obtained from different suppliers, we may have a problem connecting them. Their interfaces will most likely not be directly compatible; some redesign of at least one of the blocks may be required.

Different design teams are trying different approaches to this problem. One approach is to assume that the direct I/O to data transformation block connection will be FIFO-based, but not to provide the FIFO in either block. Rather, the system designer can design a small block with just the FIFO and two simple interfaces; one to the I/O block and the other to the data transformation block. This approach has been used successfully in a number of applications.

Another approach is to eliminate direct IP-to-IP connections altogether. Several design teams are looking at forcing all block-to-block communication to take place over the bus. This reduces the IP-to-IP interface problem to an IP to bus interface problem, greatly reducing the complexity of the overall problem. For a variety of designs, teams have shown (at least on paper) that buses can be designed with more than enough bandwidth to handle this additional communication. But once again, we do not have enough experience with this approach to know if it will be widely adopted.

Considering the conflicting approaches to solving the on-chip bus problem, we recommend the following guidelines to SoC design teams.

Rule – The design of the on-chip busing scheme that will interconnect the various blocks in an SoC design must be an integral part of the macro selection and design process. If it is done after the fact, conflicting bus designs are likely to require additional interface hardware design and could jeopardize system performance.

Guideline – There are different bus strategies for different kinds of blocks used in an SoC design. Microprocessors and microcontrollers tend to have fixed interfaces, so it is necessary to design or select peripherals that can interface to the selected microcontroller.

Because of the need to interface to a variety of buses, it is best to design or select macros that have flexible or parameterizable interfaces. FIFO-based interfaces are particularly flexible; they have simple interfaces, simple timing requirements, and can compensate for different data rates between the macro and the bus.

The PI-Bus defined by the Open Microprocessor Systems Initiative (OMI), the FISP-bus from Mentor Graphics, and the AMBA system and peripheral buses from ARM are examples of on-chip buses [9,10,11]. We believe most on-chip buses will share many of the characteristics of these standards, including:

- Separate address and data buses
- Support for multiple masters
- Request/grant protocol
- Fully synchronous, multiple-cycle transactions

3.5.5 Design for Bring-Up and Debug: On-Chip Debug Structures

Rule – The design team must develop a strategy for the bring-up and debug of the SoC design at the beginning of the design process. The most effective debug strategies usually require specific features to be designed into the chip. Adding debug features early in the design cycle greatly reduces the incremental cost of these features, in terms of design effort and schedule. Adding debug features after the basic functionality is designed can be difficult or impossible. However, without effective debug structures, even the simplest of bugs can be very difficult to troubleshoot on a large SoC design.

Guideline – Controllability and observability are the keys to an easy debug process.

- *Controllability* is best achieved by design features in the macros themselves. The system should be designed so that each macro can be effectively turned off, turned on, or put into a debug mode where only its most basic functions are operational. This can be done either from an on-chip microprocessor or microcontroller, or from the chip's test controller.

• *Observability* is best achieved by adding bus monitors to the system. These monitors check data transactions, detect illegal transactions, and provide a logic analyzer type of interface to the outside world for debugging.

For a general discussion of on-chip debug techniques, see [12]. For a description of ARM's approach to on-chip debug, see [13]. Motorola, Hitachi, Hewlett-Packard, Siemens, and Bosh Etas have formed the Nexus Global Embedded Processor Debug Interface Standard Consortium to devise a debug interface standard [14,15].

3.6   Design for Low Power

With portable devices becoming one of the fastest growing segments in the electronics market, low power design has become increasingly important. Traditionally, design teams have used full custom design to achieve low power, but this approach does not give the technology portability required for reuse-based design. In this section we discuss techniques that result in both low power and reusable designs.

The power in a CMOS circuit consists of static and dynamic power. For standard cell designs, static current is inherently low, and is primarily a function of the library rather than the design. So we will focus on techniques for lowering the dynamic power of a design.

The dynamic power of a CMOS design can be expressed as:

$$P = \sum \alpha f C V^2$$

where the sum is over all nodes, α is the switching activity for the node, f is the clock frequency, C is the capacitance of the node, and V is the supply voltage.

The basic approach to low power design is to minimize α, C, and V; f is then fixed by the required system performance.

3.6.1   Lowering the Supply Voltage

Lowering the supply voltage has the largest effect on power; lowering the voltage from 5v to 1.1v results in a 21x reduction in power. Silicon providers have been lowering the standard supply voltage with each new process from .5µ onwards. Running the core of the chip at the lowest possible voltage (consistent with correct functionality) is the first step in achieving a very low-power design.

Unfortunately, lowering the supply voltage has several adverse effects which must be overcome in other areas of design.

The primary problem with lowering the supply voltage is that it slows the timing performance of the chip. To compensate for this factor, designers typically use pipelining and parallelism to increase the inherent performance of the design. Although this increases area of the design, and thus the overall capacitance, the end result can lower power significantly [16].

I/O voltages must meet the requirements of the board design, and are usually higher than the minimum voltage that the process will support. Typical I/O voltages are 3.3v or 5v. Most designers run the I/O at the required voltage, and use a separate, lower voltage power supply for the core logic of the chip.

3.6.2   Reducing Capacitance and Switching Activity

Once we have lowered the supply voltage to the minimum, we need to reduce the capacitance and switching activity of the circuit.

The standard cell library provider can use a variety of techniques to produce a low power library. The detailed techniques are beyond the scope of this book, but are discussed in [17].

Once we have selected a good low-power library, we can use architectural and design techniques to reduce system power. In real chips, memory design, I/O cells, and the clocking network often dominate overall power. These areas deserve special attention when doing low power design.

Reducing power in I/O requires minimizing the internal, short-circuit switching current (by selecting the right I/O cell from the library) and minimizing the capacitance of the external load.

Memory Architecture

Reducing power in the on-chip memories again involves both circuit and architectural techniques. Most silicon providers have memory compilers that can produce a variety of memory designs that trade off area, power, and speed.

The memory architecture itself can reduce power significantly. Instead of using a single, deep memory, it may be possible to partition the memory into several blocks, selected by a decode of the upper or lower address bits. Only the block being accessed is powered up. This approach again produces redundant logic (in extra decode logic), so it reduces power at the expense of (slightly) increasing area. This technique is shown in Figure 3-7 and described in more detail in [16], where an 8x reduction in RAM power was achieved.

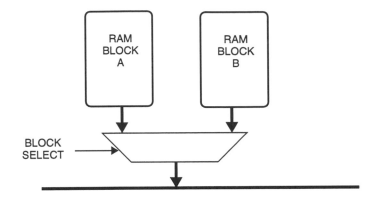

Figure 3-7   Multi-block RAM architecture

Clock Distribution

In pipelined designs, a significant portion of the overall power is in the clock, so reducing power in the clock distribution network is important. As few different clocks as possible should be used. Single clock, flop-based designs can reduce power by 50% over latch-based dual, non-overlapping clock designs.

Clock gating, by shutting down clock distribution to part of the circuit, can significantly reduce chip power. Clock gating, however, can be very technology dependent; careful design is required to ensure a portable, reusable design.

There are two basic types of clock gating: gating the clock to a block of logic, or gating the clock to a single flop.

In Figure 3-8, a central clock module provides separate gated clocks to Block A and Block B. Significant power savings are realized because whole blocks can be shut down when not being used. In addition, the entire clock distribution to the block can be shut down. Since large buffers are often used in clock distribution networks, shutting down the clock inputs to these buffers can result in significant power savings.

The actual clock gating circuit itself can be non-trivial. Disabling the clock in such a way as to avoid generating a glitch on the clock line requires careful design, and a detailed knowledge of the timing of the gates used. For this reason, the clock gating circuit itself tends to be technology dependent and not reusable.

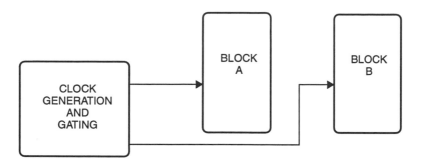

Figure 3-8   Block- level clock gating

Isolating the clock gating in a separate clock generation block allows Block A and Block B to be designed to be completely reusable. The clock generation block can be made small, so that its technology-dependent design can be manually verified for correctness.

In some cases, it may not be possible to gate the clock to an entire block, and the designer may want to gate the clock on a flop by flop basis. This case usually occurs on flops where we selectively hold data, as shown in Figure 3-9.

In Figure 3-9a, Reg A has its data selectively held by the mux. Figure 3-9b shows the equivalent circuit using clock gating instead, which results in lower power.

Guideline – Use the approach shown in Figure 3-9a. The approach in Figure 3-9b is not recommended for reusable designs, since the clock gating function is inherently technology dependent. Today's advanced power synthesis tools can detect the configuration in Figure 3-9a, and, working in conjunction with clock tree physical design tools, automatically convert it to the configuration in Figure 3-9b.

By designing and coding the circuit without clock gating, engineers can ensure that the design is technology independent and reusable.

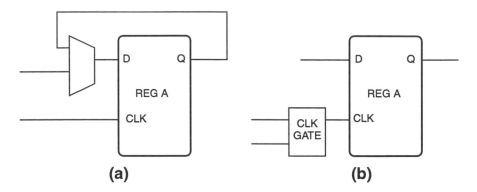

Figure 3-9   Clock gating at individual flip-flops

3.6.3   Sizing and Other Synthesis Techniques

The next major technique for reducing chip power involves optimizing the gate-level design for low power.

Gate sizing can produce a significant power savings in many designs. This technique consists of reducing the drive strength of gates to the lowest level that meets the timing requirements for the design. Synthesis tools can do this automatically, without any requirement for changing the RTL code.

Some incremental improvement can be gained by restructuring logic to reduce the number of intermediate, spurious transitions in the logic. Again, synthesis tools can do this automatically.

3.6.4   Summary

In [16] the results of several low power chip designs are reported. The results show:

*   21x reduction in power by lowering the voltage from 5v to 1.1v.
*   3–4x reduction from gate sizing, low power I/O cells, and similar gate-level optimizations.
*   2–3x improvement by clock gating.
*   8x improvement in a memory array by using the multi-block technique described above.

Thus, with a good low-power library, low power design for reuse is possible through a combination of architectural techniques and the proper use of power synthesis tools.

These techniques can produce designs that are fully reusable and are quite close to full custom designs in power consumption. Considering that overall chip power is likely to be dominated by I/O and memory, the small increase in power from the logic in the chip is more than offset by the time-to-market advantage of having reusable blocks.

3.7 Design for Test: Manufacturing Test Strategies

Manufacturing test strategies must be established at specification time. The optimal strategy for an individual block depends on the type of block.

3.7.1 System Level Test Issues

Rule – The system-level chip manufacturing test strategy must be documented.

Guideline – On-chip test structures are recommended for all blocks. It is not feasible to develop parallel test vectors for chips consisting of over a million gates. Different kinds of blocks will have different test strategies; at the top level, a master test controller is required to control and sequence these independent test structures.

3.7.2 Memory Test

Guideline – Some form of BIST is recommended for RAMs, because this provides a rapid, easy-to-control test methodology. However, some BIST solutions are not sufficient to test data retention. Some form of reasonably direct memory access is recommended to detect and troubleshoot data retention problems.

3.7.3 Microprocessor Test

Guideline – Microprocessors usually have some form of custom test structure, combining full or partial scan and parallel vectors. Often, this means that the chip-level test controller must provide the microprocessor with both a scan chain controller and some form of boundary scan.

3.7.4 Other Macros

Guideline – For most other blocks, the best choice is a full-scan technique. Full scan provides very high coverage for very little design effort. The chip-level test controller needs to manage the issue of how many scan chains are operated simultaneously, and how to connect them to the chip-level I/O.

3.7.5   Logic BIST

Logic BIST is a variation on the full scan approach. Where full scan must have its scan chain integrated into the chip's overall scan chain(s), logic BIST uses an LFSR (Linear Feedback Shift Register) to generate the test patterns locally. A signature recognition circuit checks the results of the scan test to verify correct behavior of the circuit.

Logic BIST has the advantage of keeping all pattern generation and checking within the macro. This provides some element of additional security against reverse engineering of the macro. It also reduces the requirements for scan memory in the tester and allows testing at higher clock rates than can be achieve on most testers. Logic BIST does require some additional design effort and some increase die area for the generator and checker, although tools to automate this process are becoming available.

Logic BIST is currently being used in some designs, but it is much less common than standard full-scan testing. The success of logic BIST in the long term probably depends on the ability of scan test equipment manufactures to keep up with the need for ever-increasing scan memory in the tester. If the test equipment fails to provide for scan test of large chips, logic BIST will become the test methodology of choice for SoC designs.

3.8   Prerequisites for Reuse

We conclude this chapter with a discussion of some of the prerequisites for reuse, some of the technical infrastructure that must be in place for the standard model of reuse to be successful.

3.8.1   Libraries

First of all, design teams must have access to high quality standard cell libraries. These libraries should provide a full set of views, including synthesis, physical, and power views. These libraries need to be validated in hardware so that design teams can have a high degree of confidence in their timing and power characteristics. Finally, the libraries should have accurate, validated wire load models to enable accurate synthesis and timing analysis of designs.

These libraries need to be tested in the SoC flow before they can be considered completely validated. A number of subtle problems, such as not modeling antenna rules correctly or using non-standard definitions for rise times, can bring a large chip design project to a screeching halt. Testing the libraries through the entire flow can help prevent significant delays on later projects.

These libraries should be available as early as possible. In some semiconductor companies, libraries are not available to design teams until after the process is on line. This is too late; many designs are started while the new process is being developed. In some cases design teams have designed their own libraries to allow design work to proceed. This practice can lead to the proliferation of invalid, high-defect libraries.

These libraries should also include a set of memory compilers. These memory compilers should provide for some tradeoffs between power, area, and timing performance. They should support single and multiple port configurations, and provide fully synchronous interfaces. (Generating a write pulse in standard cell logic requires technology-dependent, non-reusable design practices.)

If the target technology supports flash EPROM and/or DRAM, then the memory compilers should support these as well.

Although not always considered part of the library, certain analog blocks occur so often in chip designs that they should be provided along with the library. These include Phase Locked Loop (PLL) clock generators and basic analog-to-digital and digital-to-analog converters. PLLs, in particular, are very demanding designs, and it makes no sense to force individual design teams to develop their own.

3.8.2   Physical Design Rules

One common problem in large designs is that several pieces of hard IP are integrated from different sources. For example, an automotive group may use a processor from a computer division and a DSP from a wireless division. If these blocks have been designed with different physical design rules, and verified using different DRC decks, then physical verification at the chip level can be a major problem. The design team will be hard pressed to find or develop a DRC deck that will work for both blocks.

We strongly recommend that, for a given process, standard DRC and LVS decks be developed and validated. These decks should be used by all design teams, so that physical designs (hard IP) can be exchanged and integrated without undue effort.

References

1. Ovadia, Bat-Sheva. PalmDSPCore: An Architecture for Intensive Parallel DSP Processing, Proceedings of Microprocessor Forum, 1998.

2. Press release announcing synthesizable ARM7. http://www.arm.com/CoInfo/PressRel/15Jun98/

3. Sylvester, Dennis and Keutzer, Kurt. Getting to the Bottom of Deep Submicron. Proceedings of ICCAD, 1998.

4. Chaney, Thomas, "Measured Flip-Flop Responses to Marginal Triggering," IEEE Transactions of Computers, Volume C-32, No. 12, December 1983, pgs 1207 to 1209.

5. Horstmann, Jens U, Hans W Eichel, and Robert L Coates, "Metastability Behavior of CMOS ASIC flip-flops in theory and test," IEEE Journal of Solid-State Circuits, Volume 24, No. 1, February 1989, pgs 146 to 157.

6. Poulin, Jeffrey. *Measuring Software Reuse: Principles, Practices, and Economic Models*. Addison-Wesley, 1996.

7. Jones, Capers. *Applied Software Measurement: Assuring Productivity and Quality*. McGraw Hill, 1996.

8. VSIA: Virtual Socket Interface Alliance. http://www.vsi.org/library/specs.htm

9. PI bus: http://www.sussex.ac.uk/engg/research/vlsi/projects/pibus/index.html

10. FISPbus: http://www.mentorg.com/inventra/fispbus

11. ARM AMBAbus: http://www.arm.com/Documentation/Oveviews/AMBA_Intro/ index.html

12. Neugass, Henry. Approaches to on-chip debugging, *Computer Design*, December 1998.

13. Goudge, Liam. Debugging Embedded Systems. http://www.arm.com/Documentation/WhitePapers/DebugEmbSys.

14. Cole, Bernard. User demands shake up CPU debug traditions, EE Times. http://www.eetimes.com/sotry/OEG19990216S0009

15. Nexus website: http://www.nexus-standard.org/nexus-standard.nsf

16. Chandrakasan, Anantha and Brodersen, Robert. *Low Power Digital CMOS Design*. Kluwer Academic Publishers, 1995.

17. Chandrakasan, Anantha (editor) and Brodersen, Robert (editor). *Low Power CMOS Design*. IEEE, 1998.

CHAPTER 4

The Macro Design Process

This chapter addresses the issues encountered in designing hard and soft macros for reuse. The topics include:

- An overview of the macro design workflow
- Contents of a design specification
- Top-level macro design and partitioning into subblocks
- Designing subblocks
- Integrating subblocks and macro verification
- Productization and prototyping issues

4.1 Design Process Overview

Once the SoC design team has developed a set of specifications for the various macros in the design, these macros need to be selected from an existing library of reusable parts or designed from scratch. This chapter describes the design process for developing macros, with an emphasis on developing reusable macros.

Figure 4-1 shows the macro design process up to the point of integrating subblocks into the parent macro. Figure 4-2 shows the process of integrating the subblocks. The major steps in the macro design process are:

1. **Specification and partitioning** – The first thing the macro design team must do is to make sure the team completely understands the initial macro specification. The team then refines the specification and partitions the design into subblocks. Usually this refinement includes developing a behavioral model and testing it. This is particularly useful in algorithmic-intensive designs, where the algorithm itself must be developed in addition to the implementation. It also provides an initial testbench and test suite for the macro, and it can be used to generate a simulation model for end users of the macro.

2. **Subblock specification and design** – Once the partitioning is complete, the designer develops a functional specification for the subblock, emphasizing the timing and functionality of the interfaces to other subblocks. The specifications for all subblocks are reviewed by the team and checked for consistency. The designer then develops the RTL code, the detailed timing constraints, the synthesis scripts, and the testbench and test suite for the subblock. Once these are completed and verified, the subblock is ready for integration with the other subblocks.

3. **Testbench development** – In parallel with the subblock development, some members of the macro design team refine the behavioral testbench into a testbench that can be used for RTL testing of the entire macro.

4. **Timing checks** – In addition, the team must be checking the timing budgets of the subblocks to ensure that they are consistent and achievable.

5. **Integration** – Integrating the subblocks into the macro includes generating the top-level netlist and using it to perform functional test and synthesis. The synthesis process includes verifying that the macro meets the requirements for manufacturing testability. This usually consists of doing scan insertion and automatic test pattern generation (ATPG) and verifying test coverage.

   Once these tasks have been successfully completed, the macro is ready for productization.

6. **Productization** – During the productization phase, the team prepares the macro for use by the SoC integration team. For all macros, this involves productization as a soft macro. For some macros, additional productization is done to produce a hard macro version.

Figure 4-3 shows the activities of the various team members during the first three phases of macro design.

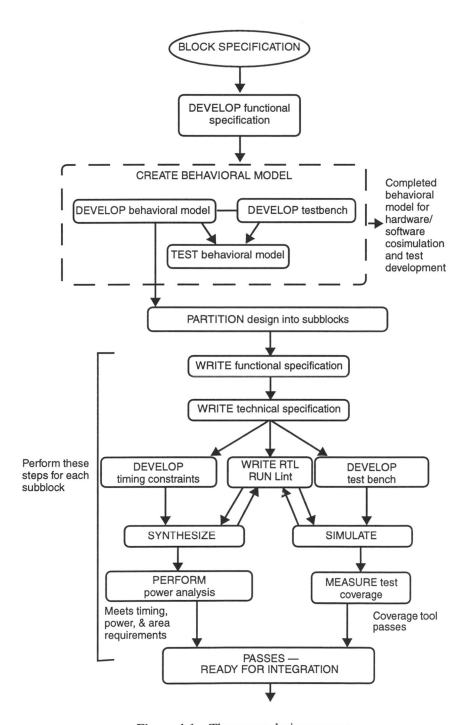

Figure 4-1 The macro design process

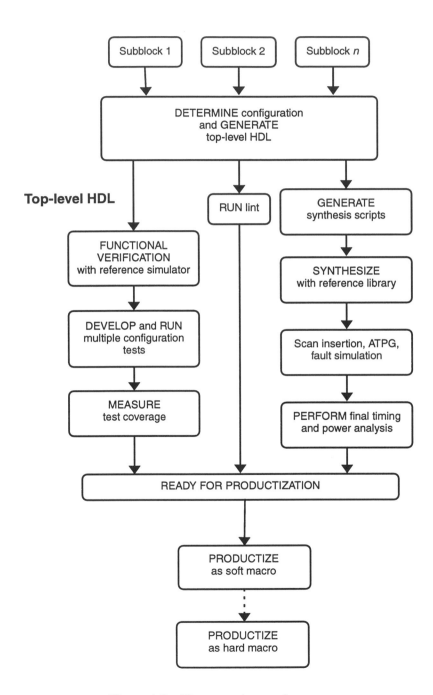

Figure 4-2   The macro integration process

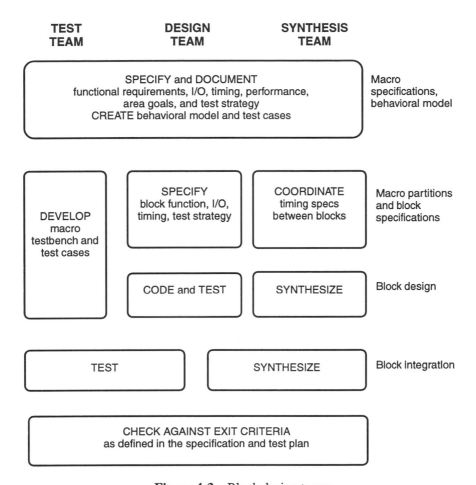

Figure 4-3   Block design teams

It is important to note that the separation of the design process into distinct phases does not imply a rigid, top-down design methodology. Frequently, some detailed design work must be done before the specification is complete, just to make sure that the design can be implemented.

A rigid, top-down methodology says that one phase cannot start until the preceding one is completed. We prefer a more mixed methodology, which simply says that one phase cannot complete until the preceding one is completed.

Methodology note – The design flow described in this chapter is the standard, RTL/synthesis flow. There are several alternate flows that use domain-specific tools such as Module Compiler. These flows are described in Chapter 6 of this manual.

4.2   Contents of a Design Specification

Specifications occur at every level in the design process. They are very general at the beginning and become progressively more focused and detailed as the design process continues. There are common elements, however, to all specifications. This section describes the archetypal structure of a good specification. When there are references to specifications later in this document, assume that the specifications contain the following elements:

Overview
This section briefly describes the technical goals for the design. In particular, if the design needs to comply with a specific standard, such as an IEEE standard, the standard must be specified here.

Functional requirements
This section describes the project from a technical perspective. Its main purpose is to describe the unit being designed as seen by the outside world: its form, fit, and function, and how it transforms the data at its inputs and outputs, based on the values of the software registers.

Physical requirements
This section describes the packaging, die size, power, and other physical design requirements of the unit being designed. For soft macros, it includes the cell libraries the design must support and the performance requirements for the design.

Design requirements
This section describes the design rules to which the design must comply. It may reference a standard design guideline document or explicitly list the guidelines. The issues addressed in this section of the specification are those described in Chapter 3 of this manual.

The block diagram
Block diagrams are essential for communicating the function of most hardware. The block diagrams must present enough detail so that the reader can understand the functionality of the unit being designed.

Interfaces to external system
This section describes the inputs and outputs of the module and how they operate:

- Signal names and functions
- Transaction protocols with cycle-accurate timing diagrams
- Legal values for input and output data
- Timing specifications
- Setup and hold times on inputs
- Clock to out times for outputs

- Special signals
- Asynchronous signals and their timing
- Clock, reset, and interrupt signals and their timing

Manufacturing test methodology

This section describes the manufacturing test methodology that the macro supports, and the chip-level requirements for supporting the test methodology. For most macros, this methodology will be full scan. Typically, the integrator will perform scan insertion and ATPG on the entire chip (or a large section of the chip) at one time, rather than doing scan insertion for the macro and then integrating it into the chip design. Any untestable regions in the design must be specified.

For some hard macros, the performance penalty of scan-based testing is not acceptable, and parallel vectors are used for test. In this case, a JTAG-based boundary scan technique is used to isolate the macro and to provide a way to apply the vectors to the block.

The software model

This section describes the hardware registers that are visible to the software. It includes complete information on which registers are read, write, and read/write, which bits are valid, and the detailed function of the register.

Software requirements

Hardware design doesn't stop until software runs on it. One of the key obligations of the hardware team is to provide the lowest level of software required to configure and operate the hardware. Once this software is provided, the software team only needs to know about these software routines, and not about the detailed behavior of the hardware or of the registers. For many hardware systems, this low-level software is referred to as the *set of software drivers for the system*. Although the drivers are often written by the software team, the hardware team is responsible for helping to specify this software and for verifying that it is correct.

The specification of this software must be included in the functional specification.

Deliverables

This section describes the deliverables for the project: what files and documents will be created, archived, and delivered at the end of the project.

Verification Plan

This section describes how the team will verify that the design requirements have been met. It describes what functional tests will be run and what tools and processes will be used. It also defines how performance will be verified, for example, what configurations will be synthesized with what technology libraries.

The deliverables and the test plan define the exit criteria for the project. When all the deliverables pass all the verification procedures defined in the verification plan, design is done.

4.3   Top-Level Macro Design

The first phase of macro design consists of refining the functional specification to the point where the design can be partitioned into subblocks small enough that each subblock can be designed, coded, and tested by one person. The key to success in this phase is a complete and clear specification for the macro and its subblocks. In particular, the interfaces between subblocks must be clearly specified, so that subblock integration will be relatively smooth and painless.

4.3.1   Top-Level Macro Design Process

Figure 4-4 shows the top-level macro design process. This phase is complete when the design team has produced and reviewed the following top-level design elements:

- Updated macro hardware specification

  All sections of the document should be updated to reflect the design refinement that occurs during the macro top-level design process. In particular, the partitioning of the macro and the specifications for the subblocks must be added to the macro specification.

- Executable specification/behavioral model

  In many cases, a behavioral model is extremely useful as an executable specification for the macro. This model allows the development and debug of testbenches and test suites during the detailed design of the macro, rather than after the design is completed. For hard macros, this behavioral model can provide a key simulation model for the end user.

  A behavioral model is particularly useful for a macro that has a high algorithmic content. For a macro dominated by state machines and with little algorithmic content, a behavioral model may be of little use, because it would have all the interesting behavior abstracted out of it.

  A behavioral model is required in the case of macros that have software content. The behavioral model provides a high-speed simulation model early in the design cycle. The software developers can use this model for software design and debug while the detailed design is being done. This approach is essential for meeting time-to-market goals with this kind of macro.

- Testbench

  A high-level, self-checking testbench with a complete set of test suites is essential
  to the successful design and deployment of the macro. Typically, the testbench
  consists of bus functional models for the surrounding system and is designed to
  allow the verification engineer to write tests at a relatively high level of abstraction.

- Preliminary specification for each subblock

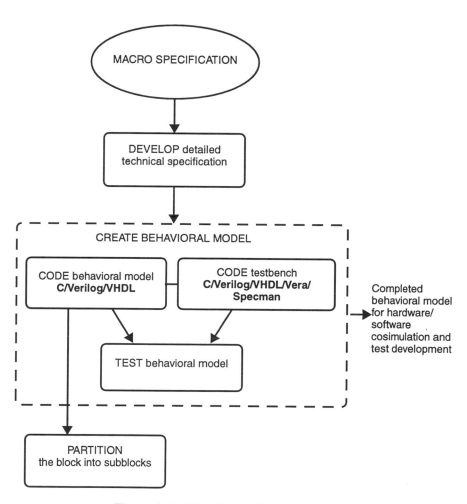

Figure 4-4   Flow for top-level macro design

4.3.2   Activities and Tools

The top-level macro design process involves the following activities and tools:

Develop algorithms and behavioral models

For most designs, the behavioral model is developed in C/C^{++}, Verilog, or VHDL; some developers are starting to use the new testbench tools Vera and Specman for creating behavioral models as well. C/C^{++} is particularly useful for designs that require significant hardware/software cosimulation, such as processor designs. Verilog, VHDL, Vera, and Specman are preferred for designs in which some of the RTL characteristics, such as I/O behavior, may be needed.

These behavioral models are all easily ported to multiple environments, either through programming language interfaces to the simulation tools, or using a commercial interface like SWIFT. In particular, through the SWIFT interface, it is possible to package the model for secure, highly portable distribution to most commercial simulators.

These behavioral models are particularly important for applications such as digital video, wireless communications, and data communication.

For example, in some digital video applications, macros are being designed around an application-specific processor. This processor controls the other blocks in the macro, simplifying hardware design and improving performance. This approach also provides an additional level of reuse through reprogramming. Such a design, however, can have significant software content. The behavioral model is essential for this kind of design.

Developing software for a processor-based macro requires significant test and debug. This, in turn, requires a model of the hardware that can be simulated at tens or hundreds of thousands of cycles per second. RTL and gate-level netlists, even when they are available, are much too slow to achieve this kind of performance, typically running at tens or hundreds of cycles per second. Only a high-level model provides the performance required for software development and testing.

Stream-driven tools such as COSSAP and SPW can be useful modeling tools for those datapath-intensive designs in which the algorithm itself, independent of the implementation, requires significant exploration and development. For example, when verifying a video compression algorithm, it may be necessary to simulate with many frames of video. The different processing blocks in the algorithm typically operate at different data rates; however, including the logic to handle these different rates can slow down simulation. With a stream or data driven simulator, each block executes as soon as the required data is received. This approach provides the kind of simulation performance and ease of modeling required for datapath-intensive designs like video processing.

COSSAP can also help generate RTL code and can assist in the hardware/software partitioning.

Develop testbenches

Testbench design and test development are essential and challenging at every level of representation — behavioral, RTL, and gate. For a full discussion of the macro testbench, refer to Chapter 7 of this manual.

4.4   Subblock Design

The second phase of macro design consists of design, RTL coding, and testing the subblocks in the macro. The key to the success of this phase is to have a complete and clear specification for each subblock before RTL coding begins, and to have a clear understanding of the deliverables needed at the end of the design phase.

4.4.1   Subblock Design Process

Subblock design, as illustrated in Figure 4-5, begins when there is a preliminary hardware specification for the subblock and a set of design guidelines for the project. The phase is complete when the design team has produced and reviewed the following subblock design elements:

- An updated hardware specification for the subblock
- A synthesis script
- A testbench for the subblock, and a verification suite that achieves 100% test coverage. See Chapter 7 for details on this requirement. In particular, note that the testbench/verification suite must provide 100% path and statement coverage as measured by a coverage tool.
- RTL that passes lint and synthesis. The final RTL code for the subblock must comply with the coding guidelines adopted by the design team. A configurable lint-like tool that verifies compliance to the guidelines is essential to ensure consistent code quality throughout the macro.

  The final RTL code must also synthesize on the target library and meet its timing constraints, using a realistic wire load model.

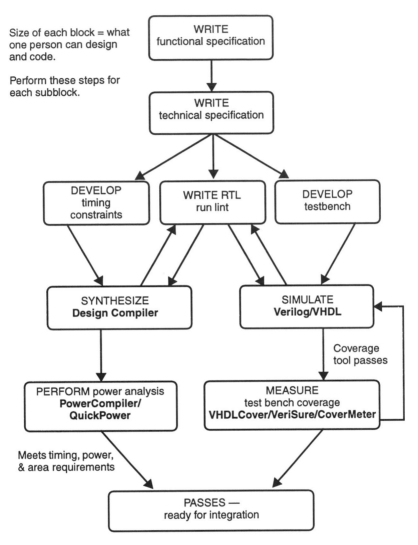

Figure 4-5   Flow for designing subblocks

4.4.2   Activities and Tools

The subblock design process involves the following activities and tools:

Develop the functional and technical specifications

The actual design of the subblock should be done before, not during, RTL coding.

The *functional specification* for the subblock describes, in detail, the aspects of the subblock that are visible to the rest of the macro: functionality, I/O, timing, area, and power. This specification can be included as part of the macro functional specification.

The *technical specification* describes the internals of the subblock and is intended to be the vehicle by which the designer captures the details of the subblock design before beginning coding. The quality of the technical specification is a key factor in determining the time required for the rest of the subblock design process. A good technical specification allows the designer to code once and to verify quickly. A poorly thought-out specification results in many iterations through the code/test/synthesis loop.

Develop RTL

In most cases, the RTL code is written directly by the designer.

For some arithmetic-intensive designs, Module Compiler provides a means of specifying the datapath and controlling the structures to be synthesized. Module Compiler generates a gate-level netlist and a simulation model for the subblock. It takes as input its own Verilog-like HDL. See "RAM and Datapath Generators" in Chapter 6 for a more detailed description of the work flow using Module Compiler.

Develop testbench

The design of the subblock-level testbench is described in Chapter 7. The critical requirements for this testbench are readability and ease of modification, so that the designer can easily create and extend the testbench, and use the testbench to detect and debug problems in the subblock.

Develop synthesis scripts and synthesize

The external timing constraints should be fully defined by the specification before coding begins. Synthesis scripts must be developed early in the design process and synthesis should begin as soon as the RTL code passes the most basic functional tests. These early synthesis runs give great insight into problem areas for timing and may significantly affect the final code.

Run lint

A lint-like tool, such as Verilint/VHDLlint from InterHDL, provides a powerful method for checking the RTL for violations of coding guidelines and other kinds of errors. It should be run often throughout the design process, since it is the fastest means of catching errors. The final code must pass all lint checks specified in the coding guidelines.

Measure testbench coverage

It is essential to catch bugs as early as possible in the design process, since the time to find and correct a bug increases by an order of magnitude at each level of design integration. A bug found early during specification/behavioral modeling is dramatically cheaper than a bug found at macro integration.

Coverage tools such as VeriSure and VHDLCover provide a means of measuring statement and path coverage for RTL designs and testbenches. A coverage tool must be run on the final design and it should indicate 100 percent statement and path coverage before the subblock is integrated with other subblocks.

Perform power analysis

If power consumption is an issue, the design team uses QuickPower or Power Compiler to analyze power and to ensure that power consumption is within specification.

4.5   Macro Integration

The third phase of macro design consists of integrating the subblocks into the top-level macro and performing a final set of tests. The key to the success of this phase is to have subblocks that have been designed to the guidelines outlined in this document. In particular, the timing and functional behavior of the interfaces between subblocks should be completely specified before subblock design and verified after subblock design. Most bugs occur at the interfaces between subblocks and as a result of misunderstandings between members of the design team.

4.5.1   Integration Process

The macro integration process, shown in Figure 4-6, is complete when:

- Development of top-level RTL, synthesis scripts, and testbenches is complete
- Macro RTL passes all tests
- Macro synthesizes with reference library and meets all timing, area, and power criteria
- Macro RTL passes lint and manufacturing test coverage

The only new criterion here is the one about meeting the manufacturing test coverage requirements. Most macros use a full scan methodology for manufacturing test, and require 95 percent coverage (99 percent is preferred). Whatever the methodology, test coverage must be measured at this point and must be proven to meet the requirements in the functional specification.

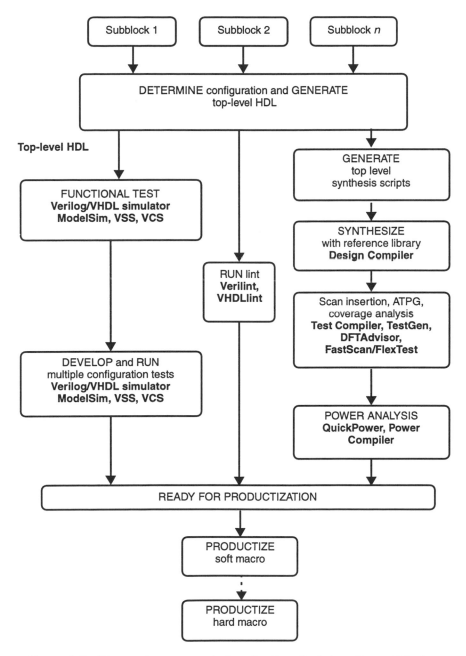

Figure 4-6   Flow and recommended applications for integrating subblocks

4.5.2   Activities and Tools

The process of integrating the subblocks into the top-level macro involves the following activities and tools:

Develop top-level RTL

Once the subblocks have all been developed, the design team needs to develop a top-level RTL description that instantiates the subblocks and connects them together. Parameterizable macros, where the number of instances of a particular subblock may vary, present a particular challenge here. It may be necessary to develop a script that will generate the appropriate instances and instantiate them in the top level RTL.

Run functional tests

It is essential to develop a thorough functional test suite and to run it on the final macro design. The design team must run this test on a sufficient set of configurations to ensure that the macro is robust for all possible configurations.

The verification strategy for the entire macro is discussed in Chapter 7 of this manual.

Develop synthesis scripts

Once the subblock-level synthesis scripts have all been developed, the design team needs to develop a top-level synthesis script. For parameterizable macros, where the number of instances of a particular subblock may vary, this presents a particular challenge. It may be necessary to provide a set of scripts for different configurations of the macro. It may also be useful to provide different scripts for different synthesis goals: one script to achieve optimal timing performance, another to minimize area.

Run synthesis

The design team must run synthesis on a sufficiently large set of configurations to ensure that synthesis will run successfully for all configurations. In general, this means synthesizing both a minimum and maximum configuration. Note that the final synthesis constraints must take into account the fact that scan will later be inserted in the macro, adding some setup time requirements to the flops.

Use Design Compiler to perform top-level synthesis.

Perform scan insertion

The final RTL code must also meet the testability requirements for the macro. Most macros will use a full scan test methodology and require 95% coverage (99% preferred).

Use a test insertion tool (for example Test Compiler, TestGen, DFTAdvisor, or FastScan/FlexTest) to perform scan insertion and automatic test pattern generation for the macro. As part of this process, the test insertion tool should also report the actual test coverage for the macro.

After scan insertion, the design team uses a static timing analysis tool to verify the final timing of the macro.

Perform power analysis
If power consumption is an issue, the design team uses QuickPower or Power Compiler to analyze power and to ensure that power consumption is within specification.

Run lint
Finally, run the lint tool on the entire design to ensure compliance to guidelines. In addition, use the lint tool to verify the translatability of the macro and testbench between Verilog and VHDL.

4.6   Soft Macro Productization

The final phase of macro design consists of productizing the macro, which means creating the remaining deliverables that system integrators will require for reuse of the macro. This chapter describes the productization of soft macros only. The development and productization of hard macros is described in Chapter 8.

4.6.1   Productization Process

The soft macro productization phase, shown in Figure 4-7, is complete when the design team has produced and reviewed the following components of the final product.

- Verilog and VHDL versions of the code, testbenches, and tests
- Supporting scripts for the design

  This includes the installation scripts and synthesis scripts required to build the different configurations of the macro.

- Documentation

  This includes updating all the functional specifications and generating the final user documentation from them.

- Final version locked in RCS

  All deliverables must be in a revision control system to allow future maintenance.

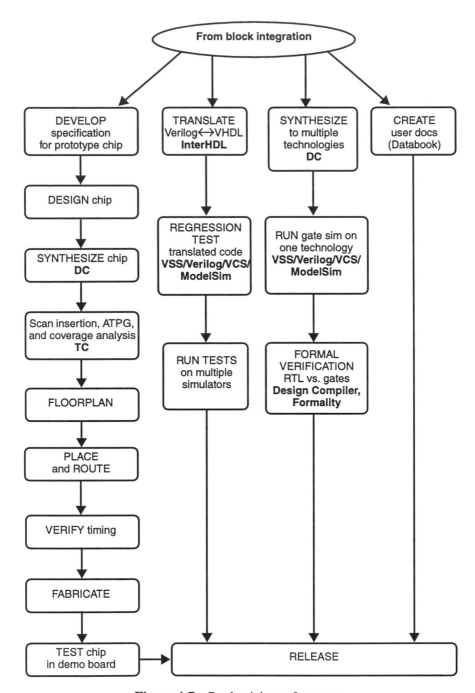

Figure 4-7   Productizing soft macros

4.6.2   Activities and Tools

The soft macro productization process involves the following activities and tools:

Develop a prototype chip

A prototype chip is essential for verifying both the robustness of the design and the correctness of the original specifications. Some observers estimate that 90 percent of chips work the first time, but only 50 percent of chips work correctly in the system.

Developing a chip using the macro and testing it in a real application with real application software allows us to:

- Verify that the design is functionally correct.
- Verify that the design complies with the appropriate standards (for example, we can take a PCI test chip to the PCI SIG for compliance testing).
- Verify that the design is compatible with the kind of hardware/software environment that other integrators are likely to use.

The process for developing the prototype chip is a simple ASIC flow appropriate for small chip design. It is assumed that the chip will be a simple application of the macro, perhaps twice the size of the macro itself in gate count.

Provide macro and testbench in both Verilog and VHDL

To be widely useful, the macro and its testbenches must be available in both the Verilog and VHDL languages. Commercial translators are available, including one from InterHDL. These translators do a reasonable job on RTL code but still present some challenge for translating testbenches.

After the code and testbenches have been translated, they must be re-verified to validate the translation.

Test on several simulators

In addition, the macro and testbenches should be run on the most popular simulators in order to ensure portability. This is particularly important for the VHDL simulators, which have significant differences from vendor to vendor.

Synthesize on multiple technologies

The macro should be synthesized using a variety of technologies to ensure portability of the scripts and to ensure that the design can meet its timing and area goals with the ASIC libraries that customers are most likely to use.

Perform gate-level simulation

Gate-level simulation must be run on at least one target technology in order to verify the synthesis scripts.

Formal verification

Using formal verification tools, such as Formality or the `compare_design` feature of Design Compiler, we can verify that the final netlist is functionally equivalent to the original RTL.

Create/update user documentation

The functional specifications created during the design process are usually not the best vehicle for helping a customer use the macro. A set of user documents must be developed that address this need. The components of this documentation are described in Chapter 9 of this manual.

CHAPTER 5

RTL Coding Guidelines

This chapter offers a collection of coding rules and guidelines. Following these practices helps to ensure that your HDL code is readable, modifiable, and reusable. Following these coding practices also helps to achieve optimal results in synthesis and simulation.

Topics in this chapter include:

- Basic coding practices
- Coding for portability
- Guidelines for clocks and resets
- Coding for synthesis
- Partitioning for synthesis
- Designing with memories
- Code profiling

5.1 Overview of the Coding Guidelines

The coding guidelines in this chapter are based on a few fundamental principles. The basic underlying goal is to develop RTL code that is simple and regular. Simple and regular structures are inherently easier to design, code, verify, and synthesize than more complex designs. The overall goal for any reusable design should be to keep it as simple as possible and still meet its functional and performance goals.

The coding guidelines detailed in this chapter provide the following general recommendations:

- Use simple constructs, basic types (for VHDL), and simple clocking schemes.
- Use a consistent coding style, consistent naming conventions, and a consistent structure for processes and state machines.
- Use a regular partitioning scheme, with all module outputs registered and with modules roughly of the same size.
- Make the RTL code easy to understand, by using comments, meaningful names, and constants or parameters instead of hard-coded numbers.

By following these guidelines, the developer should be better able to produce code that converges quickly to the desired performance, in terms of functionality, timing, power, and area.

5.2   Basic Coding Practices

The following guidelines address basic coding practices, focusing on lexical conventions and basic RTL constructs.

5.2.1   General Naming Conventions

Rule – Develop a naming convention for the design. Document it and use it consistently throughout the design.

Guideline – Use lowercase letters for all signal names, variable names, and port names.

Guideline – Use uppercase letters for names of constants and user-defined types.

Guideline – Use meaningful names for signals, ports, functions, and parameters. For example, do not use *ra* for a RAM address bus. Instead, use *ram_addr*.

Guideline – If your design uses several parameters, use short but descriptive names. During elaboration, the synthesis tool concatenates the module's name, parameter names, and parameter values to form the design unit name. Thus, lengthy parameter names can cause excessively long design unit names when you elaborate the design with Design Compiler.

Guideline – Use the name *clk* for the clock signal. If there is more than one clock in the design, use *clk* as the prefix for all clock signals (for example, *clk1*, *clk2*, or *clk_interface*).

Guideline – Use the same name for all clock signals that are driven from the same source.

Guideline – For active low signals, end the signal name with an underscore followed by a lowercase character (for example, _b or _n). Use the same lowercase character to indicate active low signals throughout the design.

Guideline – For standardization, we recommend that you use _n to indicate an active low signal. However, any lowercase character is acceptable as long as it is used consistently.

Guideline – Use the name *rst* for reset signals. If the reset signal is active low, use *rst_n* (or substitute *n* with whatever lowercase character you are using to indicate active low signals).

Rule – When describing multibit buses, use a consistent ordering of bits. For VHDL, use either (y downto x) or (x to y). For Verilog, use (x:0) or (0:x). Using a consistent ordering helps improve the readability of the code and reduces the chance of accidently swapping order between connected buses.

Guideline – Although the choice is somewhat arbitrary, we recommend using (y downto x) for multibit signals in VHDL and (x:0) for multibit signals in Verilog. We make this recommendation primarily to establish a standard, and thus achieve some consistency across multiple designs and design teams.
See Example 5-1.

Example 5-1 Using downto in port declarations

```
entity DW_addinc is
  generic(WIDTH : natural);
  port(
    A,B : in std_logic_vector(WIDTH-1 downto 0);
    CI  : in std_logic;
    SUM : out std_logic_vector(WIDTH-1 downto 0);
    CO  : out std_logic;
  );
end DW01_addinc;
```

Guideline – When possible, use the same name or similar names for ports and signals that are connected (for example, a => a; or a => a_int;).

Guideline – When possible, use the signal naming conventions listed in Table 5-1.

Table 5-1   Signal naming conventions

Convention	Use
*_r	Output of a register (for example, count_r)
*_a	Asynchronous signal (for example, addr_strobe_a)
*_p*n*	Signal used in the *n*th phase (for example, enable_p2)
*_nxt	Data before being registered into a register with the same name
*_z	Tristate internal signal

5.2.2   Naming Conventions for VITAL Support

VITAL is a gate-level modeling standard for VHDL libraries and is described in IEEE Specification 1076.4. This specification places restrictions on the naming conventions (and other characteristics) of the port declarations at the top level of a library element.

Normally, an RTL coding style document need not address gate-level modeling conventions. However, some of these issues can affect developers of hard macros. The deliverables for a hard macro include full-functional/full-timing models, where a timing wrapper is added to the RTL code. If the timing wrapper is in VHDL, then it must be VITAL-compliant.

Background

According to IEEE Specification 1076.4, VITAL libraries can have two levels of compliance with the standard: VITAL_Level0 and VITAL_Level1. VITAL_Level1 is more rigorous and deals with the architecture (functionality and timing) of a library cell. VITAL_Level0 is the interface specification that deals with the ports and generics specifications in the entity section of a VHDL library cell. VITAL_Level0 has strict rules regarding naming conventions and port/generic types. These rules were designed so that simulator vendors can assume certain conventions and deal with SDF back-annotation in a uniform manner.

Rules

Section 4.3.1 of IEEE Specification 1076.4 addresses port naming conventions and includes the following rules. These restrictions apply only to the top-level entity of a hard macro.

Rule (hard macro, top-level ports) – Do not use underscore characters (_) in the entity port declaration for the top-level entity of a hard macro.

The reason for the above rule is that VITAL uses underscores as separators to construct names for SDF back-annotation from the SDF entries.

Rule (hard macro, top-level ports) – A port that is declared in entity port declaration shall not be of mode LINKAGE.

Rule (hard macro, top-level ports) – The type mark in an entity port declaration shall denote a type or subtype that is declared in package `std_logic_1164`. The type mark in the declaration of a scalar port shall denote a subtype of `std_ulogic`. The type mark in the declaration of an array port shall denote the type `std_logic_vector`.

Rule (hard macro, top-level ports) – The port in an entity port declaration cannot be a guarded port. Furthermore, the declaration cannot impose a range constraint on the port, nor can it alter the resolution of the port from that defined in the standard logic package.

5.2.3   Architecture Naming Conventions

Guideline – Use the VHDL architecture types listed in Table 5-2.

Table 5-2   Architecture naming conventions

Architecture	Naming Convention

synthesis model	`ARCHITECTURE rtl OF my_syn_model IS`
	or
	`ARCHITECTURE str OF my_structural_design IS`

simulation model	`ARCHITECTURE sim OF my_behave_model IS`
	or
	`ARCHITECTURE tb OF my_test_bench IS`

5.2.4   Include Headers in Source Files

Rule – Include a header at the top of every source file, including scripts. The header must contain:

- Filename
- Author

- Description of function and list of key features of the module
- Date the file was created
- Modification history including date, name of modifier, and description of the change

Example 5-2 shows a sample HDL source file header.

Example 5-2 Header in an HDL source file

```
--This confidential and proprietary software may be used
--only as authorized by a licensing agreement from
--Synopsys Inc.
--In the event of publication, the following notice is
--applicable:
--
-- (C) COPYRIGHT 1996 SYNOPSYS INC.
-- ALL RIGHTS RESERVED
--
-- The entire notice above must be reproduced on all
--authorized copies.
--
-- File        : DWpci_core.vhd
-- Author      : Jeff Hackett
-- Date        : 09/17/96
-- Version     : 0.1
-- Abstract    : This file has the entity, architecture
--                and configuration of the PCI 2.1
--                MacroCell core module.
--                The core module has the interface,
--                config, initiator,
--                and target top-level modules.
--
-- Modification History:
-- Date       By    Version    Change Description
--
=========================================================
-- 9/17/96    JDH     0.1       Original
-- 11/13/96   JDH               Last pre-Atria changes
-- 03/04/97   SKC               changes for ism_ad_en_ffd_n
--                               and tsm_data_ffd_n
--
=========================================================
```

5.2.5   Use Comments

Rule – Use comments appropriately to explain all processes, functions, and declarations of types and subtypes. See Example 5-3.

Example 5-3   Comments for a subtype declaration

```
--Create subtype INTEGER_256 for built-in error
--checking of legal values.
subtype INTEGER_256 is type integer range 0 to 255;
```

Guideline – Use comments to explain ports, signals, and variables, or groups of signals or variables.

Comments should be placed logically, near the code that they describe. Comments should be brief, concise, and explanatory. Avoid "comment clutter"; obvious functionality does not need to be commented. The key is to describe the intent behind the section of code.

5.2.6   Keep Commands on Separate Lines

Rule – Use a separate line for each HDL statement. Although both VHDL and Verilog allow more than one statement per line, the code is more readable and maintainable if each statement or command is on a separate line.

5.2.7   Line Length

Guideline – Keep the line length to 72 characters or less.

Lines that exceed 80 characters are difficult to read in print and on standard terminal width computer screens. The 72 character limit provides a margin that enhances the readability of the code.

For HDL code (VHDL or Verilog), use carriage returns to divide lines that exceed 72 characters and indent the next line to show that it is a continuation of the previous line. See Example 5-4.

Example 5-4   Continuing a line of HDL code

```
hp_req <= (x0_hp_req or t0_hp_req or x1_hp_req or
    t1_hp_req or s0_hp_req or t2_hp_req or s1_hp_req or
    x2_hp_req or x3_hp_req or x4_hp_req or x5_hp_req or
    wd_hp_req and ea and pf_req nor iip2);
```

5.2.8   Indentation

Rule – Use indentation to improve the readability of continued code lines and nested loops. See Example 5-5.

Guideline – Use indentation of 2 spaces. Larger indentation (for example, 8 spaces) restricts line length when there are several levels of nesting.

Guideline – Avoid using tabs. Differences in editors and user setups make the positioning of tabs unpredictable and can corrupt the intended indentation. There are programs available, including language-specific versions of emacs, that will replace tabs with spaces.

Example 5-5   Indentation in a nested if loop

```
if (bit_width(m+1) >= 2) then
  for i in 2 to bit_width(m+1) loop
    spin_j := 0;
    for j in 1 to m loop
      if j > spin_j then
        if (matrix(m)(i-1)(j) /= wht) then
          if (j=m) and (matrix(m)(i)(j) = wht) then
            matrix(m)(i)(j) := j;
          else
            for k in j+1 to m loop
              if (matrix(m)(i-1)(k) /= wht) then
                matrix(m)(i)(k) := j;
                spin_j := k;
                exit;
              end if;
            end loop; -- k
          end if;
        end if;
      end if;
    end loop; -- j
  end loop; -- i
end if;
```

5.2.9 Do Not Use HDL Reserved Words

Rule – Do not use VHDL or Verilog reserved words for names of any elements in your RTL source files. Because macro designs must be translatable from VHDL to Verilog and from Verilog to VHDL, it is important not to use VHDL reserved words in Verilog code, and not to use Verilog reserved words in VHDL code.

5.2.10 Port Ordering

Rule – Declare ports in a logical order, and keep this order consistent throughout the design.

Guideline – Declare one port per line, with a comment following it (preferably on the same line).

Guideline – Declare the ports in the following order:

Inputs:
- Clocks
- Resets
- Enables
- Other control signals
- Data and address lines

Outputs:
- Clocks
- Resets
- Enables
- Other control signals
- Data

Guideline – Use comments to describe groups of ports. See Example 5-6.

Example 5-6   Port ordering in entity definition

```
entity my_fir is
  generic  (
    DATA_WIDTH  : positive;
    COEF_WIDTH  : positive;
    ACC_WIDTH   : positive;
    ORDER       : positive
  );
```

```
  port (
--
--          Control Inputs
--
    clk     : in std_logic;
    rst_n   : in std_logic;
    run     : in std_logic;
    load    : in std_logic;
    tc      : in std_logic;
--
--          Data Inputs
--
    data_in : in std_logic_vector(DATA_WIDTH-1 downto 0);
    coef_in : in std_logic_vector(COEF_WIDTH-1 downto 0);
    sum_in  : in std_logic_vector(ACC_WIDTH-1 downto 0);
--
--          Control Outputs
--
    start   : out std_logic;
    hold    : out std_logic;
--
--          Data Outputs
--

    sum_out : out std_logic_vector(ACC_WIDTH-1 downto 0)
        );

end my_fir;
```

5.2.11 Port Maps and Generic Maps

Rule – Always use explicit mapping for ports and generics, using named association rather than positional association. See Example 5-7.

Guideline – Leave a blank line between the input and output ports to improve readability.

Example 5-7   Using named association for port mapping

VHDL:

```
-- instantiate my_add
  U_ADD: my_add
    generic map (width => WORDLENGTH)
    port map (
      a => in1,
      b => in2,
      ci => carry_in,

      sum => sum,
      co => carry_out
    );
```

Verilog:

```
// instantiate my_add
my_add #('WORDLENGTH) U_ADD (
  .a   (in1      ),
  .b   (in2      ),
  .ci  (carry_in ),

  .sum (sum      ),
  .co  (carry_out)
);
```

5.2.12 VHDL Entity, Architecture, and Configuration Sections

Guideline – Place entity, architecture, and configuration sections of your VHDL design in the same file. Putting all the information about a particular design in one file makes the design easier to understand and to maintain.

If you include subdesign configurations in a source file with entity and architecture declarations, you must comment them out for synthesis. You can do this with the pragma translate_off and pragma translate_on pseudo-comments in the VHDL source file, as shown in Example 5-8.

Example 5-8   Using pragmas to comment out VHDL configurations for synthesis

```
-- pragma translate_off
configuration cfg_example_struc of example is
  for struc
    use example_gate;
  end for;
end cfg_example_struc;
-- pragma translate_on
```

5.2.13 Use Functions

Guideline – Use functions when possible, instead of repeating the same sections of code. If possible, generalize the function to make it reusable. Also, use comments to explain the function.

For example, if your code frequently converts address data from one format to another, use a function to perform the conversion and call the function whenever you need to. See Example 5-9.

Example 5-9   Creating a reusable function

VHDL:

```
--This function converts the incoming address to the
--corresponding relative address.

function convert_address
    (input_address, offset : integer)
  return integer is
begin

  -- ... function body here ...

end; -- convert_address
```

Verilog:

```
// This function converts the incoming address to the
// corresponding relative address.

function ['BUS_WIDTH-1:0] convert_address;
  input input_address, offset;
  integer input_address, offset;
```

```
begin
  // ... function body goes here ...
end
endfunction // convert_address
```

5.2.14 Use Loops and Arrays

Guideline – Use loops and arrays for improved readability of the source code. For example, describing a shift register, PN-sequence generator, or Johnson counter with a loop construct can greatly reduce the number of lines of source code while still retaining excellent readability. See Example 5-10.

Example 5-10   Using loops to improve readability

```
shift_delay_loop: for i in 1 to (number_taps-1) loop
  delay(i) := delay(i-1);
end loop shift_delay_loop;
```

The ARRAY construct also reduces the number of statements necessary to describe the function and improves readability. Example 5-11 is an example of a register bank implemented as a two-dimensional array of flip-flops.

Example 5-11   Register bank using an array

```
type reg_array is array(natural range <>) of
  std_logic_vector(REG_WIDTH-1 downto 0);
signal reg: reg_array(WORD_COUNT-1 downto 0);

begin
  REG_PROC: process(clk)
  begin
    if clk='1' and clk'event then
      if we='1' then
        reg(addr) <= data;
      end if;
    end if;
  end process REG_PROC;

  data_out <= reg(addr);
```

Guideline – Arrays are significantly faster to simulate than for loops. To improve simulation performance, use vector operations on arrays rather than for loops whenever possible. See Example 5-12.

Example 5-12   Using arrays for faster simulation

Poor coding style;

```
function my_xor( bbit : std_logic;
                 avec : std_logic_vector(x downto y) )
   return std_logic_vector is
variable cvec :
   std_logic_vector(avec'range-1 downto 0);
begin
   for i in avec'range loop        -- bit-level for loop
     cvec(i) := avec(i) xor bbit; -- bit-level xor
   end loop;
   return(cvec);
end;
```

Recommended coding style:

```
function my_xor( bbit : std_logic;
                 avec : std_logic_vector(x downto y) )
   return std_logic_vector is
variable cvec, temp :
   std_logic_vector(avec'range-1 downto 0);
begin
   temp := (others => bbit);
   cvec := avec xor temp;
   return(cvec);
end;
```

5.2.15   Use Meaningful Labels

Rule – Label each process block with a meaningful name. This is very helpful for debug. For example, you can set a breakpoint by referencing the process label.

Guideline – Label each process block *<name>*_PROC.

Rule – Label each instance with a meaningful name.

Guideline – Label each instance U_*<name>*.

In a multi-layered design hierarchy, keep the labels short as well as meaningful. Long process and instance labels can cause excessively long path names in the design hierarchy. See Example 5-13.

Rule – Do not duplicate any signal, variable, or entity names. For example, if you have a signal named *incr*, do not use *incr* as a process label.

Example 5-13   Meaningful process label

```
-- Synchronize requests (hold for one clock).
SYNC_PROC : process (req1, req2, rst, clk)

 ... process body here ...

end process SYNC_PROC;
```

5.3   Coding for Portability

The following guidelines address portability issues. By following these guidelines, you will create code that is technology-independent, compatible with various simulation tools, and easily translatable from VHDL to Verilog (or from Verilog to VHDL).

5.3.1   Use Only IEEE Standard Types

Rule (VHDL only) – Use only IEEE standard types.

You can create additional types and subtypes, but all types and subtypes should be based on IEEE standard types. Example 5-14 shows how to create a subtype (`word_type`) based on the IEEE standard type `std_logic_vector`.

Example 5-14   Creating a subtype from `std_logic_vector`

```
--Create new 16-bit subtype
subtype WORD_TYPE is std_logic_vector (15 downto 0);
```

Guideline (VHDL only) – Use `std_logic` rather than `std_ulogic`. Likewise, use `std_logic_vector` rather than `std_ulogic_vector`. The `std_logic` and `std_logic_vector` types provide the resolution functions required for tristate buses. The `std_ulogic` and `std_ulogic_vector` types do not provide resolution functions.

Note – Standardizing on either `std_logic` or `std_ulogic` is more important than which of the two you select. There are advantages and disadvantages to each. Most designers today use `std_logic`, which is somewhat better supported by EDA tools. In most applications, the availability of resolution functions is not required. Internal tristate buses present serious design challenges and should be used only when absolutely necessary. However, at the system level and in those extreme cases where internal tristate buses are required, the resolution functions are essential.

Guideline (VHDL only) – Be conservative in the number of subtypes you create. Using too many subtypes makes the code difficult to understand.

Guideline (VHDL only) – Do not use the types `bit` or `bit_vector`. Many simulators do not provide built-in arithmetic functions for these types. Example 5-15 shows how to use built-in arithmetic packages for `std_logic_vector`.

Example 5-15   Using built-in arithmetic functions for `std_logic_vector`

```
use ieee.std_logic_arith.all;
signal a,b,c,d:std_logic_vector(y downto x);
    c <= a + b;
```

5.3.2   Do Not Use Hard-Coded Numeric Values

Guideline – Do not use hard-coded numeric values in your design. As an exception, you can use the values 0 and 1 (but not in combination, as in 1001). Example 5-16 shows Verilog code that uses a hard-coded numerical value (7) in the "poor coding style" example and a constant (MY_BUS_SIZE) in the "recommended coding style" example.

Example 5-16   Using constants instead of hard-coded values

Poor coding style:

```
wire      [7:0] my_in_bus;
reg       [7:0] my_out_bus;
```

Recommended coding style:

```
'define MY_BUS_SIZE 8
wire      ['MY_BUS_SIZE-1:0] my_in_bus;
reg       ['MY_BUS_SIZE-1:0] my_out_bus;
```

5.3.3   Packages

Guideline (VHDL only) – Collect all parameter values and function definitions for a design into a single separate file (a "package") and name the file *DesignName*_package.vhd.

5.3.4   Include Files

Guideline (Verilog only) – Keep the `define` statements for a design in a single separate file and name the file *DesignName*`_params.v`.

5.3.5   Avoid Embedding dc_shell Scripts

Although it is possible to embed `dc_shell` synthesis commands directly in the source code, this practice is not recommended. Others who synthesize the code may not be aware of the hidden commands, which may cause their synthesis scripts to produce poor results. If the design is reused in a new application, the synthesis goals may be different, such as a higher-speed version. If the source code is reused with a new release of Design Compiler, the commands will still be supported but may be obsolete.

There are several exceptions to this rule. In particular, the synthesis directives to turn synthesis on and off must be embedded in the code in the appropriate places. These exceptions are noted in various guidelines throughout this chapter.

5.3.6   Use Technology-Independent Libraries

Guideline – Use the DesignWare Foundation Library to maintain technology independence.

The DesignWare Foundation Library contains improved architectures for the inferable arithmetic components, such as:

- Adders
- Multipliers
- Comparators
- Incrementers and decrementers

These architectures provide improved timing performance over the equivalent internal Design Compiler architectures.

The DesignWare Foundation Library also provides additional arithmetic components such as:

- Sin, cos
- Modulus, divide
- Square root
- Arithmetic and barrel shifters

These DesignWare components are all high-performance designs that are portable across processes. They provide significantly more portability than custom-designed, process-specific designs. Using these components helps you create designs that achieve high performance in all target libraries.

The DesignWare Foundation Library also includes a number of sequential components, also designed to be completely process-portable, and which can save considerable design time. These components include:

- FIFO's and FIFO controllers
- ECC
- CRC
- JTAG components and ASIC debugger

For more information about using DesignWare components, see the *DesignWare Foundation Library Databook* and the *DesignWare User Guide*.

Guideline – Avoid instantiating gates in the design. Gate-level designs are very hard to read, and thus difficult to maintain and reuse. If technology-specific gates are used, then the design is not portable to other technologies.

Guideline – If you must use technology-specific gates, then isolate these gates in a separate module. This will make it easier to modify these gates as needed for different technologies.

Guideline – The GTECH library If you must instantiate a gate, use a technology-independent library such as the Synopsys generic technology library, GTECH. This library contains the following technology-independent logical components:

- AND, OR, and NOR gates (2, 3, 4, 5, and 8)
- 1-bit adders and half adders
- 2-of-3 majority
- Multiplexors
- Flip-flops
- Latches
- Multiple-level logic gates, such as AND-NOT, AND-OR, AND-OR-INVERT

5.3.7   Coding For Translation (VHDL to Verilog)

Guideline (VHDL only) – Do not use `generate` statements. There is no equivalent construct in Verilog.

Guideline (VHDL only) – Do not use `block` constructs. There is no equivalent construct in Verilog.

Guideline (VHDL only) – Do not use code to modify `constant` declarations. There is no equivalent capability in Verilog.

5.4   Guidelines for Clocks and Resets

The following sections contain guidelines for clock and reset signals. The basic theory behind these guidelines is that a simple clocking structure is easier to understand, analyze, and maintain. It also consistently produces better synthesis results. The preferred clocking structure is a single global clock and positive edge-triggered flops as the only sequential devices, as illustrated in Figure 5-1.

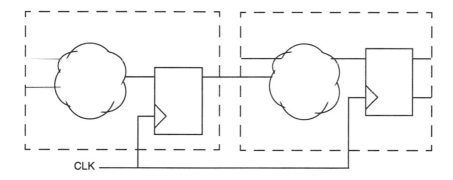

Figure 5-1   Ideal Clocking Structure

5.4.1   Avoid Mixed Clock Edges

Guideline – Avoid using both positive-edge and negative-edge triggered flip-flops in your design.

Mixed clock edges may be necessary in some designs. In designs with very aggressive timing goals, for example, it may be necessary to capture data on both edges of the clock. However, clocking on both edges creates several problems, and should be used with caution:

• The duty cycle of the clock becomes a critical issue in timing analysis, in addition to the clock frequency itself.

• Most scan-based testing methodologies require separate handling of positive and negative-edge triggered flops.

Figure 5-2 shows an example of a module with both positive-edge and negative-edge triggered flip-flops.

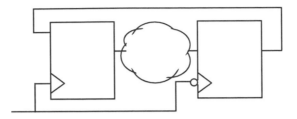

Figure 5-2   Bad example: Mixed clock edges

Rule – If you must use both positive-edge and negative-edge triggered flip-flops in your design, be sure to model the worst case duty cycle of the clock accurately in synthesis and timing analysis.

The assumption of a perfect clock with 50% duty cycle is optimistic, giving signals half the clock cycle to propagate from one register to the next. In the physical design, the duty cycle will be not be perfect, and the actual time available for signals to propagate can be much smaller.

Rule – If you must use both positive-edge and negative-edge triggered flip-flops in your design, be sure to document the assumed duty cycle in the user documentation.

In most chip designs, the duty cycle is a function of the clock tree that is inserted into the design; this clock tree insertion is usually specific to the process technology. The chip designer using the macro must check that the actual duty cycle will match requirements of the macro, and must know how to change the synthesis/timing analysis scripts for the macro to match the actual conditions.

Guideline – If you must use a large number of both positive-edge and negative-edge triggered flip-flops in your design, it may be useful to separate them into different modules. This makes it easier to identify the negative-edge flops, and thus to put them in different scan chains.

Figure 5-3 shows an example design where the positive-edge triggered flip-flops and negative-edge triggered flip-flops are partitioned into separate blocks.

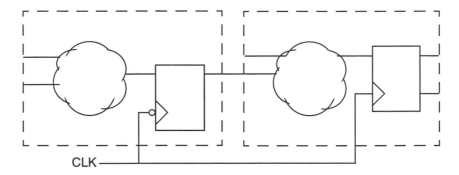

Figure 5-3 Better example: Negative-edge and positive-edge flip-flops are separated

5.4.2   Avoid Clock Buffers

Guideline – Avoid hand instantiating clock buffers in RTL code. Clock buffers are normally inserted after synthesis as part of the physical design. In synthesizable RTL code, clock nets are normally considered ideal nets, with no delays. During place and route, the clock tree insertion tool inserts the appropriate structure for creating as close to an ideal, balanced clock distribution network as possible.

5.4.3   Avoid Gated Clocks

Guideline – Avoid coding gated clocks in your RTL. Clock gating circuits tend to be technology specific and timing dependent. Improper timing of a gated clock can generate a false clock or glitch, causing a flip-flop to clock in the wrong data. Also, the skew of different local clocks can cause hold time violations.

Gated clocks also cause limited testability because the logic clocked by a gated clock cannot be made part of a scan chain. Figure 5-4 shows a design where U2 cannot be clocked during scan-in, test, or scan-out, and cannot be made part of the scan chain.

Gated clocks are required for many low-powered designs, but they should not be coded in the RTL for a macro. See section 5.4.5 for the preferred way of dealing with gated clocks. If individual flip-flops need to be gated within a design, the clock gating should be inserted by a tool such as Power Compiler, so that the RTL remains technology portable.

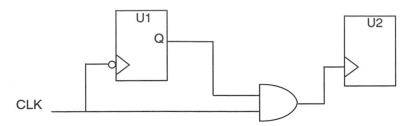

Figure 5-4   Bad example: Limited testability and skew problems because of gated
clock

5.4.4   Avoid Internally Generated Clocks

Guideline – Avoid using internally generated clocks in your design.

Internally generated clocks cause limited testability because logic driven by the internally generated clock cannot be made part of a scan chain. Internally generated clocks also make it more difficult to constrain the design for synthesis.

Figure 5-5 shows a design in which U2 cannot be clocked during scan-in, test, or scan-out, and cannot be made part of the scan chain because it is clocked by an internally generated clock. As an alternative, design synchronously or use multiple clocks.

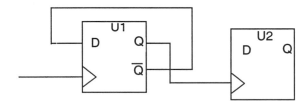

Figure 5-5   Bad example: Internally generated clock

5.4.5   Gated Clocks and Low Power Designs

Some designs, especially low-power designs, required a gated clocks. The following guidelines address this issue.

Guideline – If you must use a gated clock, or an internally generated clock or reset, keep the clock and/or reset generation circuitry as a separate module at the top level of the design. Partition the design so that all the logic in a single module uses a single clock and a single reset. See Figure 5-6.

In particular, a gated clock should never occur within a macro. The clock gating circuit, if required, should appear at the top level of the design hierarchy, as shown in Figure 5-6.

Isolating clock and reset generation logic in a separate module solves a number of problems. It allows submodules 1–3 to use the standard timing analysis and scan insertion techniques. It restricts exceptions to the RTL coding guidelines to a small module than can be carefully reviewed for correct behavior. It also makes it easier for the design team to develop specific test strategies for the clock/reset generation logic.

Guideline – If your design requires a gated clock, model it using synchronous load registers, as illustrated in Example 5-17.

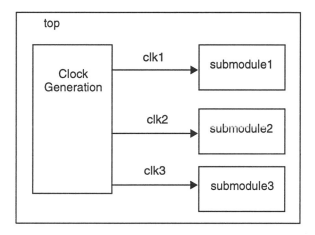

Figure 5-6   Good example: Clock generation circuitry is isolated at the top level

Example 5-17   Use synchronous load instead of combinational gating

Poor coding style:

```
clk_p1 <= clk and p1_gate;
EX17A_PROC: process (clk_p1)
  begin
    if (clk_p1'event and clk_p1 = '1') then
        .......
    end if;
  end process EX17A_PROC;
```

Good coding style:

```
EX17B_PROC: process (clk)
  begin
    if (clk'event and clk = '1') then
      if (p1_gate = '1') then
          . . .
      end if;
    end if;
  end process EX17B_PROC;
```

5.4.6   Avoid Internally Generated Resets

Make sure your registers are controlled only by a simple reset signal.

Guideline – Avoid internally generated, conditional resets if possible. Generally, all the registers in the macro should be reset at the same time. This approach makes analysis and design much simpler and easier.

Guideline – If a conditional reset is required, create a separate signal for the reset signal, and isolate the conditional reset logic in a separate module, as shown in Example 5-18. This approach results in more readable code and improves synthesis results.

Example 5-18   Isolating conditional reset logic

Poor coding style:

```
EX18A_PROC: process ( clk, rst, a, b )
  begin
    if (rst or (a and b) = '1') then
      reg_sigs <= '0';
    elsif (clk'event and clk = '1') then
        . . .
    end if;
  end process EX18A_PROC;
```

Good coding style:

```
-- in a separate reset module
    . . .

z_rst <= rst or (a and b);
    . . .
-- in the main module
```

```
EX18B_PROC: process ( clk, z_rst)
  begin
    if (z_rst = '1') then
       reg_sigs <= '0';
    elsif (clk'event and clk = '1') then
       . . .
    end if;
end process EX18B_PROC;
```

5.5   Coding for Synthesis

The following guidelines address synthesis issues. By following these guidelines, you will create code that achieves the best compile times and synthesis results, including:

- Testability
- Performance
- Simplification of static timing analysis
- Gate-level circuit behavior that matches that of the original RTL code

5.5.1   Infer Registers

Guideline – Registers (flip-flops) are the preferred mechanism for sequential logic. To maintain consistency and to ensure correct synthesis, use the following templates to infer technology-independent registers (Example 5-19 for VHDL, Example 5-20 for Verilog). Use the design's reset signal to initialize registered signals, as shown in these examples. In VHDL, do not initialize the signal in the declaration; in Verilog, do not use an `initial` statement to initialize the signal. These mechanisms can cause mismatches between pre-synthesis and post-synthesis simulation.

Example 5-19   VHDL template for sequential processes

```
-- process with synchronous reset
EX19A_PROC: process(clk)
  begin
    IF (clk'event and clk = '1') then
      if rst = '1' then
        . . .
      else
        . . .
      end if;
    end if;
```

```
    end process EX19A_PROC;

-- process with asynchronous reset
EX19B_PROC: process(clk, rst_a)
  begin
    IF rst_a = '1' then
       . . .
       elseif (clk'event and clk = '1') then
       . . .
    end if;
  end process EX19B_PROC;
```

Example 5-20   Verilog template for sequential processes

```
// process with synchronous reset
always @(posedge clk)
  begin : EX20A_PROC
    if (reset == 1'b1)
      begin
         . . .
      end
    else
      begin
         . . .
      end
  end // EX20A_PROC

// process with asynchronous reset
always @(posedge clk or posedge rst_a)
  begin : EX20B_PROC
    if (reset == 1'b1)
      begin
         . . .
      end
    else
      begin
         . . .
      end
  end // Ex20b_proc
```

5.5.2 Avoid Latches

Rule – Avoid using any latches in your design.

As an exception, you can instantiate technology-independent GTECH D latches. However, all latches must be instantiated and you must provide documentation that lists each latch and describes any special timing requirements that result from the latch.

Large registers, memories, FIFOs, and other storage elements are examples of situations in which D latches are permitted. Also, for 2-phase clocked synchronous RAM, you may want to use D latches to latch the address.

Note – To check your design for latches, compile the design (with no constraints for a quick compile) and use the `all_registers -level_sensitive` command, which will list all level sensitive elements, such as latches, in your design.

Example 5-21 illustrates a VHDL code fragment that infers a latch because there is no `else` clause for the `if` statement. Example 5-22 illustrates another VHDL code fragment that infers a latch because the z output is not assigned for the `when others` condition.

Example 5-21 Poor coding style: Latch inferred because of missing `else` condition

```
EX21_PROC: process (a, b)
begin
  if (a = '1') then
    q <= b;
  end if;
end process EX21_PROC;
```

Example 5-22 Poor coding style: Latch inferred because of missing z output assignment

```
EX22_PROC: process (c)
begin
  case c is
    when '0' => q <= '1'; z <= '0';
    when others => q <= '0';
  end case;
end process EX22_PROC;
```

Example 5-23 illustrates a Verilog code fragment that infers latches because of missing s output assignments for the 2'b00 and 2'b01 conditions and a missing 2'b11 condition.

Example 5-23   Poor coding style: Latches inferred because of missing assignments
                and missing condition

```
always @ (d)
begin
  case (d)
    2'b00: z <= 1'b1;
    2'b01: z <= 1'b0;
    2'b10: z <= 1'b1; s <= 1'b1;
  endcase
end
```

Guideline – You can avoid inferred latches by using any of the following coding techniques:

- Assign default values at the beginning of a process, as illustrated for VHDL in Example 5-24.
- Assign outputs for all input conditions, as illustrated in Example 5-25.
- Use else (instead of elsif) for the final priority branch, as illustrated in Example 5-26.

Example 5-24   Avoiding a latch by assigning default values

```
COMBINATIONAL_PROC : process (state, bus_request)
begin
  -- intitialize outputs to avoid latches
  bus_hold <= '0';
  bus_interrupt <= '0'
  case (state) ...
  ................
  ................
end process COMBINATIONAL_PROC;
```

Example 5-25 Avoiding a latch by fully assigning outputs for all input conditions

Poor coding style:

```
EX25A_PROC: process (g, a, b)
begin
  if (g = '1') then
    q <= 0;
  elsif (a = '1') then
    q <= b;
  end if;
end process EX25A_PROC;
```

Recommended coding style:

```
EX25B_PROC: process (g1, g2, a, b)
begin
  q <= '0';
  if (g1 = '1') then
    q <= a;
  elsif (g2 = '1') then
    q <= b;
  end if;
end process EX25B_PROC;
```

Example 5-26 Avoiding a latch by using else for the final priority branch
          (VHDL)

Poor coding style:

```
MUX3_PROC: process (decode, A, B)
begin
  if (decode = '0') then
    C <= A;
  elsif (decode = '1') then
    C <= B;
  end if;
end process MUX3_PROC;
```

Recommended coding style:

```
MUX3_PROC: process (decode, A, B)
begin
  if (decode = '1') then
    C <= A;
  else
    C <= B;
```

```
        end if;
    end process MUX3_PROC;
```

5.5.3   If you must use a latch

In some designs, using a latch is absolutely unavoidable. For instance, in a PCI design, the team found that it was impossible to comply with the PCI specification for reset behavior without having a latch in the design. In order to achieve testability, the team used the approach in Figure 5-7. They used a mux to provide either the normal function or the input from an I/O pad as data to the mux. The mux was selected by the test mode pin used to enable scan.

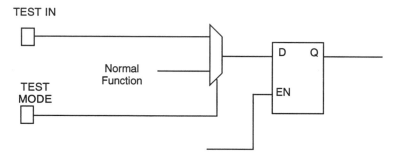

Figure 5-7   Making a latch testable

5.5.4   Avoid Combinational Feedback

Guideline – Avoid combinational feedback; that is, the looping of combinational processes. See Figure 5-8.

BAD: Combinational processes are looped

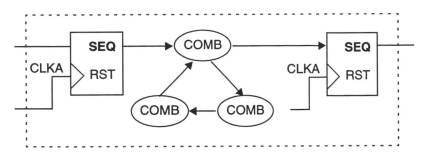

GOOD: Combinational processes are not looped

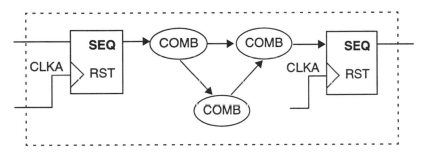

Figure 5-8   Avoiding combinational feedback

5.5.5   Specify Complete Sensitivity Lists

Rule – Include a complete sensitivity list in each of your process (VHDL) or always (Verilog) blocks.

If you do not use a complete sensitivity list, the behavior of the pre-synthesis design may differ from that of the post-synthesis netlist, as illustrated in Figure 5-9.

Design Compiler, as well as InterHDL's Verilint and VHDLlint, detect incomplete sensitivity lists and issue a warning when you elaborate the design.

VHDL

```
process (a)
begin
  c <= a or b;
end process
```

Verilog

```
always @ (a)
  c <= a or b;
```

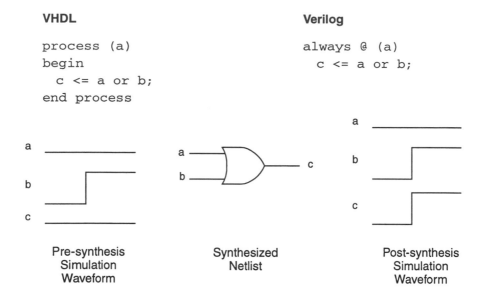

| Pre-synthesis Simulation Waveform | Synthesized Netlist | Post-synthesis Simulation Waveform |

Figure 5-9   Bad example: Simulation mismatch because of incomplete sensitivity list

Combinational Blocks

For combinational blocks (blocks that contain no registers or latches), the sensitivity list must include every signal that is read by the process. In general, this means every signal that appears on the right side of an assign (<=) statement or in a conditional expression. See Example 5-27.

Example 5-27   Good coding style: Sensitivity list for combinational process block

VHDL:

```
COMBINATIONAL_PROC : process (a, inc_dec)
begin
  if inc_dec = '0' then
    sum <= a + 1;
  else
    sum <= a - 1;
  end if;
end process COMBINATIONAL_PROC;
```

Verilog:

```
always @(a or inc_dec)
begin : COMBINATIONAL_PROC
  if (inc_dec == 0)
    sum = a + 1;
  else
    sum = a - 1;
end  // COMBINATIONAL_PROC
```

Sequential Blocks

For sequential blocks, the sensitivity list must include the clock signal that is read by the process, as shown in Example 5-28. If the sequential process block also uses a reset signal, include the reset signal in the sensitivity list.

Example 5-28   Good coding style: Sensitivity list in a sequential process block

VHDL:

```
SEQUENTIAL_PROC : process (clk)
begin
  if (clk'event and clk = '1') then
    q <= d;
  end if;
end process SEQUENTIAL_PROC;
```

Verilog;

```
always @(posedge clk)
begin : SEQUENTIAL_PROC
  q <= d;
end  // SEQUENTIAL_PROC
```

Sensitivity List and Simulation Performance

Guideline – Make sure your process sensitivity lists contain only necessary signals, as defined in the sections above. Adding unnecessary signals to the sensitivity list slows down simulation.

5.5.6   Blocking and Nonblocking Assignments (Verilog)

In Verilog, there are two types of assignment statements: blocking and nonblocking. Blocking assignments execute in sequential order, nonblocking assignments execute concurrently.

Rule (Verilog only) – When writing synthesizable code, always use nonblocking assignments in `always @ (posedge clk)` blocks. Otherwise, the simulation behavior of the RTL and gate-level designs may differ.

Example 5-29 shows a Verilog code fragment that uses a blocking assignment where *b* is assigned the value of *a*, then *a* is assigned the value of *b*. The result is the circuit shown in Figure 5-10, where Register A just loops around and reassigns itself every clock tick. Register B is the same result one time unit later.

Example 5-29   Poor coding style: Verilog blocking assignment

```
always @ (posedge clk)
begin
  b = a;
  a = b;
end
```

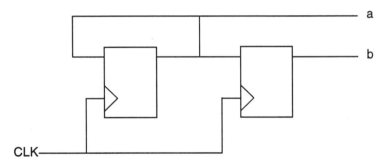

Figure 5-10   Bad example: Circuit built from blocking assignment

Example 5-30 shows a Verilog code fragment that uses a nonblocking assignment. *b* is assigned the value of *a* and *a* is assigned the value of *b* at every clock tick. The result is the circuit shown in Figure 5-11.

Example 5-30   Recommended coding style: Verilog nonblocking assignment

```
always @ (posedge clk)
begin
  b <= a;
  a <= ~b;
end
```

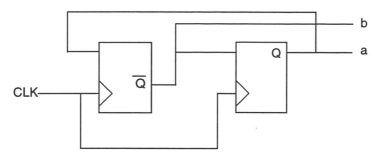

Figure 5-11   Circuit built from nonblocking assignment

5.5.7   Signal vs. Variable Assignments (VHDL)

In VHDL simulation, signal assignments are scheduled for execution in the next simulation cycle. Variable assignments take effect immediately, and they take place in the
order in which they appear in the code. Thus, they present some of the same problems
as blocking assignments in Verilog. VHDL variables are not as problematic as Verilog
blocking assignments because the interfaces between modules in VHDL are required
to be signals, so these interfaces are well-behaved. The order dependencies of variables are thus strictly local, so it is reasonable easy to develop correct code.

Guideline (VHDL only) – When writing synthesizable code, we suggest you use
signals instead of variables to ensure that the simulation behavior of the pre-synthesis
design matches that of the post-synthesis netlist. If you feel that simulation speed will
be significantly improved by using variables, then it is certainly appropriate to do so.
Just exercise caution in creating order-dependent behavior in the code.

Example 5-31   VHDL variable assignment in synthesizable code

Poor coding style:

```
EX31_PROC: process (a,b)
variable c : std_logic;
begin
   c := a and b;
end process EX31_PROC;
```

Recommended coding style:

```
signal c : std_logic;
EX31_PROC:process (a,b)
begin
   c <= a and b;
end process EX31_PROC;
```

5.5.8   Case Statements versus if-then-else Statements

In VHDL and Verilog, a case statement infers a single-level multiplexer, while an if-then-else statement infers a priority-encoded, cascaded combination of multiplexers.

Figure 5-12 shows the circuit built from the VHDL if-then-else statement in Example 5-32.

Figure 5-13 shows the circuit built from the VHDL case statement in Example 5-33.

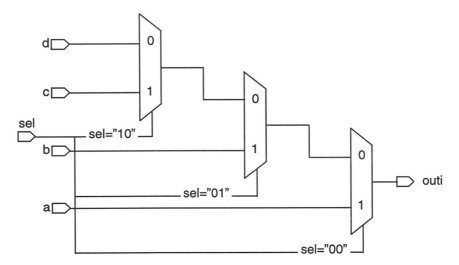

Figure 5-12   Circuit built from if-then-else statement

Example 5-32   Using a VHDL if-then-else statement

```
EX32_PROC: process (sel,a,b,c,d)
begin
  if (sel = "00") then
    outi <= a;
  elsif (sel = "01") then
    outi <= b;
  elsif (sel = "10") then
    outi <= c;
  else
    outi <= d;
  end if;
end process EX32_PROC;
```

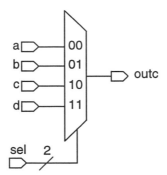

Figure 5-13   Circuit built from the case statement

Example 5-33   Using a VHDL case statement

```
EX33_PROC:process (sel,a,b,c,d)
begin
  case sel is
    when "00" => outc <= a;
    when "01" => outc <= b;
    when "10" => outc <= c;
    when others => outc <= d;
  end case;
end process EX33_PROC;
```

Guideline – The multiplexer is a faster circuit. Therefore, if the priority-encoding structure is not required, we recommend using the case statement rather than an if-then-else statement. Note that an if-then-else statement can be useful if you have a late arriving signal; this signal can then be connect to the "a" input in Figure 5-13 for the fastest path through the selection function.

In a cycle-based simulator, the case statement also simulates faster than the if-then-else statement.

A conditional signal assignment may also be used to infer a multiplexer. For large multiplexers, a case statement will simulate faster than a conditional assignment on most simulators, and especially on cycle-based simulators. For small muxes, the relative speed of the two constructs varies with different simulators.

Example 5-34 illustrates how to use a conditional assignment to infer a mux.

Example 5-34   Using a conditional assignment to infer a mux

VHDL:

```
z1 <= a when sel_a = '1' else
      b when sel_b = '1' else
      c;

z2 <= d when sel_a = '1' else
      e when sel_b = '1' else
      f;
```

Verilog:

```
assign z1 = (sel_a) ? a : (sel_b) ? b : c;

assign z2 = (sel_a) ? d : (sel_b) ? e : f;
```

5.5.9   Coding State Machines

Observe the following guidelines when coding state machines:

Guideline – Separate the state machine HDL description into two processes, one for the combinational logic and one for the sequential logic.

Guideline – In VHDL, create an enumerated type for the state vector. In Verilog, use `define` statements to define the state vector.

Guideline – Keep FSM logic and non-FSM logic in separate modules. See "Partitioning for Synthesis" later in this chapter for details.

Guideline – Assign a default state for the state machine. This is useful to implement graceful entry into the idle state if no other state is initiated. For VHDL, assign a state for the `others` condition, as shown in Example 5-35. For Verilog, assign a `default` state, as shown in Example 5-36.

For more information about coding state machines, read the Optimizing Finite State Machines chapter of the *Design Compiler Reference Manual*.

Example 5-35   VHDL FSM coding example

```
library IEEE, STD;
use IEEE.std_logic_1164.all;
use IEEE.std_logic_components.all;
use IEEE.std_logic_misc.all;
entity fsm is
```

```vhdl
  port (
    x     : in  std_logic;
    rst   : in  std_logic;
    clock : in  std_logic;
    z     : out std_logic);
end fsm;

architecture rtl of fsm is
type state is (STATE_0, STATE_1, STATE_2, STATE_3);
signal current_state, next_state : state;
begin

-- combinational process calculates next state

  COMBO_PROC : process(x, current_state)
  begin
    case (current_state) is
    when STATE_0 =>
      z <= '0';
      if x = '0' then
        next_state <= STATE_0;
      else
        next_state <= STATE_1;
      end if;
    when STATE_1 =>
      z <= '0';
      if x = '0' then
        next_state <= STATE_1;
      else
        next_state <= STATE_2;
      end if;
    when STATE_2 =>
      z <= '0';
      if x = '0' then
        next_state <= STATE_2;
      else
        next_state <= STATE_3;
      end if;
    when STATE_3 =>
      if x = '0' then
        z <= '0';
```

```
        next_state <= STATE_3;
      else
        z <= '1';
        next_state <= STATE_0;
      end if;
  when others =>
      next_state <= STATE_0;
    end case;
  end process COMBO_PROC;

-- synchronous process updates current state

  SYNCH_PROC : process(rst,clock)
  begin
    if (rst ='1') then
      current_state <= STATE_0;
    elsif (clock'event and clock ='1') then
      current_state <= next_state;
    end if;
  end process SYNCH_PROC;
end rtl;
```

Example 5-36   Verilog FSM coding example

```
module fsm(clock, rst, x, z);
input clock, rst, x;
output z;
reg [1:0] current_state;
reg [1:0] next_state;
reg z;
parameter [1:0]
  STATE_0 = 0,
  STATE_1 = 1,
  STATE_2 = 2,
  STATE_3 = 3;

// combinational process calculates next state

always @ (current_state or x)
case(current_state) //synopsys parallel_case full_case
  STATE_0 : begin
    if (x) begin
```

```
          next_state <= STATE_1;
          z <= 1'b0;
        end else begin
          next_state <= STATE_0;
          z <= 1'b0;
        end
    end
  STATE_1 : begin
    if (x)
      begin
      next_state <= STATE_2;
      z <= 1'b0;
      end
    else
      begin
      next_state <= STATE_1;
      z <= 1'b0;
      end
  end
  STATE_2 : begin
    if (x)
      begin
      next_state <= STATE_3;
      z <= 1'b0;
      end
    else
      begin
      next_state <= STATE_2;
      z <= 1'b0;
      end
  end
  STATE_3 : begin
    if (x)
      begin
      next_state <= STATE_0;
      z <= 1'b1;
      end
    else
        begin
        next_state <= STATE_3;
        z <= 1'b0;
```

```
            end
        end
        default  :  begin
            next_state <= STATE_0;
            z <= 1'b0;
            end
      endcase
   always @ ( posedge clock or negedge rst_na)
      begin
      if (!rst_na)
        current_state <= STATE_0;
      else
        current_state <= next_state;
      end
   endmodule
```

5.6   Partitioning for Synthesis

Good synthesis partitioning in your design provides several advantages including:

• Better synthesis results
• Faster compile runtimes
• Ability to use simpler synthesis strategies to meet timing

The following sections illustrate several recommended synthesis partitioning techniques.

5.6.1   Register All Outputs

Guideline – For each block of a hierarchical design, register all output signals from the block.

Registering the output signals from each block simplifies the synthesis process because it makes output drive strengths and input delays predictable. All the inputs of each block arrive with the same relative delay. Output drive strength is equal to the drive strength of the average flip-flop.

Figure 5-14 shows a hierarchical design in which all output signals from each block are registered; that is, there is no combinational logic between the registers and the output ports.

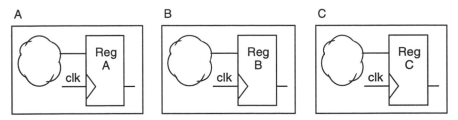

Figure 5-14   Good example: All output signals are registered

5.6.2   Locate Related Combinational Logic in a Single Module

Guideline – Keep related combinational logic together in the same module.

Design Compiler has more flexibility in optimizing a design when related combinational logic is located in the same module. This is because Design Compiler cannot move logic across hierarchical boundaries during default compile operations.

Figure 5-15 shows an example design where the path from register A to register C is split across three modules. Such a design inhibits Design Compiler from efficiently optimizing the combinational logic because it must preserve the hierarchical boundaries in the design.

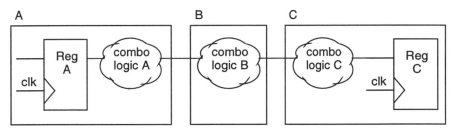

Figure 5-15   Bad example: Combinational logic split between modules

Figure 5-16 shows a similar design in which the related combinational logic is grouped into a single hierarchical block. This design allows Design Compiler to perform combinational logic optimization on the path from register A to register C.

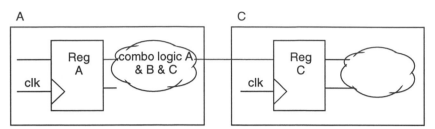

Figure 5-16   Better example: Combinational logic grouped into same module

Figure 5-17 shows an even better design where the combinational logic is grouped into the same module as the destination register. This design provides for improved sequential mapping during optimization because no hierarchical boundaries exist between the sequential logic and the combinational logic that drives it.

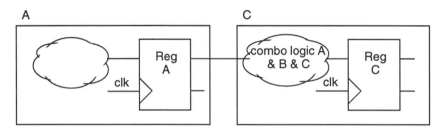

Figure 5-17   Best example: Combinational logic grouped with destination register

Keeping related combinational logic in the same module also eases time budgeting and allows for faster simulation.

5.6.3   Separate Modules That Have Different Design Goals

Guideline – Keep critical path logic in a separate module from noncritical path logic so that Design Compiler can optimize the critical path logic for speed, while optimizing the noncritical path logic for area.

Figure 5-18 shows a design where critical path logic and noncritical path logic reside in the same module. Optimization is limited because Design Compiler cannot perform different optimization techniques on the two groups of logic.

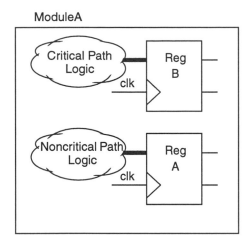

ModuleA

Figure 5-18   Bad example: Critical path logic grouped with noncritical path logic

Figure 5-19 shows a similar design where the critical path logic is grouped into a separate module from the noncritical path logic. In this design, Design Compiler can perform speed optimization on the critical path logic, while performing area optimization on the noncritical path logic.

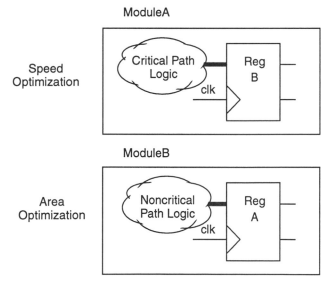

Figure 5-19   Good example: Critical path logic and noncritical path logic
grouped separately

5.6.4   Asynchronous Logic

Guideline – Avoid asynchronous logic.

Asynchronous logic is more difficult to design correctly and to verify. Correct timing and functionality may be technology dependent, which limits the portability of the design.

Guideline – If asynchronous logic is required in the design, partition the asynchronous logic in a separate module from the synchronous logic.

Isolating the asynchronous logic in a separate module makes code inspection much easier. Asynchronous logic need to be reviewed carefully to verify its functionality and timing.

5.6.5   Arithmetic Operators: Merging Resources

A resource is an operator that can be inferred directly from an HDL, as shown in the following code fragment:

```
if ctl = '1' then
  z <= a + b;
else
  z <= c + d;
end if;
```

Normally, two adders are created in this example. If only an area constraint exists, however, Design Compiler is likely to synthesize a single adder and to share it between the two additions. If performance is a consideration, the adders may or may not be merged.

For Design Compiler to consider resource sharing, all relevant resources need to be in the same level of hierarchy; that is, within the same module.

Figure 5-20 is an example of poor partitioning. In this example, resources that can be shared are separated by hierarchical boundaries.

Figure 5-21 is an example of good partitioning because the two adders are in the same module. This partitioning allows Design Compiler full flexibility when choosing whether or not to share the adders.

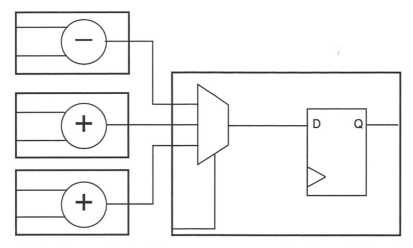

Figure 5-20 Poor partitioning: Resources area separated by hierarchical boundaries.

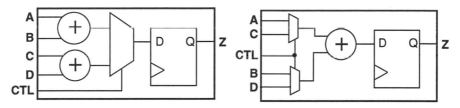

Figure 5-21 Good partitioning: Adders are in the same hierarchy

5.6.6 Partitioning for Synthesis Runtime

In the past, most synthesis guidelines have recommended keeping modules relatively small in order to reduce synthesis runtime. Improvements to Design Compiler, increases in workstation performance, and more experience with large designs has changed this.

The most important considerations in partitioning should be the logic function, design goals, and timing and area requirements. Grouping related functions together is much better than splitting functions artificially, and creating complex inter-block timing dependencies. Good timing budgets and appropriate constraints can have a larger impact on synthesis runtime than circuit size. In one test case, synthesis went from nine hours to 72 hours when the critical range was increased from 0.1 ns to 10 ns.

By grouping logic by design goals, the synthesis strategy can be focused, reducing synthesis runtime. For example, if the goal for a particular block is to minimize area, and timing is not critical, then the synthesis scripts can be focused on area only, greatly reducing runtime.

Overconstraining a design is one of the biggest causes of excessive runtime. A key technique for reducing runtimes is to develop accurate timing budgets early in the design phase and design the macro to meet these budgets. Then, develop the appropriate constraints to synthesize to this budget. Finally, by developing a good understanding of the Design Compiler commands that implement these constraints, you can achieve an optimal combination of high quality of results and low runtime.

For more information on synthesizing large designs, including the test case mentioned above, see "Synthesis Methodology for Large Designs – Design Compiler 1997.01 Release" from Synopsys.

5.6.7   Avoid Point-to-Point Exceptions and False Paths

A point-to-point exception is a path from the output of one register to the input of another that does not follow the standard objective of having the data traverse the path in one clock cycle. A multicycle path is the prime example of a point-to-point exception.

Multicycle paths are problematic because they are more difficult to analyze correctly and lend themselves to human error. They must be marked as exceptions to the static timing analysis tool; it is all too easy to mark a path as an exception by mistake and not perform timing analysis. Most static timing analyzers work much better on standard paths than on exceptions.

Guideline – Avoid multicycle paths in your design.

Guideline – If you must use a multicycle path in your design, keep point-to-point exceptions within a single module, and comment them well in your RTL code.

Isolating point-to-point exceptions (for example, multicycle paths) within a module improves compile runtime and synthesis results. Also, the `characterize` command has limited support for point-to-point exceptions that cross hierarchical boundaries.

Figure 5-22 shows a good partitioning example where the start and end points of a multicycle path occur within a single module.

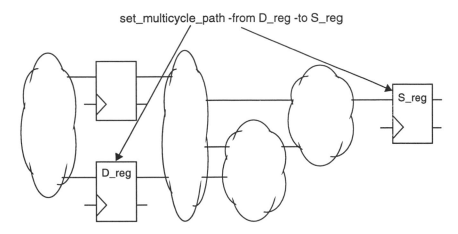

set_multicycle_path -from D_reg -to S_reg

Figure 5-22   Good example: Isolating a point-to-point exception to a single module

Guideline – Avoid false paths in your design.

False paths are paths that static timing analysis identifies as failing timing, but that the designer knows are not actually failing.

False paths are a problem because they require the designer to ignore a warning message from the timing analysis tool. If there are many false paths in a design, it is easy for the designer to accidently ignore valid warning message about actual failing paths.

5.6.8   Eliminate Glue Logic at the Top Level

Guideline – Do not instantiate gate-level logic at the top level of the design hierarchy.

A design hierarchy should contain gates only at leaf levels of the hierarchy tree. For example, Figure 5-23 shows a design where a NAND gate exists at the top level, between two lower-level design blocks. Optimization is limited because Design Compiler cannot merge the NAND with the combinational logic inside block C.

Top

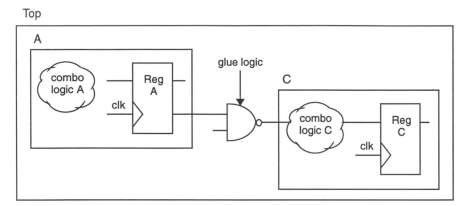

Figure 5-23   Bad example: Glue logic existing at top level

Figure 5-24 shows a similar design where the NAND gate is included as part of the combinational logic in block C. This approach eliminates the extra CPU cycles needed to compile small amount of glue logic and provides for simpler synthesis script development. An automated script mechanism only needs to compile and characterize the leaf-level cells.

Top

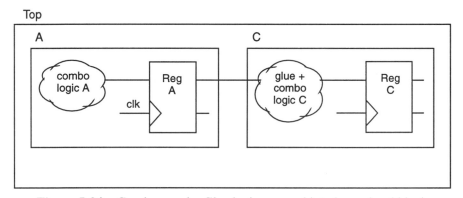

Figure 5-24   Good example: Glue logic grouped into lower-level block

5.6.9   Chip-Level Partitioning

Figure 5-25 shows the partitioning recommendation for the top level of an ASIC.

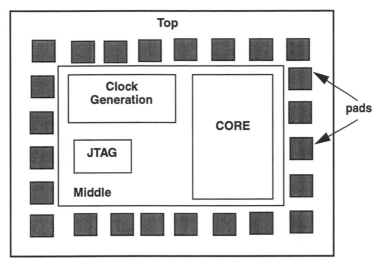

Figure 5-25 Top-level partitioning for an ASIC

Guideline – Make sure that only the top level of the design contains an I/O pad ring. Within the top level of hierarchy, a middle level of hierarchy contains IEEE 1149.1 boundary scan (JTAG) modules, clock generation circuitry, and the core logic. The clock generation circuitry is isolated from the rest of the design as it is normally hand crafted and carefully simulated. This hierarchy arrangement is not a requirement, but allows easy integration and management of the test logic, the pads, and the functional core.

5.7 Designing with Memories

Memories present special problems for reusable design, since memory design tends to be foundry specific. Macros must be designed to deal with a variety of memory interfaces. This section outlines some guidelines for dealing with these issues, in particular, designing with synchronous and asynchronous memories.

Synchronous memories present the ideal case, and their interfaces are in the general form shown in Figure 5-26. Figure 5-27 shows the equivalent asynchronous RAM design.

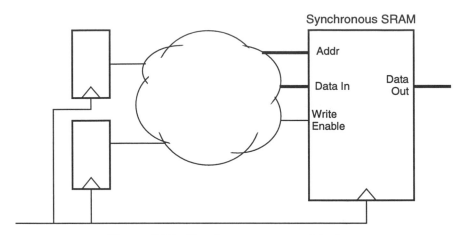

Figure 5-26   Synchronous memory interface

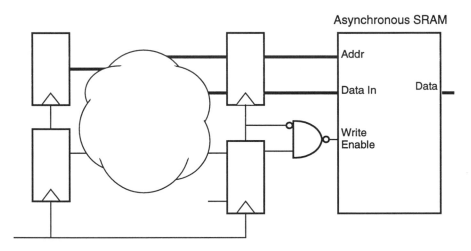

Figure 5-27   Asynchronous memory interface

Guideline – Partition the address and data registers and the write enable logic in a separate module. This allows the memory control logic to work with both asynchronous and synchronous memories. See Figure 5-28.

In the design shown in Figure 5-28, the interface module is required only for asynchronous memories. The functionality in the interface module is integrated into the synchronous RAM.

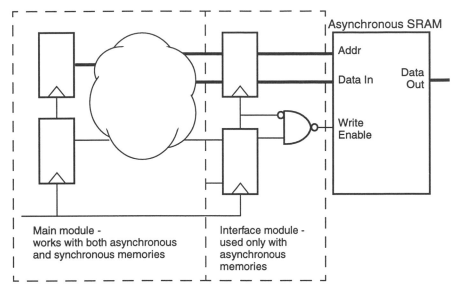

Figure 5-28 Partitioning memory control logic separately

5.8 Code Profiling

In some cases, *code profiling* can assist you in optimizing your code. Some simulators, and several third-party code coverage tools, provide the capability of tracking how often each line of code is executed during a given simulation run.

Profiling is a valuable tool that can reveal bottleneck areas in the model. However, you must keep in mind that the profiler looks only at the frequency with which a line is executed, not at how expensive that construct is in terms of machine cycles. For example, performing a variable assignment statement differs a great deal from performing a signal assignment.

Code coverage tools that measure path coverage as well as statement coverage can be very useful for analyzing how well a given test vector set exercises the model and for checking redundancies in the model itself. For example, if some parts of the model receive no execution coverage at all, either the vectors are failing to exercise the model fully or that portion of the model is redundant. See Chapter 7 for more discussion of code coverage tools.

| CHAPTER 6 | *Macro Synthesis Guidelines* |

This chapter discusses strategies for developing macro synthesis scripts that enable the integrator to synthesize the macro and meet timing goals. The topics include:

- Overview of the synthesis problem
- Synthesis strategies for reusable macros
- High-performance synthesis
- RAM and datapath generators
- Coding guidelines for synthesis scripts

6.1 Overview of the Synthesis Problem

There are some special problems associated with the synthesis of parameterizable soft macros:

- The macro and synthesis scripts must allow the integrator to synthesize the macro and meet timing goals in the final chip.
- The macro must meet timing with the integrator's gate array or standard cell library.
- The macro must meet timing in the integrator's specific configuration of the macro.

This chapter presents a set of tools and methodologies for achieving these goals.

The synthesis guidelines in this chapter are based on many of the same fundamental principles guiding the previous chapter. First and foremost, synthesis and timing design must start at the beginning of the macro design cycle.

That is:

- Functional specifications for the macro must describe the timing, area, wire load model, and power requirements for the design.
- Detailed technical specifications for the macro and its various subblocks must describe the timing requirements and interfaces in detail, including specifications for input and output delays.
- RTL needs to be coded from the outset to meet both the functional and the timing requirements of the design. Coding for functionality first, and then fixing timing problems later, causes significant delays and poor overall performance in many designs.

If these fundamental guidelines are followed, then synthesis is a straightforward issue. Each synthesizable unit or module in the design has a timing budget. Once each module meets this timing budget, the macro is ensured of meeting its overall timing goals. Synthesis problems become localized, so the difficult problems can be solved on small modules, where they are the most tractable.

6.2 Macro Synthesis Strategy

The recommended synthesis strategy for macros is to develop a set of constraints for the macro early in the design process and to use a bottom-up synthesis strategy.

6.2.1 Macro Timing Budget

Rule – The basic timing budget for the macro must be developed as part of the specification process, before the design is partitioned into blocks and before coding begins. This timing budget must be reviewed regularly during the design process to ensure that it is still reasonable and consistent.

The macro timing budget must specify:
- Clock definition
- Setup time requirements for all signals going into the macro
- Clock to output delay requirements for all synchronous outputs of the macro
- Input and output delays for all combinational paths through the macro
- Loading budget for outputs and driving cell for inputs

- Operating conditions, including temperature and voltage

Note that combinational paths through the macro are discouraged, because they create non-local synthesis problems that can be very difficult to resolve. The combinational paths must be carefully documented and their timing budgets closely examined to make sure the design constraints can be met. The preferred method for specifying these combinational delays is to specify the input arrival times and the required output time with respect to the clock, assuming the clock is present in the block

6.2.2 Subblock Timing Budget

Rule – The basic timing budget must be developed for each subblock in the macro. This budget must be developed at the time that the design is partitioned into sub-blocks, and before coding begins. The budget must be reviewed regularly during the design process to ensure that it is still reasonable and consistent.

The subblock timing budget must specify:

- Clock definition
- Wire load model
- Setup time requirements for all signals going into the subblock
- Clock to output delay requirements for all synchronous outputs of the subblock
- Input and output delays for all combinational paths through the subblock
- Loading budget for outputs and driving cell for inputs
- Operating conditions, including temperature and voltage

A good nominal starting point for the loading and driving specifications is to use a two-input NAND gate as the driving cell and a flip-flop data input pin as the output load.

Combinational paths through subblocks are discouraged, just as they are at the macro level. In our experience, most synthesis problems arise from these combinational paths.

6.2.3 Synthesis in the Design Process

Synthesis starts as the individual designers are developing the subblocks of the macro, and is initially performed with a single technology library. Later, during the producti-zation phase, the entire macro is synthesized to multiple libraries to ensure portability.

The designer should start running synthesis as soon as the RTL passes the most basic simulation tests. Performing synthesis at this stage allows the designer to identify and fix timing problems early. Because fixing the tough timing problems usually means modifying or restructuring the RTL, it is much better to deal with these problems before the code is completely debugged.

Early synthesis also allows the designer to identify the incremental timing costs of new functionality as it is added to the code.

The target at this early stage of synthesis should be to get to within about 10-20% of the final timing budget. This should be close enough to ensure that the RTL code is structured correctly. The additional effort to achieve the timing budget completely is not worth the effort until the code is passing all functional tests. This additional effort will most likely consist of modifying the synthesis scripts and refining the timing budgets.

The subblocks should meet all timing budgets, as well as meeting all functional verification requirements, before being integrated into the macro.

6.2.4   Subblock Synthesis Process

Guideline – The subblock synthesis process consists of three phases:

1. Perform a compile on the subblock, using constraints based on the budget.
2. Perform a characterize-compile on the whole subblock, to refine the timing constraints and re-synthesize the subblock.
3. Iterate if required.

The characterize-compile strategy in step 2 is documented in the *Design Compiler Reference Manual.*

6.2.5   Macro Synthesis Process

When the subblocks are ready for integration, we are ready to perform macro-level synthesis.

Guideline – The macro synthesis process consists of three phases:

1. Perform a compile on each of the subblocks, using constraints based on the budget.
2. Perform a characterize-compile on the whole macro to improve timing and area.
3. If necessary to meet the timing goals, perform an incremental compile.

The characterize-compile in step 2 is needed to develop accurate estimates of the loading effects on the inputs and outputs of each subblock. Initially, the drive strength of the cells driving inputs, and the loading effects of cells driven by the outputs, are estimated and set manually. The set_driving_cell and set_load commands are used for this purpose. The characterize-compile step derives actual drive strengths and loading from the rest of the macro. Clearly, this requires an initial synthesis of the entire macro in order to know what cells are driving/loading any specific subblock input/output.

6.2.6 Wire Load Models

Wire load models estimate the loading effect of metal interconnect upon cell delays. For deep submicron designs, this effect dominates delays, so using accurate wire load models is critical.

The details of how a given technology library does wire load prediction varies from library to library, but the basic principles are the same. A statistical wire length is determined based on the physical size of the block. From this statistical wire length and the total input capacitance of the nodes on the net, the synthesis tool can determine the total load on the driving cell.

The most critical factor in getting an accurate statistical wire length is to estimate accurately the size of the block that will be placed and routed as a unit. Typically, a macro will be placed and routed as a single unit, and the individual subblocks that make up the macro will be flattened within the macro. Thus, the appropriate wire load model is determined by the gate count (and thus area) of the entire macro at the top level.

When we synthesize a subblock, we must use the wire load model for the full macro, not just the subblock. If we use just the gate count of the subblock to determine the wire load model, we will get an optimistic model that underestimates wire delays. When we then integrate the subblocks into the macro and use the correct wire load model, we can run into significant timing problems.

6.2.7 Preserve Clock and Reset Networks

Clock networks are typically not synthesized; we rely on the place and route tools to insert a balanced clock tree with very low skew. Asynchronous reset networks are also typically treated as special networks, with the place and route tools inserting the appropriate buffers. These non-synthesized networks need to be identified to the synthesis tool.

Guideline – Set dont_touch_network on clock and asynchronous reset networks. Include the required dont_touch_network commands in the synthesis scripts for the design. See Example 6-1.

Example 6-1   Using `dont_touch_network` on clocks and reset networks

```
dont_touch_network {clk rst}
```

6.2.8   Code Checking Before Synthesis

Several checks should be run before synthesis. These checks can spot potential synthesis problems without having to perform a complete compile.

Lint Tools

Lint-like tools (InterHDL's Verilint and VHDLlint, for example) can quickly check for many different potential problems, including:

- Presence of latches
- Non-synthesizable constructs like "===" or `initial`
- Whether a `case` statement was inferred as a mux or a priority encoder
- Whether all bits in a bus were assigned
- Unused macros, parameters, or variables

dc_shell

Once the RTL passes lint, the elaboration reports from Design Compiler should be examined to check:

- Whether sequential statements were inferred as flip-flops or latches
- Whether synchronous or asynchronous reset was inferred

A clean elaboration of the design is a critical first step in performing synthesis.

6.2.9   Code Checking After Synthesis

After synthesis, a number of Design Compiler checks can be run to identify potential problems:

Loop Checking
Run `report_timing  -loops` to determine whether there are any combinational loops.

Checking for Latches
Run `all_registers  -level_sensitive` to get a report on latches in the design.

Check for Design Rule Violations

Run check_design to check for missing cells, unconnected ports, and inputs tied high or low.

Verify Testability

Run check_test to verify that there are scan versions of all flops, and to check for any untestable structures. Soft macros are typically not shipped with scan flops inserted because scan is usually done on a chip-wide basis rather than block-by-block. Thus, it is essential to verify that scan insertion and automatic test pattern generation (ATPG) will be successful.

As part of the productization phase of the macro development process, full ATPG is run.

Verify Synthesis Results

Use Formality to verify that the RTL and the post-synthesis netlist are functionally equivalent.

6.3 High-Performance Synthesis

As chip size and complexity increase, it becomes more critical to have some interactivity between the synthesis and layout phases of chip design. Currently, some alternatives to the standard sequence are becoming available.

6.3.1 Classical Synthesis

In standard ASIC design, the synthesis phase has no automated interaction with the subsequent layout phase. Synthesis must generate the netlists without any feedback from floorplanning and place-and-route tools, and there is no opportunity to modify synthesis based on findings during layout. Hand iteration between synthesis and placement is slow and painful. If resynthesis is necessary, layout generally has to be redone from scratch. While this lack of interactivity between the synthesis and layout stages is manageable for smaller chip sizes, it is problematic and distinctly not optimal for today's large SoC designs.

The problems produced by this lack of interactivity between synthesis and layout are exacerbated because, as transistors and cells become faster, cell delays decrease and the percentage of delay due to loading factors increases. Information about physical placement becomes more important for synthesis.

6.3.2   High-Performance Synthesis

New tools, such as Synopsys' Links-to-Layout and Floorplan Manager, provide inter-activity between the synthesis and placement phases of design. Such tools allow *high-performance synthesis* by forward-annotating constraints such as timing and net priorities to a floorplanner or place and route tool, and back-annotating physical information such as net delays, net capacitance, and physical grouping to the synthesis tool. This interactivity greatly improves the speed and accuracy of synthesis and layout by speeding the iterations, and because synthesis and layout are both performed with actual values rather than estimates.

6.3.3   Tiling

In some cases, the designer knows that certain elements will fit together — "tile" — into a compact pattern that can then be repeated. Floorplanning and place and route tools are not likely to detect the possibility of such compact configurations. Historically, the designer has had to lay out such areas by hand, and then provide the floorplanner with a "black box" macro for these areas. Such hand crafting produces highly compact layout, but is costly in terms of time spent. Tools for automating this hand-crafted tiling process are becoming available.

6.4   RAM and Datapath Generators

Memories and datapaths present a special set of problems for design reuse. Historically, memories and high performance datapaths have been designed at the physical level, making them very technology dependent.

6.4.1   Memory Design

There is almost no logical design content to (most) memory design. There are single port vs. multi-port and synchronous vs. asynchronous memories, but what truly differentiates a good memory design from a bad one is the size, power, and speed of the memory. The extreme regularity of memory determines the design methodology. A memory cell is developed, hopefully as small and fast and low power as possible. The memory cell is then replicated in a regular tiling fashion. Unfortunately, the optimal cell design is very dependent on the underlying fabrication process. Thus, each silicon vendor has tended to develop a unique memory compiler tailored to the specific requirements of the target silicon technology.

The result is that memory designs are not portable or reusable. This situation places a significant burden on the developer of reusable designs. In Chapter 5, we described some approaches for dealing with memories in designing reusable macros, and later in this chapter we describe the integration flow for using macros with memory modules in chip-level designs. But first, we discuss datapath design, which, until recently, shared many of the same problems as memory design.

6.4.2 Datapath Design

In those datapaths that are dominated by arithmetic functions, the functionality of the design is usually straightforward. The functionality of a 32-bit multiply-accumulate block, for example, is clear and does not help differentiate a design. In order to have a 32-bit MAC that is superior to a competitor's, it is necessary to exploit hardware structure to achieve a faster, smaller, or lower-power design. Historically, this approach has led to tools and methodologies designed to exploit the structural regularity in the datapath, and thus derive a superior physical layout.

Datapath Design Issues

There are three major problems with traditional approaches to datapath design. First, irregular structures like Wallace tree multipliers can outperform regular structures. Second, the datapath designs produced are not portable to new technologies and do not lend themselves to reuse. Third, great majority of modern applications are poor candidates for the traditional approach, which is best suited to datapaths that are relatively simple (few number of operations) and highly regular (uniform bit-widths).

If we look at the history of datapath design, a typical datapath in 1988 would be a simple, regular datapath, such as a CPU ALU. Regular structures like muxes and adders dominated; bit slicing was used extensively, and was effective in deriving dense, regular layouts. A 32-bit MAC was a separate chip.

In 1998, graphics, video, and digital signal processing applications are the most common datapath designs. Blocks like IDCTs, FIRs, and FFTs are common datapath elements, and a 32-bit MAC is just a small component in the datapath. The significant increase in applications for complex datapaths, along with intense pressures to reduce development time, has resulted in a desire to move datapath design to a higher level of design abstraction as well as to leverage design reuse techniques.

Datapath design tools and methodologies are rapidly evolving to meet this need.

Datapath Design Tool Evolution

In the past, designers predominately designed datapaths by handcrafting the design. They captured structural information about the design in schematics and then developed a physical layout of the design. The physical design was laid out for a single bit-slice of the datapath, then replicated. For regular datapaths dominated by muxes and adders, this approach produced dense, regular physical designs. These handcrafted designs exhibit:

- High performance because the methodology effectively exploited the regular structure of the logic
- Low productivity because of the amount of handcrafting required
- Poor portability because the results were design and technology specific

In the more recent past, designers started using layout-oriented datapath design tools. With these tools, structural descriptions of the design are entered either in schematic form or in HDL, but with severe constraints limiting the subset of the language that can be used. These tools automate much of the handcrafting that was done before, such as developing bit-slice layouts and regular structures. The designs result in:

- High performance for regular structures
- Poor performance for irregular, tree-based structures like Wallace-tree multipliers
- Poor performance for structures with varying bit widths, a common characteristic of graphics designs such as IDCTs, digital filters, or any other design employing techniques like saturation, rounding, or normalization
- Moderate productivity because of the automation of design tasks
- Poor portability because designs were still design and technology specific

A number of datapath designers have used conventional synthesis to improve the technology portability of their designs. Conventional synthesis uses generic operators with structures that are expressed in a generic library; during synthesis, the designed is then mapped onto the specific technology library. Designs using conventional synthesis have:

- Moderate performance for complex datapaths, very good performance on simple ones
- Moderate productivity for complex datapaths, very good productivity on simple ones
- Good portability

Today's most advanced datapath design tools, like Module Compiler, approach the problem of datapath design differently. With these tools, the designer enters the structural description for the design in a flexible HDL. The tool then performs synthesis to generate an optimal netlist for the entire datapath. The designer has the flexibility to manipulate the structural input to guide or control the synthesis. Because the functionality for even relatively complex datapaths is well known, the designer can focus on the implementation structure to differentiate the datapath design solution.

The key realization behind these new tools is that good datapath design starts with a good netlist, not with a bit-slice physical design. Today's datapaths are dominated by tree structures that have little of the regularity of earlier datapaths. For these structures, automatic place and route tools do at least as good a job as hand design, and often better. The key to performance is to develop the best possible detailed structure (the netlist) and then map it onto the available technology (through place and route). And unlike conventional synthesis, these specialized tools use algorithms that are specific for datapath synthesis, producing better netlists in shorter time.

One of the key benefits of these tools is that they are significantly faster than any other design method, often an order of magnitude or more faster than conventional synthesis. One advantage of this speed is that many different implementations for the design can be developed and evaluated. For instance, when designing an IDCT, the designer can experiment with different saturation algorithms, different numbers of multipliers, and different numbers of pipelines. As a result of this exploration, a superior architecture can be developed. This improved architecture can more than compensate for any loss in performance compared to a handcrafted design.

Because they allow superior, technology-independent designs, these tools provide the first opportunity to develop reusable datapath designs without sacrificing performance. This capability is essential for the design of reusable blocks for complex chips in datapath-intensive domains such as video, graphics, and multimedia.

With these tools, designs have:

- High performance – implementation exploration allows superior designs
- High productivity – extremely fast synthesis times allow very rapid development of very complex designs
- High portability – because the source is technology independent and can be parameterized, it is very portable across technologies and from design to design

The next step in the evolution of datapath tools is to extend these specialized synthesis tools to include links to physical design. Although irregular structures tend to dominate most large datapaths today, there are still many designs that have substantial portions that are very regular. Exploiting this regularity could even further improve the performance of datapath circuits. Also, like any synthesis tool, links to physical design can help improve circuit performance and reduce the iterations between logic design and physical design.

6.4.3   Design Flow Using Module Compiler

Module Compiler (MC) is a Synopsys datapath synthesis and optimization tool that provides an alternative method of designing and synthesizing complex arithmetic datapaths. For such datapaths, MC offers better quality of results and much faster compile times than general purpose synthesis tools. The compile times are so much faster (1-2 orders of magnitude) than standard synthesis that it is possible to quickly code and synthesize alternative implementations. Designers can quickly evaluate tradeoffs between timing, power, and area, and converge on optimal designs much faster than by conventional handcrafting or general RTL-based synthesis.

In Module Compiler, you describe the datapath in the Module Compiler Language (MCL), a Verilog-like datapath description language. MC produces:

- A Verilog or VHDL gate-level netlist
- A Verilog or VHDL simulation model
- Area and timing reports
- Placement guidance information for layout

Some of Module Compiler's highlights are:

Interfaces
Module Compiler supports both GUI and a command-line modes.

Inputs
The inputs are a high-level description of the datapath in MCL and some design constraints. MCL has the look and feel of the Verilog hardware description language, but is better suited to the task of describing the synthesis and optimization of datapaths. The design constraints can be entered from the GUI or embedded in the description.

Work flow
MC is designed to support two work flows: the "exploration loop" and the "debugging loop" (Figure 6-1). The two flows are typically interleaved, with one feeding into the other.

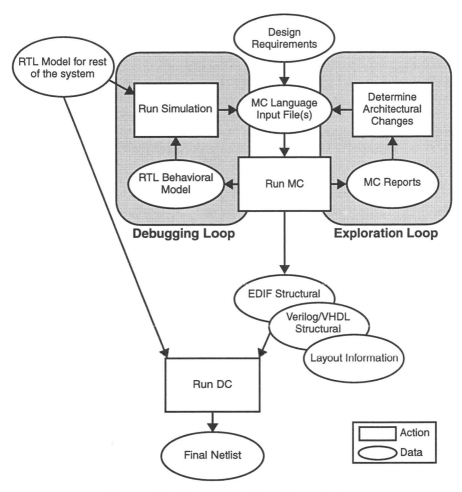

Figure 6-1   The Module Compiler work flow

The typical MC work flow is as follows:

- In the exploration loop, the designer explores the timing and area performance of alternate datapath designs. The designer codes the prospective datapath and uses MC to synthesize the input and generate reports on area, timing, and power. The designer uses these reports to optimize the macro architecture.

- In the debugging loop, MC synthesizes and optimizes the input and generates a Verilog or VHDL behavioral model and netlist. Simulation on these outputs confirms the accuracy of the network description and that latency is acceptable.

- After exploration and debug are completed, the designer uses MC to generate the final datapath netlist.

- If the datapath is part of a larger design, the designer reads both the datapath netlist and the RTL for the rest of the design into the synthesis tool. The datapath netlist can be "dont_touch'ed" so that no additional optimizations are performed on it. This option results in the fastest compile time. On the other hand, the designer can have the synthesis tool re-optimize the netlist. On some designs, some incremental improvement in timing and/or area can be achieved by this approach.

6.4.4   RAM Generator Flow

The typical RAM generator work flow, shown in Figure 6-2, is similar to that of datapath generators such as Module Compiler. With RAM compilers, the designer:

- Describes the memory configuration, through either a GUI or a command-line interface. The designer selects the family of memory, typically trading off power and area versus speed.
- Invokes the memory compiler, which produces a simulation model and a synthesis model for the memory.
- Performs simulation with models for the rest of the system to verify the functionality of the memory interfaces.
- Performs synthesis with the synthesis model for the RAM and the RTL for the rest of the system. The synthesis model for the RAM is key in determining overall chip timing and allowing optimal synthesis of the modules that interface to the RAM.

6.4.5   Design Reuse with Datapath and RAM Compilers

The input to a GUI on a RAM generator is not reusable by itself. However, the generator is a reuse tool. Most of the knowledge required to design the RAM resides in the tool, not the inputs to the tool. It is so easy to create new configurations using the RAM compiler that memory design becomes very straightforward for the chip designer. The difficult aspects of RAM design have all been encapsulated by the tool and are hidden from the user.

Module Compiler provides similar reuse capabilities. By encapsulating the difficult parts of datapath design, such as adder and multiplier tree structures and merging of arithmetic operators, MC reduces the input requirements for describing the datapath to an absolute minimum. The tool itself is the key to datapath reuse.

Unlike RAM compilers, however, the MCL code describing the datapath does have a significant design content. This code can be reused for many designs. One of the strengths of an encapsulating tool like MC is that the datapath description in MCL code is extremely simple and easy to understand. These features, of course, are the fundamental requirements for reusability.

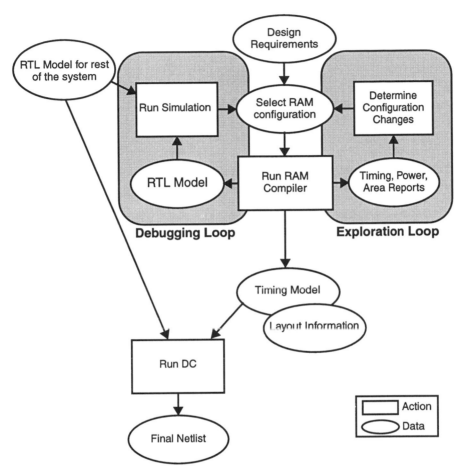

Figure 6-2 RAM generator work flow

RAM compilers and datapath compilers like MC offer a challenge to the design reuse community: Are there other domains where sufficient design expertise can be encapsulated in a tool, so that significant design reuse can be obtained from the tool itself?

6.5   Coding Guidelines for Synthesis Scripts

Many of the coding guidelines described in Chapter 5 apply equally well to all scripts, including synthesis scripts.

The following rules and guidelines apply particularly to synthesis scripts:

Rule – All scripts, including synthesis scripts, should begin with a header describing the file, its purpose, its author, and its revision history.

Rule – Comments should be used extensively to describe the synthesis strategy being executed.

Rule – All scripts used to build the design should be under revision control and a bug tracking system, just as the source code is.

Guideline – Keep the line length to 72 characters or less.

Lines that exceed 80 characters are difficult to read in print and on standard terminal width computer screens. The 72 character limit provides a margin that enhances the readability of the code.

For `dc_shell` commands, use a backslash (\) to continue the statement onto the next line if the command exceeds 72 characters and begin the next line with an indent.

Rule – No hard-coded numbers, data values, or filenames should be buried in the body of the script. Variables should be used in the body of the script and their values set at the top of the script.

Rule – No hard-coded paths should appear in any scripts. Scripts with hard-coded paths are not portable because hard-coded paths prevent the script from being reused in other environments.

Rule – Scripts should be as simple as they can be and still meet their objectives. Synthesis scripts that use only the most common commands are more easily understood and modified.

Rule – Common commands such as those defining the library and search paths should reside in a single setup file for the design, usually in the `.synopsys_dc.setup` file or in a file that can be included in `.synopsys_dc.setup`. All other synthesis scripts should perform only those unique tasks for which they were written. Having libraries or search paths defined in multiple files makes modification difficult.

Rule — Synthesis scripts for parameterized soft macros need to be tested as thoroughly as any source code. In particular, all statements and all paths through the script must be tested. Some scripting bugs appear only when the script is used to compile the macro in a particular configuration; these bugs must be uncovered before shipping the script to a customer.

Guideline — Run the syntax checker on Design Compiler scripts before running the script. The syntax checker can spot many of the scripting errors that can cause DC to halt or produce useless results.

The following example shows how to use the Design Compiler syntax checker:

```
dc_shell -syntax_check -f ./scripts/my_compile.scr
```

CHAPTER 7   *Macro Verification Guidelines*

The goal of macro verification is to ensure that the macro is 100 percent correct in its functionality and timing. In particular, the behavior of the macro must exactly match the functionality and timing described in the functional specification. This chapter discusses issues in simulating and verifying macros, including the importance of reusable testbenches and test suites, and timing verification. The topics are:

- Overview of macro verification
- Testbench design
- Timing verification

7.1   Overview of Macro Verification

Design verification is consistently one of the most difficult and challenging aspects of design. Parameterized, soft macros being designed for reuse present some particular challenges:

- The verification goal must be for zero defects because the macro may be used in anything from a computer game to a mission-critical aerospace application.
- The goal of zero defects must be achieved for all legal configurations of the macro, and for all legal values of its parameters.
- The integration team must be able to reuse the macro-level testbenches and test suites because the macro must be verified both as a standalone design and in the context of the final application.

- Because the macro may be substantially redesigned in the future, the entire set of testbenches and test suites must be reusable by other design teams.
- Because some testbenches may be used in system testing, the testbenches must be compatible with the verification tools used throughout the system testing process.

7.1.1   Verification Plan

Because of the inherent complexity and scope of the functional verification task, it is essential that comprehensive functional verification plans be created, reviewed, and followed by the design team. By defining the verification plan early, the design team can develop the verification environment, including testbenches and verification suites, early in the design cycle. Having a clear definition of the criteria that the macro verification must meet before shipment helps to focus the verification effort and to clarify exactly when the macro is ready to ship.

The specific benefits of developing a verification plan early in the design cycle include:

- The act of creating a functional verification plan forces designers to think through what are typically very time-consuming activities prior to performing them.
- A peer review of the functional verification plan allows a pro-active assessment of the entire scope of the task.
- The team can focus efforts first on those areas in which verification is most needed and will provide the greatest payoff.
- The team can minimize redundant effort.
- The engineers on the team can leverage the cumulative experience and knowledge of the entire team.
- A functional verification plan provides a formal mechanism for correlating project requirements to specific verification tests, which, in turn, allows the completeness (coverage) of the test suite to be assessed.
- Early identification of verification tests allows their development to be tracked and managed more effectively.
- A functional verification plan may serve as documentation of the verification tests and testbench – a critical element for the reuse of these items during regression testing and on subsequent projects. This documentation also reduces the impact of unexpected personnel changes midstream during a project.
- The information contained in the functional verification plan enables a separate verification support team to create a verification environment in parallel with the design capture tasks performed by the primary design team. This can significantly reduce the design cycle time.

The verification environment is the set of testbench components such as bus functional models, bus monitors, memory models, and the structural interconnect of such components with the design-under-test. Creation of such an environment may involve in-house development of some components and/or integration of off-the-shelf models.

The verification plan should be fully described either in the functional specification for the macro or in a separate verification document. This document will be a living document, changing as issues arise and strategies are refined. The plan should include:

- A description of the test strategy, both at the subblock and the top level.
- A detailed description of the simulation environment, including a block diagram.
- A list of testbench components, such as bus functional models and bus monitors. For each component, there should be a summary of key required features. There should also be an indication of whether the component already exists, can be purchased from a third party, or needs to be developed.
- A list of required verification tools, including simulators and testbench creation tools.
- A list of specific tests, along with the objective and estimated size of each. The size estimate can help in estimating the effort required to develop the test.
- An analysis of the key specifications of the macro, and identification of which tests verify each of these specifications.
- A specification of what functionality of the macro will be verified at the subblock level, and what will be verified at the macro level.
- A specification of the target code coverage for each subblock, and for the top-level macro.
- A description of the regression test environment and regression procedure. The regression tests are those verification tests that are routinely run to verify that the design team has not broken existing functionality while adding new functionality.
- A results verification procedure, specifying what criteria will be used to determine when the verification process has been successfully completed.

7.1.2 Verification Strategy

The verification of a macro consists of three major phases:

- Verification of individual subblocks
- Macro verification
- Prototyping

The overall verification strategy is to achieve a very high level of test coverage at the subblock level, and then to focus the macro-level verification at the interfaces between blocks, overall macro functionality, and corner cases of behavior. This bottom-up verification approach is based on the concept of locality; it is much easier to detect and fix bugs on small modules than on large modules.

This approach is different from the traditional approach ASIC designers have tended to use. These designers have typically designed a module for an ASIC, verified the most basic functionality at the module level, and then integrated it into the overall chip for full verification. The advantage of this approach is that the other blocks form a testbench for the module, and since we need a full verification suite for the chip anyway, why not do all the real verification at the chip level. Testing at the block level seems a great deal of redundant effort.

When designing a reusable macro, ASIC designers are tempted to take the same approach: do perfunctory testing at the subblock level, and do most of the verification at the macro level. The problem with this approach is that:

- Observability and controllability of internal nodes becomes harder with the size of the circuit. Achieving 100 percent coverage is much easier with smaller blocks.
- Debugging at the macro level can be much more difficult and time consuming than debugging at the subblock level.

On the other hand, a pure bottom-up approach to verification, like any waterfall model for development, never really works. In real projects, a spiral approach involving iteration, works best. The team does very thorough subblock testing, getting as close to 100 percent coverage as possible. They then integrate the subblock into the macro and do macro verification. Inevitably the team finds additional bugs, usually involving interfaces or interactions between blocks. They then go back and modify the subblock design, do some more subblock verification, and then go back to macro-level testing.

Realistically, this approach gains high but not 100 percent confidence in the macro's functional correctness. Building a rapid prototype of the macro allows the team to run significant amounts of real application code on the macro, greatly increasing confidence in the robustness of the design.

At each phase of the verification process, the team needs to decide what kinds of tests to run, and what verification tools to use to run them.

The basic types of verification tests include:

Compliance testing

These tests verify that the design complies with the specification. For an industry standard design, like a PCI interface or an IEEE 1394 interface, these tests also verify compliance to the published specification. In all cases, compliance to the functional specification for the design is checked as fully as possible.

Corner case testing

These tests try to find the complex scenarios, or corner cases, that are most likely to break the design. They focus on the aspects of the design that are most complex, involve the most interaction between blocks, or are the least clearly specified.

Random testing

For many designs, such as processors or complex bus interfaces, random tests can be a useful complement to compliance and corner case testing. Focused tests like the compliance and corner case tests are limited to the scenarios that the engineers anticipate. Random tests can create scenarios that the engineers do not anticipate, and often uncover the most obscure bugs in a design.

Real code testing

One of the most important parts of verifying any design is running the design in a real application, with real code. It is always possible for the hardware design team to misunderstand a specification, and design and test their code to an erroneous specification. Running the real application code is a useful way to uncover these errors.

Regression testing

As tests are developed, they should be added to the regression test suite. This regression test suite can then be run on a regular basis during the verification phase of the project. One of the typical problems in verification is that, in the process of fixing a bug, another bug can be inadvertently introduced. The regression test suite can help verify that the existing baseline of functionality is maintained as new features are added and bugs are fixed. It is particularly important that, whenever a bug is detected, the test case for the bug is added to the regression suite.

The verification tools available to the macro design team include:

Simulation

Most of the macro verification is performed by simulating the RTL on an event-driven simulator. Event-driven simulators give a good compromise between fast compile times and good simulation speed at the RTL level, and provide a good debug environment. For large macros, the run-time for simulation may become a problem, especially for regression tests, random tests, and real code testing.

VHDL in particular can present a problem here. VHDL uses a two-list simulation algorithm compared to Verilog's one-list algorithm [1], and so tends to be inherently slower than Verilog. In this case, it may be worthwhile to use a VHDL cycle-based simulator, which can provide improved runtime performance.

Although most simulation should be done at the RTL level, some simulation should be run at the gate level. Typically, this is done late in the design cycle, once the RTL is stable and well-verified. Some initialization problems are masked at the RTL level, since RTL simulation uses a more abstract model for registers, and thus does not propagate X's as accurately as gate-level simulation. Usually only the reset sequence and a few basic functional tests need to be run at the gate level to verify correct initialization.

Testbench Automation Tools

Testbench automation tools such as Vera and Specman Elite can dramatically aid the task of creating reusable testbenches. These tools essentially extend VHDL and Verilog by providing powerful constructs for generating stimulus and checking response. For example, the designer can check that an event occurred some time within a window of clock cycles. They provide mechanisms for generating random tests and for checking test coverage. They also provide mechanisms for communication between testbench objects; this feature can be used to coordinate multiple bus functional models.

Code Coverage Tools

Code coverage tools, such as VHDLCover, VeriSure, VeriCov, and CoverMeter provide the ability to assess the quality of the verification suite. They can provide information about what parts of the code have been tested, as well as what states and arcs of a finite state machine have been tested. Code coverage is discussed in more detail in a later section of this chapter.

Hardware modeling

A hardware modeler provides an interface between a physical chip and the software simulator, so that stimulus can be applied to the chip and responses monitored within the simulation environment. Hardware modelers allow the designer to compare the simulation results of the RTL design with those of an actual chip. This verification method is very effective for designs where there is a known-good chip whose functionality is being designed into the macro.

Emulation

Emulation provides very fast run times but long compile times. It is significantly more expensive and more difficult to use than simulation. It is an appropriate tool for running real code on a large design, but is not a very useful tool for small macro development.

Prototyping

Building an actual prototype chip using the macro is key to verifying functionality. A prototype allows execution of real code in a real application at real-time speeds. A physical chip is not as easy to debug as a simulation of the design, so prototyping should only occur late in the design phase. Once a problem is detected using a prototype, it is usually best to recreate the problem in the simulation environment, and perform the debug there.

7.1.3   Subblock Simulation

Subblock verification is generally performed by the creator of the subblock, using a handcrafted testbench. This testbench typically consists of algorithmically-generated stimulus and a monitor to check outputs. The goal at this stage is 100 percent statement and path coverage, as measured with a commercial code coverage tool. This level of coverage is usually achievable with a reasonable effort because the subblocks are small. It is essential that this level of coverage be achieved at the subblock level because high levels of coverage become increasingly more difficult at higher levels of integration. Of course, good judgement needs to be used when applying this guideline. For example, if a datapath and its control block are initially designed as separate subblocks, then it may be impossible to get high coverage testing them separately. It may be much more appropriate to integrate the two and then perform verification.

Whenever possible, the outputs of the subblock should be checked automatically. The best way to do this is to add checking logic to the testbench. Of course, the checking logic needs to be even more robust than the macro code it is checking.

Automated response checking is superior to visual verification of waveforms because:

* It is less error-prone.
* It enables checking of longer tests.
* It enables checking of random tests.

Rule – All response checking should be done automatically. It is not acceptable for the designer to view waveforms and determine whether they are correct.

Guideline – All subblock test suites should achieve 100 percent statement and path coverage as measured by a test coverage tool such as VeriSure or VHDLCover. Subblock testing is the easiest place to detect design errors. With high coverage at this level, integration-level errors should be limited to interfacing problems.

7.1.4   Macro Simulation

If the subblocks have been rigorously tested, then the major source of errors at the macro integration level will either be interface problems or the result of the designer misunderstanding the specification. Macro-level tests focus on these areas. At the macro level, 100 percent coverage is no longer a practical goal. The emphasis at this stage is on testing the interaction between the component subblocks and the interfaces of the macro with its environment. Testing random cases of inputs and outputs is a crucial element of macro verification.

The design of testbenches for macro simulation is discussed in the section, "Testbench Design."

7.1.5   Prototyping

The design reuse methodology encourages rapid prototyping to complement simulation, and to compensate for the less-than-100 percent coverage at the macro verification stage. Achieving the final small percent of coverage at the macro level is generally extremely costly in time and still does not detect some of the bugs that will become apparent in prototype operation.

For many macros, it is possible to build a prototype chip and board and thus test the design in the actual target environment. Current FPGA and laser prototyping technologies do not provide the gate-count or the speed of state-of-the-art ASIC technology, but do provide the ability to create prototypes very rapidly. For designs that fit in these technologies and that can be verified at the speeds they provide, these technologies are very useful debugging mechanisms.

Building a prototype ASIC is required for macros that must be tested at speeds or gate counts exceeding those of FPGA and laser technologies. For some projects, this may mean that the prototype chip for the macro is the first SoC design in which it is used. In this case, the team must realize that the chip is a prototype, and that there is a high likelihood that it will have to be turned in order to achieve fully functional silicon.

7.1.6   Limited Production

Even after robust verification and prototyping, we cannot be sure that there are no remaining bugs in the design. There may be testcases that we did not run, or configurations that we did not prototype. Fundamentally, we have done a robust design but we have not used the macro in a real SoC design. For this reason, we recommend a period of limited production for any new macro. Typically, limited production involves working with just a few (1–4) customers and making sure that they are successful using the macro, before releasing the macro to widespread distribution. We have found this cautious approach very beneficial in reducing the risk of support problems.

7.2   Inspection as Verification

All of the books on code quality state that the fastest, cheapest, and most effective way to detect and remove bugs is by careful inspection of the design and code. Design reviews and code reviews play a key part in the drive towards zero defects.

Unfortunately, almost all of the research on code quality has been done in the area of software rather than hardware. But the software data we have is compelling and is likely to apply, in some general form, to hardware.

In Applied Software Measurement [2], Capers Jones reports that code inspections can be twice as effective as any other method in removing defects. In particular, code inspections are much more effective than test and debug for finding bugs. Jones states:

"Inspections tend to benefit project schedules and effort as well as quality. They are extremely efficient at finding interface problems between components and in using the human capacity for inductive reasoning to find subtle errors that testing will miss."

In our experience, we have found the same to be true for hardware designs as well. Finding bugs by code inspection is much faster than finding the same bugs by debugging the code during simulation.

There are many styles of design and code review, and a number of authors offer data on the advantages of different styles [2,3]. The following paragraphs describe a typical approach to performing design and code reviews.

A design review is a presentation by the designer (or design team) to the rest of the team. The size of the review team can be quite large. The designer provides the specification document to the reviewers ahead of time, so they can read it and come to the meeting well informed. At the meeting the designer reviews the requirements for the design, and describes in some detail how the design meets these requirements.

Design reviews take place at many points during the design cycle; from the beginning, where the specification is clear but the design is just being defined, up to release of the final design. The level of detail varies at each stage. The purpose of the design review is to review the approach to solving the problem, and to make sure that it is sound. There is no useful way to review the detailed implementation with a large number of people simultaneously.

Code reviews, on the other hand, are reviews of the details of the implementation. They typically involve the designer and a very small number of reviewers, often just a single reviewer. The object of the code review is to do a detailed peer review of the code. The reviewer and the designer go through the code line by line, and the reviewer is expected to fully understand the implementation. Often, teams will insist that reviewers are not managers, to maintain the sense of a supportive, collegial review. Teams have found that reviews work best when the designer knows that the purpose of the review is to help drive quality, and not for assessment of the designer's performance.

Pressman [3] gives results of some interesting studies assessing the optimal number of reviewers for code walkthroughs.

Code reviews are usually done after a subblock has been designed and verified by the designer, and before it is integrated into the macro.

Static analysis tools such as linting tools can also help spot defects before going to simulation. Linting tools such as Verilint, VHDLlint, and tools from Leda S.A. and Escalade can check for a variety of potential sources of error. For example, they can check for uninitialized variables or incomplete sensitivity lists. New versions of the linting tools are becoming available to check many of the guidelines in this book. Linting tools are very fast to run and should be run often.

Thus, there is a whole series of static verification methods that can effectively reduce the number of bugs before even starting dynamic, simulation-based verification. In addition, several software methodology books recommend single stepping through code in a debugger as the first step in dynamic verification. This approach is a combination of dynamic and static verification. By stepping through the code, the designer clearly sees how the code actually behaves in great detail, and can spot bugs as they are executed.

We have very limited experience in using this approach in hardware verification, but encourage readers to try it and see if they find it effective. Single stepping through code clearly works only relatively small blocks; stepping through a million gate design that requires thousands of cycles to do anything interesting is clearly not a useful exercise. But for subblocks of a macro, this could be an effective verification tool.

7.3   Adversarial Testing

Hardware and software teams have found that having a dedicated team of verification specialists can significantly improve the quality of the final product. Subblock or unit testing is done by the designer, and typically much of the macro verification is done by the design team. However, designers often are focused on proving that the design works correctly.

A separate team of verification experts can take a different view; they can focus on trying to prove that the design is broken. The combination of these two approaches usually gives the best results.

It is also useful to have some members of the team who are verification specialists, and who spend time keeping up with the latest tools and methodologies in verification. In the last few years there has been a proliferation of new point tools targeting verification, from the large EDA companies and from start-ups. Just keeping current on these tools, much less integrating them into the design flow, can be a challenge for the design team.

7.4 Testbench Design

Testbench design differs depending on the function of the macro. For example, the top-level testbench for a microprocessor macro would typically execute test programs, while that of a bus interface macro would typically use bus functional models and bus monitors to apply stimulus and check the results. There are also significant differences between subblock testbench design and top-level macro testbench design. In all cases, it is important to make sure that the test coverage provided by the testbench is adequate.

7.4.1 Subblock Testbench

Testbenches for subblocks tend to be rather ad hoc, developed specifically for the subblock under test. At some abstract level, though, they tend to look like Figure 7-1.

Because subblocks will almost never have bidirectional interfaces, we can develop a simple testbench that generates a set of inputs to the input ports and checks the outputs at the output ports. The activity at these ports is not random; in most digital systems, there will be a limited set of *transactions* that occur on a given port. These transactions usually have to do with reading or writing data to some storage element (registers, FIFOs, or memories) in the block.

Figure 7-1   Typical testbench for a subblock

Stimulus Generation

When we design the subblock, we can specify the transaction types that are allowed to occur on a given input port; for example, a register write consists of one specific sequence of data, address, and control pins changing, and no other sequence of actions on these pins is legal. As we design the macro, of course, we need to make sure that no block driving this port can ever generate any transactions other than the legal transactions at this port.

Once we have defined the legal set of transaction types on the input ports, we need to generate sequences of these transactions with the appropriate data/address values for testing the subblock. We start by analyzing the functionality of the subblock to determine useful sequences that will verify that the subblock complies with the specification. Then we search for the corner cases of the design: those unique sequences or combinations of transactions and data values that are most likely to break the design.

Once we have developed all the tests we can in this manner, we run a code coverage tool. This tool gives us a good indication of the completeness of the test suite. If additional testing is required to achieve 100 percent coverage, then we can develop additional focused tests or we can create a random test generator to generate random patterns of transactions and data. Random testing is effective for processors and bus interfaces because of the large number of transaction types make it difficult to manually generate all of the interesting combinations of transactions.

Output Checking

Generating test cases is, of course, just the first part of verification. We must check the responses of the design to verify that it is working correctly. This checking can be done manually, by monitoring the outputs on a waveform viewer and verifying that the waveforms are correct. However, this process is very error-prone and, therefore, an automatic output checker is a necessary part of the testbench. The design of this checker is unique to the subblock being tested, but there are some common aspects to most checkers:

- We can verify that only legal transactions are generated at the output port of the design. For example, if the read/write line is always supposed to transition one clock cycle before data and be stable until one clock cycle after data transitions, then we can check this automatically.

- We can verify that the specific transactions are correct responses to the input transactions generated. This requires a detailed analysis of the design. Clearly, the simpler the design, the simpler this checking is. This provides another reason to keep the design as simple as possible and still meet function and performance goals.

7.4.2   Macro Testbench

We can extend the concepts used in the subblock testbench to the testbench used for checking the macro. Once the subblocks have been integrated into the macro, we construct a testbench that again automatically generates transactions at the macro input ports and checks transactions at the output ports. There are several reasons why we want to develop a more powerful and well-documented testbench at this level:

- The design is now considerably more complex, and so more complex test scenarios will be required for complete testing.

- More people will typically be working on verification of the macro, often the entire team that developed the subblocks.

- The testbench will be shipped along with the macro so that the customer can verify the macro in the system design.

The testbench can take several forms. An interface macro, such as a PCI interface, might have a testbench like the one shown in Figure 7-2. This testbench is coded using a testbench generation tool, such as Vera or Specman Elite.

The PCI macro provides an interface between the PCI bus, with its complex protocol, and two application buses: the master application bus, which can initiate PCI transactions, and the slave application bus, which is the target of PCI transactions.

In this testbench, PCI bus functional models are used to create transactions on the PCI bus, and thus to the PCI macro. A PCI bus monitor checks the transactions on the PCI bus, and thus acts as a transaction checker. The monitor produces a log file, where address and data information for each transaction is recorded, and an error message generated if the basic PCI protocol is violated.

Multiple instances of the PCI BFM are used to generate complex test scenarios, with colliding traffic in both directions. Because testbench creation tools are object-oriented, creating and managing these multiple instances is very straightforward.

Because the PCI macro acts as a bridge between the PCI bus and the application buses, we need bus functional models and bus monitors for the application buses as well.

The bus monitors are very useful for checking the correctness of the basic protocol, but are not adequate to check the full functionality of the PCI macro. For this, we need the On-the-Fly Checker. This block monitors all read and write transactions initiated on any of the three buses. When a write to address A occurs on the PCI bus, this transaction is written to a software FIFO in the checker. When a write appears on the slave application bus, this is also written to a software FIFO in the checker. The checker then compares the contents of the software FIFOs to make sure that transactions correctly propagated through the PCI macro, and in the correct number of cycles.

Because of the complexity of the PCI protocol, the exact number of cycles for the write to propagate through the macro is essentially non-deterministic. It depends strongly on the other transactions occurring at about the same time. The testbench generations tools deal with this elegantly, allowing us to specify a window of time during which the write must appear on the application slave bus.

One requirement for a complex testbench such as that shown in Figure 7-2 is that actions of the BFMs must be coordinated. The testbench tools provide a message passing mechanism so that commands from a central command file can drive all of the BFMs.

Thus, when this testbench is fully assembled, we have the ability to generate and check any sequence of transactions at any port of the PCI macro.

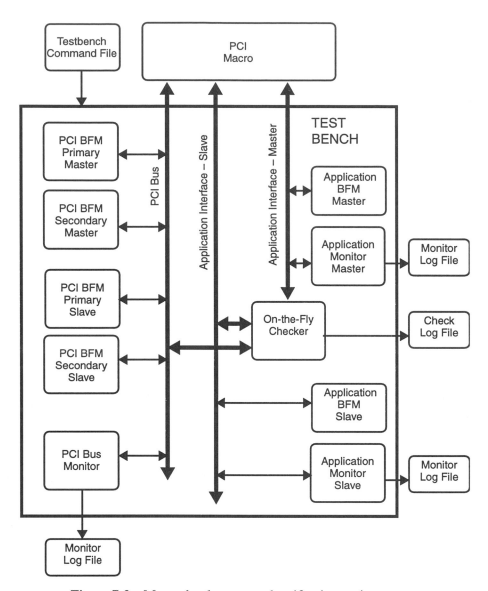

Figure 7-2   Macro development and verification environment

A more complex testbench is shown in Figure 7-3. Here, the actual software application is the source of commands for the PCI bus functional model. This application can run on the workstation that is running the simulator; device driver calls that would normally go to the system bus are redirected through a translator to the simulator, using a programming language interface such as Verilog's PLI or ModelSim's FLI. A hardware/software cosimulation environment can provide an effective way to set up this testbench and a convenient debug environment.

The actual transactions between the application and the PCI macro under test are a small percentage of the cycles being simulated; many cycles are spent generating inputs to the bus functional model. Also, real code tends to repeat many of the same basic operations many times; extensive testing of the macro requires the execution of a considerable amount of application code. Thus, software-driven simulation is an inherently inefficient test method, but it does give the opportunity of testing the macro with real code. For large macros, this form of testing is most effective if the simulation is running on a very high-speed simulator, such as a cycle-based simulator or an emulator.

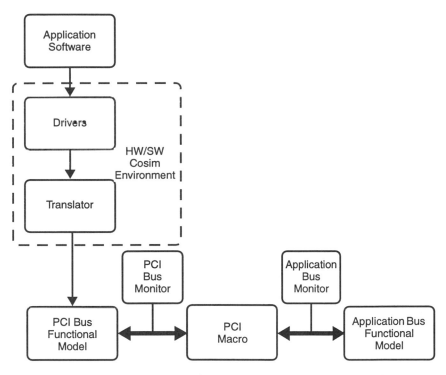

Figure 7-3   Software-driven testbench for macro-level testing

7.4.3   Bus Functional Models

The bus functional models (BFM) used in the examples above are a common method of creating testbenches. Typically they are written in RTL, a testbench automation tool, or in C/C++, and use some form of command language to create sequences of transactions on the bus. The intent of these models is to model only the bus transactions of an agent on the bus. They do not model any of the functionality of an agent on the bus; each read and write transaction is specified by the test developer explicitly.

Because of their simplicity, these models place little demand on simulator performance; simulation speeds are mostly determined by the macro itself.

Well-designed BFMs allow the test developer to specify the transactions on the bus at a relatively high level of abstraction. Instead of controlling individual signals on the bus, the test developer can specify a read or write transaction, with the associated data, or an interrupt. The developer may well also want to generate an error condition, such as forcing a parity error; therefore, the BFM should include this capability as well.

Many testbenches require multiple BFMs, as in the PCI example above. In this case, it is best to use a single command file to coordinate the actions of the various models. The models must be written so that they can share a common command file. Many commercial BFMs offer this capability.

BFMs are also extremely useful for system-level simulation, as described in Chapter 11. For example, a PCI BFM can be used to generate transactions to an SoC design that has a PCI interface block. Similarly, the PCI monitor can be used to verify output transactions to the PCI bus. For this reason, the BFM and monitor are considered two of the macro deliverables.

Because they are part of the deliverables that will ship with the product, the BFM and monitor must be designed and coded with the same care as the macro RTL. The designer also needs to provide full documentation on how to use the BFM and monitor.

7.4.4   Automated Response Checking

In the previous examples, the automated response checking for the testbench was provided by the bus monitors and checkers. This approach is useful for bus interfaces, but for other types of macros there are some other techniques that may be useful.

One effective technique is to compare the output responses of the macro to those of a reference design. If the macro is being designed to be compatible with an existing chip (for example, a microcontroller or DSP), then the chip itself can be used as a reference model. A hardware modeler can be used to integrate the physical chip as a model in the simulation environment. Figure 7-4 shows a such a configuration.

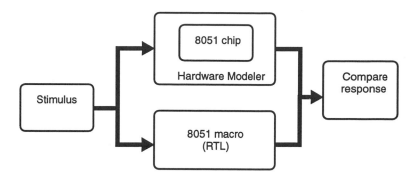

Figure 7-4   Self-checking testbench using a hardware modeler

If a behavioral model for the design was developed as part of the specification process, then this behavioral model can be used as the reference model, especially if it is cycle accurate.

One approach often used by microprocessor developers is to develop an Instruction Set Architecture (ISA) model of the processor, usually in C. This ISA model is defined to be the reference for the design, and all other representations of the design must exhibit the same instruction-level behavior. As RTL is developed for the design, its behavior is constantly being compared to the reference ISA model.

In some sense, the "On-the-Fly Checker" in the PCI example is a reference design for the PCI macro. The intent is for the checker to look at every input to the PCI macro from the BFMs, look at the PCI macro's response to this input, and determine if the response is correct. The difficulty lies in making the BFM, checker, and test suite rich enough to test the macro completely.

7.4.5   Verification Suite Design

Once we have built the testbench, we can develop a set of tests to verify the correct behavior of the macro. Developing a verification environment that can completely verify a macro is every bit as difficult as specifying or designing the macro in the first place, because it presents essentially the same problem: how to completely describe the expected behavior of the design.

Functional Testing

The first step in developing the verification suite is to perform functional testing; that is, verifying that the macro implements the functions described in the specification. This usually involves going through the functional specification essentially line by line, and verifying that there is a test for each required function. Testbench automation tools can help by providing powerful constructs for describing this functionality, but deciding how the macro should behave is essentially a human activity.

If the specification is an executable specification (for example, a C++ behavioral model), then functional verification involves showing that the behavior of the specification and that of the macro are the same. That is, we need to completely exercise the executable specification, and show that under the same stimulus, the macro produces the same results. The trick here is to *completely* exercise the executable specification. Running a coverage tool on the executable specification can help to determine the completeness of these tests.

These functional tests are necessarily a subset of a complete verification of the macro. The specification does not contain all (and in many cases does not contain any) of the implementation details of the macro. For example, an ISA model for a microprocessor is instruction set accurate, but not cycle accurate. The cycle-by-cycle behavior of the RTL must be verified in addition to its ability to execute the instruction set correctly.

Corner Case Testing

Corner case testing is intended to test the implementation details not covered in the functional testing. Designers can often spot corner cases manually. For example, in some microprocessor designs two 32-bit registers can sometimes be used as one 64-bit register. The point where bits roll over from the first 32-bit register to the second is a corner case.

Another typical set of corner cases involve designs with shared resources, such as a bus arbiter, or a block that has multiple agents accessing the same FIFO. For these designs it is useful to create contention for the resources, to ensure that the conflicts are handled correctly.

Code Coverage and Random Testing

Once the designer has exhaustively tested all the anticipated corner cases, there are two useful techniques for completing the verification suite: code coverage and random testing.

Code coverage is discussed in more detail in the next section, but it basically indicates what parts of the code have been tested, and what parts have not. This information allows the designer to create focused tests for these untested sections of code.

When manually adding new tests has become tedious or impractical, random testing can help improve test coverage. Constraint-driven random test capabilities in the test-bench automation tools are particularly useful for creating random tests with the desired distribution of activities. For processor testing, we can specify that a certain percentage of instructions should be arithmetic instructions and a different percentage should be load and store, and so on.

Random testing greatly enhances our verification capabilities, but it does have limitations. Runtimes can get very long for achieving very high coverage. And, since the designer is human, the parameters of the random test may omit some critical tests.

A number of tool providers are working on automatic test generators to help solve this problem. These tools would examine the circuit, determine what (if any) parts of the circuit have already been tested, and then automatically generate additional tests to achieve 100 percent coverage. These tools are (at the time of writing) still under development, but, once mature, they could have a dramatic impact on verification.

Still, automatic generation of vectors is not a panacea for the verification challenge. We still need to create automatic checkers that can tell us if the response of the macro is correct to this 100 percent complete set of stimuli. And no tools will ever tell us if we left out a function completely. Verification will always remain a fundamentally human activity, because it requires us to specify the expected behavior of the design. However, we start to see a much more promising picture of being able to complement this human activity with much more powerful tools to ensure higher quality designs.

Code Examples – Testbench Automation Tools

Example 7-1 and Example 7-2 show some typical uses of Vera to create BFMs and checkers. Example 7-1 shows a PCI bus monitor snooping the PCI bus to detect writes to the target (slave) bus on the application interface. When a write occurs, it is posted to a mailbox in the target bus monitor. Example 7-2 shows the target bus monitor snooping the target bus, and comparing actual writes to those received in the mailbox. That is, it checks that the writes that are initiated on the PCI bus actually propagate through the PCI macro to the target bus.

Example 7-3 shows a typical use of Specman Elite to verify a simple CPU.

Example 7-1 Vera code fragment for PCI monitor

```
class pci_snooper {
pci_port    my_port ;        // DUT port
pci_data_class   pci_data; // class structure for PCI
bit msg[255:0] msg;          //unpack pci_data to msg
task pci_monitor() {
    while(!end_of_test) {
      pci_data = snoop_pci_bus with my_port();
      pci_data.unpack(msg);
      mailbox_send(mboxId, msg);   // mboxId - addr of
                                   // target mailbox
    }
    } // end of monitor
}    // end of class pci_snooper.
```

Example 7-2 Vera code fragment for PCI application bus monitor

```
class target_snooper {
target_port    my_port ;      // DUT port
pci_data_class   pci_data;  // class structure for PCI
bit msg[255:0] msg;           //unpack pci_data to msg
task target_monitor() {
    while(!end_of_test) {
      msg = mailbox_receivekl(WAIT, msg); // block for
                                          //message
      expected_pci_data.pack(msg);        // pack
                                   // message to class
      actual_pci_data = snoop_target_bus with
              my_port();
      compare(actual_pci_data, expected_pci_data);
} // end of monitor
}    // end of class target_snooper.
```

Example 7-3   Specman Elite code fragment for verifying a CPU

```
// Four typical steps in verifying a simple CPU,
// using Specman Elite (TM):

// 1. Describing the device under test (the DUT).
//    The CPU spec says: "A CPU instruction consists of
//    an opcode and two operands. The first operand is
//    a CPU register, the second is a byte"
type command_type   :   [ LOAD, STORE, ADD, SUB,
                            JMP, JMPC, CALL, RET ];
type register_type  :   [ REG0, REG1, REG2, REG3 ];

struct instruction {
    opcode      :   command_type;
    operand1    :   register_type;
    operand2    :   byte;

    // 2. Defining constraints for generating legal
    //    instructions, as part of the instruction
    //    definition. The CPU spec says: "the LOAD
    //    instruction should not use register zero"

    keep (opcode == LOAD) => (operand1 != REG0);
};



// 3. Requesting interesting stimuli for a specific test,
//    by adding constraints on the instruction. The test
//    plan says: "Generate JMPC opcodes (JMP-on-Carry)
//    60% of the times that the carry bit is set in the
//    model (i.e., respond to model state)"
extend instruction {
    keep ('/dut/cpu/carry' == 1) =>
            // i.e., if "carry" is set in the HDL,
            // then select opcode according to ratios:
        soft opcode == select {
            60  :   JMPC;           // 60% JMPC opcode
            40  :   others;         // 40% any other opcode
    };
};
```

```
// 4. Checking a temporal rule (timing & sequence).
//    The memory protocol spec states Interface Rule #4:
//    "After data was requested, there should be at most
//    MAX_WAIT cycles till data is ready. During those
//    cycles, no other data request should be issued."
struct memory_monitor {
    // events tied to HDL
    event data_req is rise('/dut/memory/request');
    event data_ready is rise('/dut/memory/ready');

    expect @data_req =>
        {[0..MAX_WAIT] * not @data_req; @data_ready}
    else dut_error("Violation of Memory i/f rule #4: ",
                   "data_req was not followed by ",
                   "data_ready in due time");
};
```

7.4.6   Code Coverage Analysis

Verifying test coverage is essential to the verification strategy; it is the only way to assess, quantitatively, the robustness of the test suite. Several commercial tools are available that provide extensive coverage capabilities.

Types of Coverage Tests

We describe here some of the capabilities of the TransEDA VHDLCover tool, which is representative of the better coverage tools currently available.

The coverage tool provides the following metrics:

- Statement coverage
- Branch coverage
- Condition coverage
- Path coverage
- Toggle coverage
- Triggering coverage

Statement coverage gives a count, for each executable statement, of how many times it was executed.

Branch coverage verifies that each branch in an if-then-else or case statement was executed.

Condition coverage verifies that all branch sub-conditions have triggered the condition branch. In Example 7-4, condition coverage means checking that the first line was executed with $a = 1$ and that it was executed with $b = 0$, and it gives a count of how many times each condition occurred.

Example 7-4   Condition coverage checks branch condition

```
if (a = '1' or b = '0') then
  c <= '1';
else
  c <= '0';
endif;
```

Path coverage checks which paths are taken between adjacent blocks of conditional code. For example, if there are two successive if-then-else statements, as in Example 7-5, path coverage checks the various combinations of conditions between the pair of statements.

Example 7-5   Path coverage

```
if (a = '1' or b = '0') then
  c <= '1';
else
  c <= '0';
endif;

if (a = '1' and b = '1') then
  d <= '1';
else
  d <= '0';
endif;
```

There are several paths through this pair of if-then-else blocks, depending on the values of a and b. Path coverage counts how many times each possible path was executed.

Triggering coverage checks which signals in a sensitivity list trigger a process.

Trigger coverage counts how many times the process was activated by each signal in the sensitivity list changing value. In Example 7-6, trigger coverage counts how many times the process is activated by signal *a* changing value, by signal *b* changing value, and by signal *c* changing value.

Example 7-6   Trigger coverage

```
process (a, b, c)
```

. . . . .

Toggle coverage counts how many times a particular signal transitions from '0' to '1', and how many times it transitions from '1' to '0'.

Achieving high code coverage with the macro testbench is a necessary but not sufficient condition for verifying the functionality of the macro. Code coverage does nothing to verify that the original intent of the specification was executed correctly. It also does not verify that the simulation results were ever compared or checked. Code coverage only indicates whether the code was exercised by the verification suite.

On the other hand, if the code coverage tool indicates that a line or path through the code was not executed, then clearly the verification suite is not testing that piece of code.

We recommend targeting 100 percent statement, branch, and condition coverage. Anything substantially below this number may indicate significant functionality that is not being tested.

Path, toggle, and triggering coverage can be used as a secondary metric. Achieving very high coverage here is valuable, but may not be practical. At times it may be best to examine carefully sections of code that do not have 100 percent path, toggle, or trigger coverage, to understand why the coverage was low and whether it is possible and appropriate to generate additional tests to increase coverage.

One of the limitations of current code coverage tools is in the area of path coverage. Path coverage is usually limited to adjacent blocks of code. If the design has multiple, interacting state machines, this adjacency limitation means that it is unlikely that the full interactions of the state machines are checked.

Recent Progress in Coverage Tools

Coverage tool providers continue to enhance tool performance on state machines. Tools now can recognize state machines in the RTL, and give the designer useful information about what nodes have been covered, as well as what arcs have been traversed. The tools can also examine pairs of state machines and indicate what pairs of states/arcs have been exercised. This coverage is, of course, limited by the computational power of workstations and the complexity of the state machines, but offers an important step forward.

Tool providers also have provided capabilities for using coverage to minimize regression test suites. One of the historical problem with regression tests is that the tend to grow until runtimes significantly affect the team's ability to verify modifications to the design. Many of the new tests add little incremental coverage over existing tests.

Code coverage can be used to prune the overall test suite, eliminating redundant tests and ordering tests so that the first tests run provide the highest incremental coverage. TransEDA reports [4] that on a project with Hewlett Packard, this test pruning approach reduced regression test runtime by 91 percent. Code coverage tools are still limited in their coverage; see the comments on path coverage above. So, it may be worthwhile running the full regression suite on the final version of the design. But running the pruned suite at a 10x savings in simulation time seems like a very reasonable approach during most of the development cycle of a design.

7.5   Timing Verification

Static timing verification is the most effective method of verifying a macro's timing performance. As part of the overall verification strategy for a macro, the macro should be synthesized using a number of representative library technologies. Static timing analysis should then be performed on the resulting netlists to verify that they meet the macro's timing objectives.

The choice of which libraries to use is a key one. Libraries, even for the same technology (for example, .5μ), can have significantly different performance characteristics. The libraries should be chosen to reflect the actual range of technologies in which the macro is likely to be implemented.

For macros that have aggressive performance goals, it is necessary to include a trial layout of the macro to verify timing. Pre-layout wire load models are statistical and actual wire delays after layout may vary significantly from these models. Doing an actual layout of the macro can raise the confidence in its abilities to meet timing.

Gate-level simulation is of limited use in timing verification. While leading gate-level simulators have the capacity to handle 500k or larger designs, gate-level simulation is slow. The limited number of vectors that can be run on a gate-level netlist cannot exercise all of the timing paths in the design, so it is possible that the worst case timing path in the design will never be exercised. For this reason, gate-level timing simulation may deliver optimistic results and is not, by itself, sufficient as a timing verification methodology.

Gate-level simulation is most useful in verifying timing for asynchronous logic. We recommend avoiding asynchronous logic, because it is harder to design correctly, to verify functionality and timing, and to make portable across technologies and applications. However, some designs may require a small amount of asynchronous logic. The amount of gate-level, full timing simulation should be tailored to the requirements of verifying the timing of this asynchronous logic.

Static timing verification, on the other hand, tends to be pessimistic unless false paths are manually defined and not considered in the analysis. Because this is a manual process, it is subject to human error. Gate-level timing simulation does provide a coarse check for this kind of error.

Guideline – The best overall timing verification methodology is to use static timing analysis as the basis for timing verification. You can then use gate-level simulation as a second-level check for your static timing analysis methodology (for example, to detect mis-identified false paths).

References

1. Abramovici, Miron. *Digital Systems Testing and Testable Design*. IEEE, 1998.

2. Jones, Capers. *Applied Software Measurement: Assuring Productivity and Quality*. McGraw Hill Text, 1996

3. Pressman, Roger. *Software Engineering: A Practitioner's Approach*. McGraw Hill Text, 1996.

4. http://www.transeda.com/resources_area/100_issue_5.pdf

CHAPTER 8

Developing Hard Macros

This chapter discusses issues that are specific to the development of hard macros. In particular, it discusses the need for simulation, layout, and timing models, as well as the differing productization requirements and deliverables for hard macros. The topics are:

- Overview
- Hard macro design issues
- Hard macro design process
- Physical design for hard macros
- Block integration
- Productization
- Model development for hard macros
- Portable hard macros

8.1 Overview

Hard macros are macros that have a physical representation, and are delivered in the form of a GDSII file. As a result, hard macros are more predictable than soft macros in terms of timing, power, and area. However, hard macros do not have the flexibility of soft macros; they cannot be parameterized or user-configurable. The porting process of the two forms can also be quite different.

In some sense, however, the distinction between hard and soft macros is artificial. Every macro starts out as soft, for RTL has to be the reference implementation model. Every macro ends up in GDSII, and thus in hard form. The only real distinction between hard and soft macros is at which stage of design the developer hands the macro over to the chip designer. In a very real sense, hard macros are just soft macros that have been taken to GDSII before this handoff.

In this book, we assume the following model for hard macros:

- The macro developer delivers GDSII and a full set of models to the silicon vendor.
- The silicon vendor does the physical design for the chip, including integration of the hard macro. Thus, only the silicon provider actually uses, or has access to, the GDSII for the macro.
- The silicon vendor provides the timing and functional models to the chip designer.
- The chip designer uses the timing and functional models for the hard macro while designing the rest of the chip. Typically, these models do not include RTL for the macro. Thus, the models must provide all of the functional and physical information needed to design the chip and verify its timing and functionality.

In a large semiconductor company, the macro developer, silicon vendor, and chip designer may just be different groups within the company. Some large systems houses that do their own physical design may purchase a hard macro directly from a third party provider, thus getting both the GDSII and the models. In this case, the systems house is acting as both the chip designer and as the (fabless) silicon provider. However, the case outlined above is general enough to show the issues and challenges involved in developing high-quality hard macros.

8.1.1   Why and When to use Hard Macros

Developers typically provide hard versions of macros for any one of several reasons:

- The design is pushing performance to the limit of the silicon process, and thus the physical design must be done by the designer, who knows exactly how to get optimal performance from the design.
- The design requires some full custom design, and so cannot be delivered in soft (that is, synthesizable) form.
- The value of the macro is so great that the macro provider does not want the chip designers to have access to the RTL. That is, hard macros can provide a greater degree of IP protection for the IP provider.
- The macro provider wishes to prevent the possibility of the user modifying the macro.

In the case of processors, all of these conditions are often the case. For this reason, processors are the most common macros to be delivered in hard form.

There is also a case in which soft macros are used as virtual hard macros. In some very large chips, the design team will use a divide-and-conquer approach to physical design. Each major block, including each soft macro, is placed and routed independently of the other blocks. Chip-level physical design then consists of placing these blocks and wiring them up. In such cases, most of the issues for hard macros described below apply to these independent blocks. In particular, timing and functional models for each of the major blocks can provide more abstract representations of the timing and functionality of the block. These models can provide a faster path to timing convergence and functional verification.

8.1.2   Design Process for Hard vs. Soft Macros

Hard macro development is essentially an extension to soft macro development. The extra steps for hard macros are primarily:

- Generating a physical design
- Developing models for simulation, layout, and timing.

These requirements stem from the fact that hard macros are delivered as a physical database rather than RTL. Integrators require these models to perform system-level verification, chip-level timing, floorplanning, and layout.

Guideline – It is recommended that the design process itself be kept identical with the design process for soft macros except for the productization phase. The following sections describe how the design process for hard macros differs from the design process for soft macros.

8.2   Design Issues for Hard Macros

There are several key design issues that are unique to hard macros. These issues affect the design process, and are described in the following sections.

8.2.1   Full Custom Design

Unlike soft macros, hard macros offer the opportunity to include some full custom design in a reusable form. However, advances in synthesis, libraries, and timing-driven place and route have largely eliminated the performance advantage for full custom design. And since full custom design imposes a significant cost in terms of development schedule, it should only be used in a few, specific circumstances.

Memory is the first and most natural candidate for full custom implementation. Memory compilers can produce much smaller, faster, lower-power memories than synthesized flop-based memories. We expect all memories except very small FIFOs to be generated from a memory compiler.

For some datapath elements such as barrel shifters, full custom design techniques can yield slightly smaller designs than synthesizable versions. For the most cost-sensitive designs, it may be worth replacing the synthesized version of these blocks with a full custom version.

There is considerable advantage in minimizing the amount of full custom logic in a hard macro. Not only does custom logic slow development time, but it also limits the options for porting the design to different processes. Fully synthesizable designs can be ported either by physical porting tools or by repeating synthesis, place and route. Full custom macros, or full custom components within macros, need to be ported by physical design tools or by repeating the manual design, place, and route.

8.2.2   Interface Design

As in most design, good interface design is critical to producing high quality, easy to integrate hard macros.

Guideline – We strongly recommend registering all of the inputs and outputs of the macro, and clocking them from a single edge of a single clock. In general, the output drivers should be the same for all output pins, and input setup times should be the same for all input pins.

This technique provides a simple and consistent interface for chip designers using the macro, and thus can speed up integration significantly. In addition, consistent timing on ports can simplify synthesis and timing verification scripts for the rest of the chip, reducing the chance of a human error, and speeding up timing convergence.

Registering inputs and outputs can also eliminate some difficult problems in IP security, manufacturing test, and timing modeling, as described later in this chapter.

An additional challenge in interface design is choosing the right output drive strength for output ports. Using too strong a drive strength wastes power and area; for lightly loaded outputs, they can also be slower due to increased intrinsic delay over a smaller buffer. Using too small a drive strength, of course, can result in unacceptable delays when driving long wires to other blocks. Ultimately, this choice is a judgement call, but we recommend erring on the side of too strong a drive strength rather than too weak. Wire delays are only getting greater as technologies shrink.

Registering all outputs helps make designs less sensitive to output drive strengths, especially if the other blocks in the chip register their inputs. In this case, signals have an entire clock cycle to travel from block to block. For large chip designs, where cross-chip delays can be multiple nanoseconds and clock speeds can be hundreds of megahertz, this approach can make the difference between meeting timing and not meeting timing.

8.2.3   Design For Test

Hard macros pose some unique test issues not found in soft macros. With soft macros, the integrator can choose from a variety of test methodologies: full scan, logic BIST, or application of parallel vectors through boundary scan or muxing out to the pins of the chip. The actual test structures are inserted at chip integration, so that the entire chip can have a consistent set of test structures.

Hard macros do not provide this flexibility; test structures must be built into each hard macro. The integrator then must integrate the test strategy of the hard macro with the test strategy for the rest of the chip. It is the task of the hard macro developer to provide an appropriate test structure for the hard macro that will be easy to integrate into a variety of chip-level test structures.

The hard macro developer must choose between full scan, logic BIST, or application of parallel vectors through boundary scan or muxing out to the pins of the chip.

Full scan offers very high test coverage and is easy to use. Tools can be used to insert scan flops and perform automatic test pattern generation. Fault simulation can be used to verify coverage. Thus, scan is the preferred test methodology for hard macros as long as the delay and area penalties are acceptable. For most designs, the slight increase in area and the very slight increase in delay are more than compensated for by the ease of use and robustness of scan.

For some performance-critical designs, such as a microprocessor, a "near full scan" approach is used, where the entire macro is full scan except for the datapath, where the delay would be most costly. For the datapath, only the first and last levels of flops are scanned.

Logic BIST is a variation on the full scan approach. Where full scan must have its scan chain integrated into the chip's overall scan chain(s), logic BIST uses an LFSR (Linear Feedback Shift Register) to generate the test patterns locally. A signature recognition circuit checks the results of the scan test to verify correct behavior of the circuit.

Logic BIST has the advantage of keeping all pattern generation and checking within the macro. This provides some element of additional security against reverse engineering of the macro. It also reduces the requirements for scan memory in the tester. Logic BIST does require some additional design effort and some increase in die area for the generator and checker, although tools to automate this process are becoming available.

Parallel vectors are used to test only the most timing or area critical designs. A robust set of parallel vectors is extremely time-consuming to develop and verify. If the macro developer selects parallel vector testing for the macro, boundary scan must be included as part of the macro. Boundary scan provides an effective, if slow, way of applying the vectors to the macro without requiring muxing the macro pins out to the chip pins. Requiring the integrator to mux out the pins places an unreasonable burden on the integrator and restricts the overall chip design.

Note that for the hard macro test to be fully self-contained, the inputs and the outputs of the macro must be registered. For example, if there is combinational logic on an input to the macro, then the stimulus to test this logic must come from the outside logic. In Figure 8-1, for example, the scan chain of Block A needs to provide inputs to the hard macro. With current tools, this means that ATPG must be done on Block A and the hard macro concurrently.

One major problem with this approach is that the engineer doing the ATPG has to have access to the gate-level netlist of the hard macro. For many third party IP providers, this is a major security concern.

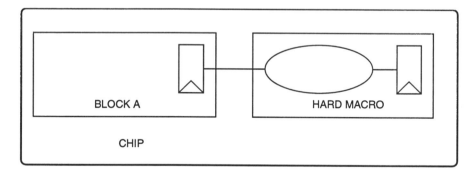

Figure 8-1   Scan chains are not independent

8.2.4   Clock and Reset

The hard macro designer has to implement a clock and reset structure in the hard macro without knowing in advance the clocking and reset structure of the chip in which the macro will be used. The designer should provide full clock and reset buffering in the hard macro, and provide a minimal load on the clock and reset inputs to the macro.

To ease the integration of the macro onto the chip, the designer should provide a buffered, precisely aligned copy of the clock as an output of the macro. This clock is then available to synchronize the signals going to/from the hard macro.

The problem, of course, is that the hard macro will have a clock tree insertion delay; that is, the delay from the clock input pin of the macro, through the clock buffers, before the clock arrives at the internal flops. This delay affects the setup and hold times at the macro's inputs and its clock-to-output delays. The chip designer needs to account for this when integrating the macro into the chip.

The macro designer can help simplify the integration process by registering the inputs and outputs of the macro. The clock-to-output delay is then just the clock tree delay plus the clock-to-q delay of the flops. For most designs, this is fast enough; if necessary, the chip designer can register the outputs immediately. This approach allows a complete clock cycle for the insertion delay, flop delay, and wire delay.

Registering the inputs of the hard macro does not entirely solve the problem. If the clock tree delay is substantial, the macro will exhibit large hold time requirements. This problem can be solved by adding buffers to the hard macro's inputs, providing sufficient delay to produce a zero hold time requirement.

Another way to deal with clock tree insertion delay is for the hard macro developer to calculate the clock tree insertion delay of the hard macro and to provide that information to the macro integrator. The macro integrator can then provide the hard macro an early version of the chip's clock signal, thereby aligning the macro's internal timing with that of the rest of the chip.

8.2.5   Aspect Ratio

The aspect ratio of the hard macro affects the floorplan and routability of the final chip. Thus, it is an important factor affecting the ease with which the macro can be integrated into the final chip. A large hard macro with an extreme ratio can present significant problems in placing and routing an SoC design. In most cases, an aspect ratio close to 1:1 minimizes the burden on the integrator. Aspect ratios of 1:2 and 1:4 are also commonly used.

Note also that a non-square aspect ratio (for example, a tall, narrow block), means that there will be more routing in vertical direction than in the horizontal. This asymmetric demand on routing resources can lead to problems during place and route. This is another reason why macro designers typically try for a 1:1 aspect ratio.

8.2.6   Porosity

Hard macros can present real challenges to the integrator if they completely block all routing. Some routing channels through the macro should be made available to the integrator, if it is possible to do so without affecting the macro's performance.

Another approach is to limit the number of used metal layers to less than the total available in the process. For processes with more than two metal layers available for signal routing, this can be an effective approach to providing routing through the hard macro.

Both of these approaches, however, pose problems. A hard macro or memory is typically characterized for the case where no extra wires are running through or over it. The resulting timing model is used by the chip design team to calculate delays and determine if the chip will meet timing.

Routing additional wires through the block adds capacitance that can slow down adjacent signals. Unfortunately, the only way to factor these additional delays into the timing model for the macro or memory is to completely re-characterize the macro or memory. In most cases, this re-characterization is not practical. The chip design team has little choice except to hope the additional capacitance does not affect a critical timing path.

For these reasons, designers of leading edge microprocessors, where each block is treated as a hard macro, leave routing channels between blocks and always route around rather than through blocks.

Rule – At the very least, the macro deliverables must include a blockage map to identify areas where over-cell routing will not cause timing problems.

8.2.7   Pin Placement

Pin placement of the macro can have a significant effect on the floorplan and top-level routing of the chips that use it. Without knowing in detail the target chip design, it is hard to ensure an optimal pin placement. However, common sense suggests that buses and other related signals should be grouped together so that top-level wire lengths can be roughly matched.

A floorplanning model is one of the deliverables of a hard macro. Among other things, this model describes the pin placement, size, and grid.

8.2.8   Power Distribution

Power and ground busing within the macro must be designed to handle the peak current requirements of the macro at maximum frequency. The integrator using the macro must provide sufficient power busing to the macro to limit voltage drop, noise, and simultaneous output switching noise to acceptable levels. The specification of the hard macro must include sufficient information about the requirements of the macro and the electrical characteristics of the power pin contacts on the macro.

8.3   The Hard Macro Design Process

The hard macro design process is shown in Figure 8-2. For the hard macro, we expand the macro specification to include physical design issues. The target library is specified, and timing, area, and power goals are described.

The macro specification also addresses the issues described in the previous section: design for test, clock and reset, aspect ratio, porosity, pin placement, and power distribution. The specification describes the basic requirements for each of these. The specification also describes the porting plan: what techniques and tools will be used to port the macro to different processes.

The macro specification also describes the models that will provided as part of the final deliverables. These models include the simulation model(s), timing model(s), and floorplanning model.

Concurrent with the functional specification and behavioral model development, we develop a more detailed physical specification for the macro, addressing all of the issues mentioned above, describing how each requirement of the macro specification will be met. From this specification, we develop a preliminary floorplan of the macro. This floorplan and the physical requirements of the macro help drive the partitioning of the macro into subblocks.

Once the macro is partitioned into subblocks, the design of the individual subblocks follows the same process as for soft macros.

For some very high performance designs, the designer may elect to not to use automated synthesis for some critical subblocks. Instead, the designer may use a datapath compiler or may handcraft the subblock. The goal of these alternate synthesis methods is the same: to meet the timing, area, and power requirements of the macro specification while ensuring that the detailed design is functionally equivalent to the RTL.

Note that even with manual synthesis and handcrafting, the RTL for the subblock is the "golden" reference. For all synthesis methods, automated and manual, formal verification should be used to ensure the equivalence between the final physical design and the RTL.

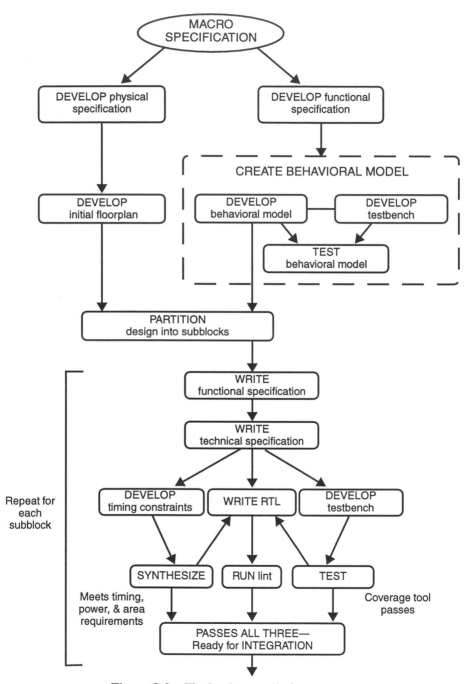

Figure 8-2   The hard macro design process

8.4   Block Integration for Hard Macros

The process of integrating the subblocks into the macro is much the same for both hard and soft macros. This process is described in Figure 8-3.

Because a hard macro is available only in a single configuration, functional test is somewhat simplified; no multiple-configuration testing is required, as it is for soft macros.

As described in the previous section, manufacturing test presents additional challenges to hard macro design. Based on the requirement for the macro, a test methodology must be selected and implemented.

Synthesis needs to target only the target technology library. Because porting is done at the physical level, after synthesis, there is no requirement to produce optimal netlists in a variety of technologies.

Synthesis of the macro is an iterative process that involves refining the floorplan based on synthesis results, updating the wire load models based on the floorplan, and repeating synthesis. With a good initial floorplan, good partitioning of the design, and good timing budgets, this process will converge rapidly. As the process starts to converge, an initial placement of the macro that produces an estimated routing can further improve the wire load models used for synthesis.

8.5   Productization of Hard Macros

Productization of hard macros involves physical design, verification, model development, and documentation.

8.5.1   Physical Design

The first step in productizing the hard macro is to complete the physical design. Figure 8-4 shows the basic loop of floorplanning and incremental synthesis, place and route, and timing extraction. In the first pass of this loop, the final floorplan and synthesized netlist provide the inputs to the place and route tools. After the initial place and route, actual resistance and capacitance values are extracted from the physical design and delivered back to the static timing analysis tool. We can then perform static timing analysis to determine if the design meets our timing goals. If necessary, we can also perform power analysis to see if the design meets the power goals.

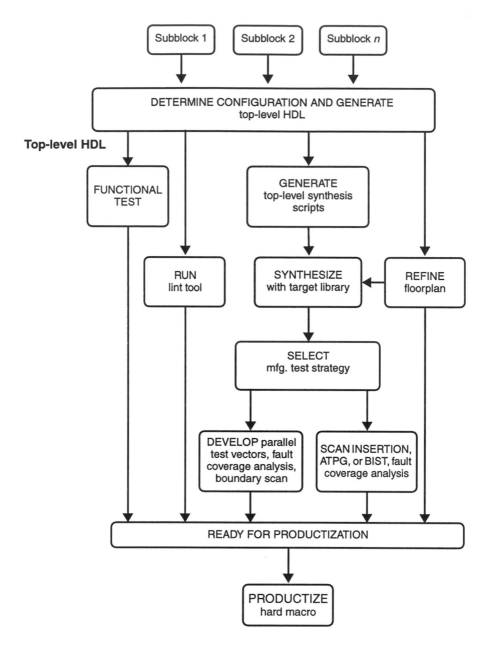

Figure 8-3   Flow for integrating subblocks into the hard macro

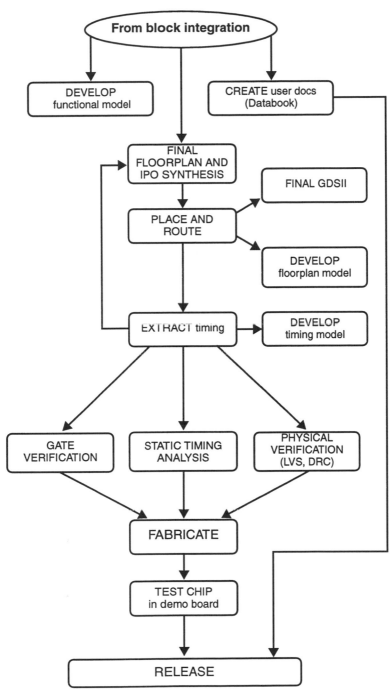

Figure 8-4   Productizing hard macros

If the physical design does not meet timing, we have two choices. If timing, power, or area is far from meeting specification, we may need to go back to the design phase and iterate as required. If we are reasonably close to meeting specification, however, we can focus on synthesis only. We first try using the IPO (In Place Optimization) feature of the synthesis tool. IPO modifies as little of the design as possible, focusing on resizing buffers. We then provide the updated netlist to the place and route tool and do an incremental place and route, where only the updated gates are modified in the physical design. By retaining as much of the original place and route as possible, we optimize our chances of rapidly converging on a good place and route.

One key to successful physical design is to have a high quality standard cell library. The library should have been fully characterized to ensure that the timing models are accurate. The library should also have all the views required to complete the design, including power modeling.

A single library, or a consistent set of libraries, should be used for all aspects of the design, including memory. For example, some libraries use a 30%-50% rise time, others use 20%-80%. Mixing these two different values in a single design can cause the static timing analysis tools to give incorrect post-extraction timing results.

8.5.2   Verification

Once we achieve our physical design goals with a place and route, we perform a series of verifications on the physical design:

Gate verification

We use formal verification to prove that the final gate-level netlist is equivalent to the RTL. For hand-crafted blocks, we use a combination of LVS (Layout vs. Schematic), to verify transistor to gate netlist equivalence, and formal verification. We also run full-timing, gate-level simulation to verify any asynchronous parts of the design.

In this book, we strongly recommend fully synchronous design, with no timing exceptions or multicycle paths and as few clock domains as possible. Following these rules makes static timing analysis very straightforward. If these rules are violated, however, it becomes necessary to develop fairly complex scripts to perform timing analysis correctly. These scripts, like all complex scripts, are subject to human error. For these designs, significant gate-level simulation may be necessary as a second check that the design meets timing.

Static Timing Analysis

We perform a final static timing analysis to verify that the design meets timing.

Physical Verification

We use LVS and DRC (Design Rule Checking) tools to verify the correctness of the final physical design.

The DRC and LVS decks are an important consideration in physical design. These decks provide the physical design rules used in physical verification of the final design. These decks need to be consistent between all the blocks in a chip design; integrating different blocks that use different decks can cause a physical verification nightmare. Typically, the hard macro designer gets these decks from the library provider; it is important that the chip design team uses the same decks for the rest of the chip, and in particular for any other hard macros used in the chip.

8.5.3   Models

In addition to the physical design database, we need to develop the models that the integrator will use to model the macro in the system design:

- The functional simulation model is developed from the final RTL.
- The floorplan model is developed as part of the floorplanning process.
- The timing model is developed using the extracted timing values.

The process and tools for developing these models are discussed later in this chapter.

8.5.4   Documentation

Finally, we need to create a complete set of user documentation to guide the integrator in using these models to develop the chip design. In addition to the requirements for a soft macro, the documentation for a hard macro includes:

- Footprint and size of the macro
- Detailed timing and power specification
- Routing restrictions and porosity
- Power and ground interconnect guidelines
- Clock and reset timing guidelines

8.6   Model Development for Hard Macros

The set of models provided to the integrator is the key to the usability of a hard macro. For most hard macros, the desired models include:

- Behavioral or ISA (Instruction Set Architecture) model for fast simulation. These models are typically used by the software team to develop the embedded software for the chip.
- Bus functional model for assisting system-level verification. Bus functional models can be used to create the system-level testbench and to test the rest of the chip.
- Full functional, cycle-accurate model for accurate simulation; this model is required for functional verification of the chip.
- Timing model; this model is required to perform full-chip timing analysis
- Floorplanning model for physical design
- Functional model for emulation (optional)

We can minimize the additional effort to create these models by leveraging the models that are created as part of the macro development process.

8.6.1   Functional Models

Hard macros are typically of high value and high complexity; only this kind of design justifies the additional effort to create a hard version. Because of this complexity, the RTL for these designs tends to simulate quite slowly, creating a bottleneck in the design process. Often, hard macros are processors, requiring significant application code to be developed while the chip is being designed. The software developers clearly need a very fast model of the processor to develop this software. On the other hand, the chip designers need a very accurate functional model to be sure that the entire chip will function correctly.

Because of these conflicting needs, it is usually necessary to provide a variety of functional models for a hard macro. These models make various tradeoffs between accuracy and speed to meet the various needs of the hardware and software design teams.

Most of these functional models are created as part of the macro design process. However, the method for packaging and delivering these models tends to be somewhat ad hoc. There are some tools, and some new emerging tools, for automating some aspects of model generation.

Model Security

One of the critical issues in developing a modeling process is determining the level of security required for the models. All the functional models described in this section are either C (or C++) models or HDL models. HDL source code for these models can be shipped directly to the customer if security is not a concern. This is often the case for bus functional models, which contain little information about the detailed functionality of the macro. If security is a concern, then some form of protection must be used. Often this security is achieved by providing a compiled version of the model.

One common form of protection is to compile the model and the simulation kernel into a single, stand-alone executable. An RTL wrapper is used to provide a simple timing and functional interface to the RTL for the rest of the chip. The Verilog PLI and VHDL language interfaces provide a reasonably straightforward mechanism for tying this kind of model into the simulator. By delivering object code, the designer ensures a high level of security.

Some commercial tools, such as VMC and SWIFT from Synopsys, and Visual IP from Summit can help automate the compilation of these models and provide a standard interface to the major commercial simulators.

Behavioral and ISA Models

Extensive hardware/software cosimulation is critical to the success of many SoC design projects. In turn, effective hardware/software cosimulation requires very high performance models for large system blocks. Behavioral and ISA models provide this level of performance by abstracting out many of the implementation details of the design.

Most processor design teams develop a high-level C/C++ model of the processor as they define the processor architecture. This model accurately reflects the instruction-level behavior of the processor while abstracting out implementation details. It is then used as a reference against which the detailed design is compared. This high level model is often referred to as an ISA (Instruction Set Architecture) or ISS (Instruction Set Simulator) model.

Because of their high level of abstraction, ISA models allow for very fast simulation.

The SoC designer using the processor core in a chip design can then use the ISA model to verify the software and the rest of the system design. The hardware/software cosimulation environment provides an interface between this model and the RTL simulation of the rest of the hardware, as shown in Figure 8-5.

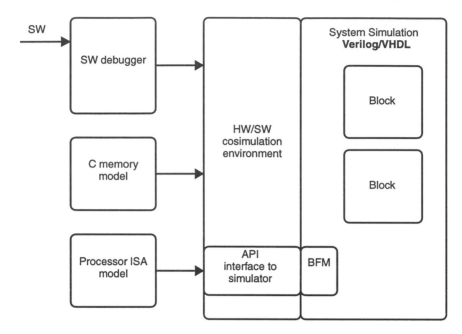

Figure 8-5   Hardware/software cosimulation using an ISA model

Behavioral models are the equivalent of ISA models for non-processor designs. Behavioral models represent the algorithmic behavior of the design at a very high level of abstraction, allowing very high speed simulation. For example, for a design using an MPEG macro, using a behavioral model instead of an RTL model can provide orders of magnitude faster system simulation.

Behavioral models can be written in C/C++, Verilog, or VHDL, and they may be protected or unprotected. Behavioral models can also be written using the new testbench generation tools VERA and Specman Elite.

A representative flow for compiling the behavioral Verilog/VHDL models is shown in Figure 8-6. A substantially equivalent flow is possible with Visual IP. VMC (Verilog Model Compiler) compiles the Verilog model and the simulation kernel into a VCS-compatible object format. VFM then adds the SWIFT interface, allowing the model to work with all major simulators.

In the flow shown in Figure 8-6, if the model is coded in VHDL, then it must first be translated to Verilog, because VMC does not yet support VHDL. (A VHDL version of VMC, VhMC, is under development.) The translation to Verilog can be done with commercial translation tools available from a number of vendors, including Inter-

HDL. These translation tools are not yet perfected, especially for behavioral code. However, they provide an initial translation that can be completed manually.

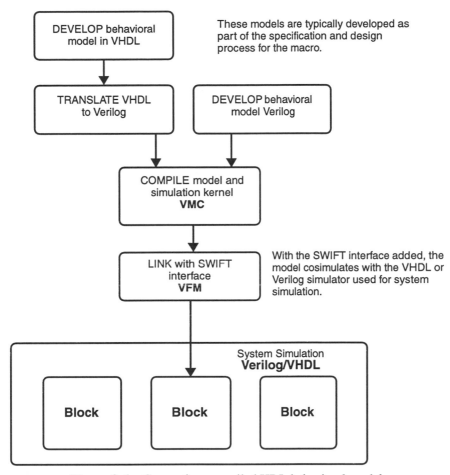

Figure 8-6   Generating compiled HDL behavioral models

Bus Functional Models

Bus functional models abstract out all the internal behavior of the macro, and only provide the capability of creating transactions on the output buses of the macro. These models are useful for system simulation when the integrator wants to test the rest of the system, independent of the macro. By abstracting out the internal behavior of the macro, we can develop a very fast model that still accurately models the detailed behavior of the macro at its interfaces.

In the past, bus functional models have usually been developed in Verilog or VHDL, and distributed in source code. Because so little of the detailed behavior of the macro is modeled, security is not a major concern.

The new testbench automation tools such as VERA and Specman Elite provide powerful features for creating bus functional models. In particular, they provide communication mechanisms to facilitate coordination between multiple BFMs. They also provide a richer semantics than either Verilog or VHDL for checking transactions on ports and buses. With these tools, it is relatively simple to create bus monitors to check the behavior of the rest of the chip as it interacts with the hard macro BFM.

Full Functional Models

Although more abstract models are useful for system-level verification, final verification of the RTL must be done using full functional models for all blocks in the design. Full functional models provide the detailed, cycle-by-cycle behavior of the macro. The RTL for the macro is a full functional model, and is the easiest full functional model to deliver to the integrator. Because the model is available in RTL, the flow shown in Figure 8-7 can be used. This flow is essentially the same as that for behavioral models coded in Verilog or VHDL.

Because the RTL for the macro is synthesizable, the requirement to translate VHDL to Verilog is much less of a problem than for behavioral models. Commercial translators do a reasonably good job of this translation.

Some hard macro providers choose to deliver a C-based model rather than an RTL-based model. The C-based model is a cycle-accurate, bit-accurate model of the macro, but written in C or C++ rather than Verilog or VHDL. The compilation process is essentially the same, however. The C model and the simulator kernel are compiled into a single executable, and an RTL wrapper provides the external interface.

The major problem with full functional models is that they are slow to simulate.

Full Functional Models with Timing

For some hard macros, it is necessary to provide a full functional model that contains detailed timing information. If the macro does not comply with the guidelines in this book, in particular if inputs and outputs are not registered, then static timing analysis may not be sufficient to ensure timing performance of the overall chip design. Also, if the macro exhibits asynchronous behavior, a full timing model may be required. Of course, asynchronous design is not recommended because it is much harder to verify.

We can develop a full functional, full timing simulation model from the back-annotated netlist obtained from place and route. The same compilation scheme shown in

Figure 8-7 can be used. The drawback of this approach is that simulation is extremely slow.

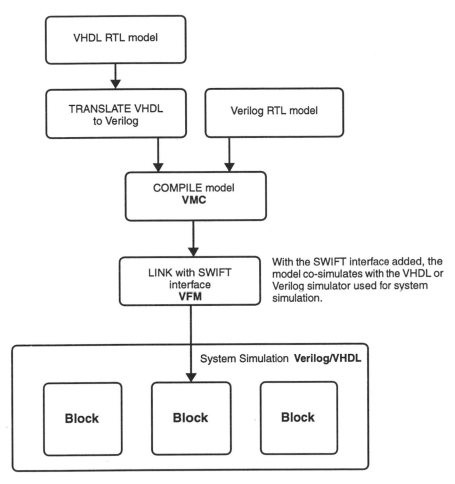

VHDL RTL model

TRANSLATE VHDL to Verilog

Verilog RTL model

COMPILE model
VMC

LINK with SWIFT interface
VFM

With the SWIFT interface added, the model co-simulates with the VHDL or Verilog simulator used for system simulation.

System Simulation **Verilog/VHDL**

Block

Block

Block

Figure 8-7   Generating full functional models

Figure 8-8 shows how to develop a full functional, full timing model with much better simulation performance. This approach takes the full functional model developed from the RTL (or C/C++) and adds a timing wrapper; that is, a set of structures on the inputs and outputs that can be used to model the actual delays (and setup and hold requirements) of the macro. The timing information for these buffers can be derived from the extracted timing information from place and route. This approach can be very effective provided that the macro is designed so that it does not have state dependent timing.

State dependent timing occurs when the timing characteristics of the block depend on the value of the inputs or on the internal state of the block. For example, asynchronous RAMs have different timing for read and write modes. On the other hand, synchronous RAMs have exactly the same timing regardless of mode, and thus are easier to characterize. Using a fully synchronous design style ensures that the macro will have no state dependent timing.

It can be extremely burdensome to develop timing shells for blocks with state dependent timing, to the point where this approach is not practical.

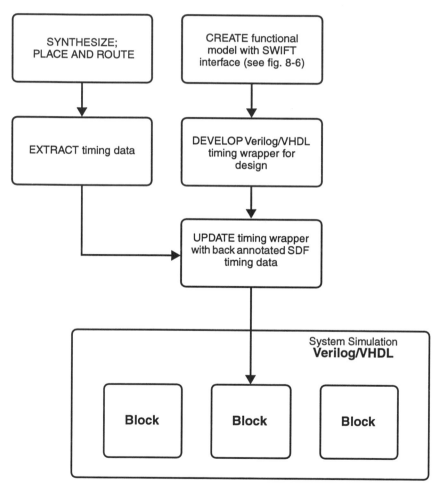

Figure 8-8   Generating full functional models with timing

Emulation Models

One of the major problems with full functional models is the slow simulation speeds achieved with them. Emulation is one approach to addressing the problem of slow system-level simulation with full functional models.

Emulation requires that the model for the macro be compiled into a gate-level representation. We can provide the RTL directly to the integrator, who can then use the emulator's compiler to generate the netlist, but this does not provide any security.

An alternate approach is to provide a netlist to the integrator. This approach provides some additional security for the macro. A separate synthesis of the macro, compiling for area with no timing constraints, will give a reasonable netlist for emulation without providing a netlist that meets the full performance of the macro.

Some emulation systems have more sophisticated approaches to providing security for hard macro models. See Chapter 11 for a brief discussion on this subject.

Hardware Models

Hardware models provide an alternate approach for providing highly secure full functional models. Because the hard macro design process requires that we produce a working test chip for the macro, this approach is often a practical form of model generation.

Hardware modelers are systems that allow a physical device to interface directly to a software simulator. The modeler is, in effect, a small tester that mounts the chip on a small board. When the pins of the device are driven by the software simulator, the appropriate values are driven to the physical chip. Similarly, when the outputs of the chip change, these changes are propagated to the software simulator.

Rapid prototyping systems, such as those from Aptix, also allow a physical chip to be used in modeling the overall system. These systems are described in Chapter 11.

Some emulators, including those from Mentor Graphics, allow physical chips to be used to model part of the system. Thus, the test chip itself is an important full functional model for the macro.

In all these cases, it is important that the physical chip reflect exactly the functionality of the macro. For example, with a microprocessor, one might be tempted to make the data bus bi-directional on the chip, to save pins, even though the macro uses unidirectional data buses. This approach makes it much more difficult to control the core and verify system functionality with a hardware modeler or emulator.

8.6.2   Synthesis and Floorplanning Models

The timing and floorplanning models can be generated from the design database.

From the final place and route of the macro, we can extract the basic blockage information, pin locations, and pin layers of the macro. This information can then used by the integrator when floorplanning the SoC design. This information is typically delivered in the LEF format.

Figure 8-9 shows the process for developing a static timing analysis model for the hard macro. From the SDF back-annotated netlist for the macro, the PrimeTime timing analysis tool extracts a black-box timing model for the macro. This model provides the setup and hold time requirements for input pins and the clock-to-output delays for the output pins. This model is delivered as a Synopsys standard format .db file. During static timing analysis on the entire chip, PrimeTime uses the context information, including actual ramp rates and output loading, to adjust the timing of the hard macro model to reflect the macro's actual timing in the chip.

For this black-box model to work, of course, the design must have no state-dependent timing. For blocks that do have state-dependent timing, a gray box timing model must be used; this model retains all of the internal timing information in the design. The entire back-annotated netlist can be used as a gray-box model, but it will result in slower static timing analysis runtimes.

If the hard macro has any blocks that are handcrafted at the transistor level, we need another approach to extract this timing information. Figure 8-10 shows a flow for this case. After parasitic extraction, the CoreMill static timing analysis tool verifies that the timing requirements for the design are met. Through a configuration file, the designer provides the input ramp rates and output loading information, as well as identification of input, output, and clock pins. When timing has been successfully verified, CoreMill can generate a black box timing model for the design in Stamp format. If desired, additional characterization information can be provided to the tool, and CoreMill will develop a table of timing values based on different input ramp rates and output loading. PrimeTime uses this Stamp model to develop the final timing model in the .db format.

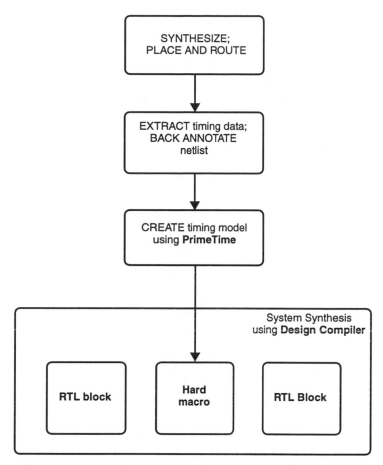

Figure 8-9   Generating static timing models for standard cell designs

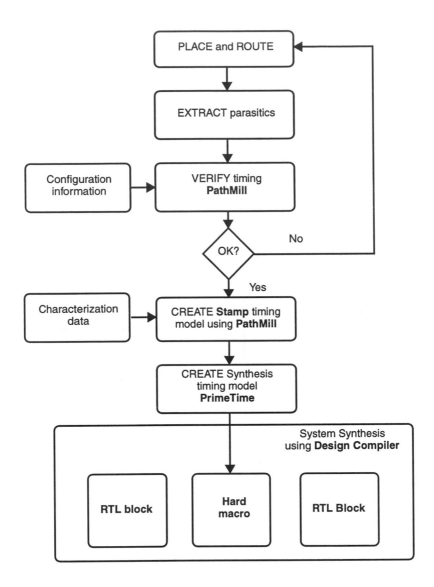

Figure 8-10   Generating static timing models for full custom designs

8.7   Porting Hard Macros

One of the challenges for hard macro provider is to port the macro rapidly from one process to another.

For hard IP that was completely synthesized, the porting strategy is quite straightforward. We just resynthesize, targeting the new technology library, and repeat the physical design and timing model generation. If we have saved the scripts from our initial physical design, and these scripts were written to be as technology-independent as possible, then this is a reasonably painless process.

For those sections of the design that are full custom, we have the choice between manual porting and automated porting. Under certain circumstances, automatic porting tools such as Segantec's DREAM can be effective. These tools operate at the polygon level, automatically mapping transistors and interconnect from one set of design rules to another, and shrinking the design as much as possible.

This polygon mapping works quite well on cell libraries, and reasonably well on small blocks, perhaps hundreds of gates. As the blocks get larger, the chances increase that we will run into problems that require significant manual intervention. These problems can slow down the porting process dramatically. This is another reason why we recommend reserving full custom design only for the most critical subblocks of the design.

The problems typically encountered in automated porting include clocking and hold time problems. As the technology shrinks, circuits speed up, and the acceptable clock skew becomes smaller, and minimum delays from flop to flop become less. These problems can be difficult to resolve, and can require adding or resizing gates and buffers.

One of the time-consuming aspects of using the porting tools is establishing the corresponding design rules for the source and target technologies. One way of reducing the risk of porting problems with automatic porting tools is to use lambda rules in the initial full custom design. With these rules, all the physical constraints of the process are described as multiples of lambda, a unit length representative of the technology. If the design constraints of both the source and target libraries are both described as lambda rules, and the original macro design complies with the source library lambda rules, then automatic mapping is significantly easier.

CHAPTER 9 — *Macro Deployment: Packaging for Reuse*

This chapter discusses macro deployment issues, including deliverables for hard and soft macros and the importance of keeping a design archive. The topics are:

- Delivering the complete product
- The contents of the user guide

9.1   Delivering the Complete Product

Once a macro has been designed according to the guidelines detailed in the preceding chapters, the macro must be packaged and delivered to the customer. The packaging of the macro depends on how it will be delivered.

Soft macros require:

- The RTL code
- Support files
- Documentation

Hard macros require:

- A rich set of models for system integration
- Documentation support for integration into the final chip

In addition, all files associated with the development of the macro must be stored together in a design archive so that all necessary information is available when it is time to modify or upgrade the macro.

As described in Chapter 4, a physical prototype of the macro is built as part of the verification phase of the macro development. Many third party vendors make this prototype available to customers either as a demonstration of capability or as an evaluation unit. Evaluation prototypes are particularly helpful with programmable macros like microcontrollers and microprocessors; application code can be developed and run on the prototype to verify functionality and performance.

9.1.1   Soft Macro Deliverables

Table 9-1 lists the deliverables for soft macros.

Table 9-1   Deliverables for soft macros

Group	Deliverables
Product files	• Synthesizable Verilog for the macro and its subblocks • Synthesizable VHDL for the macro and its subblocks • Application notes, including Verilog/VHDL design examples that instantiate the macro • Synthesis scripts and timing constraints • Scripts for scan insertion and ATPG • CBA or other reference library • Installation scripts
Verification files	• Bus functional models/monitors used in testbench • Testbench files, including representative verification tests
Documentation files	• User guide/functional specification • Datasheet
System Integration files	• Bus functional models of other system components • Cycle-based/emulation models as appropriate to the particular macro and/or its testbenches and BFMs • Recommendation of commercially available software required for hardware/software cosimulation and system integration, as appropriate for the particular macro

Product Files

In addition to the RTL in Verilog and VHDL, we must include the synthesis and installation scripts. We include the reference CBA library so that the customer can synthesize the design and verify that the installation was completed successfully. In addition, providing the reference library, scripts, and verification environment allows the user the recreate the developer's environment. This allows the user to verify many of the claims of the developer, in terms of timing, power, area, and testability of the macro.

The CBA reference library is also very helpful in identifying library problems in the integrator's environment. Synthesis libraries vary considerably. If the integrator encounters synthesis problems with the vendor's library, the integrator can synthesize exactly the same configuration with the same scripts using the CBA library. This process helps the integrator identify whether the problem is in the macro (and its scripts) or in the vendor's technology library.

Application notes that show exactly how to instantiate the design are also useful. If the application notes are available in soft form, the integrator can cut and paste the instantiation example, avoiding typographical errors and ensuring correct port names.

Verification files

The entire verification environment, including any bus functional models, bus monitors, or other models, and some set of verification test cases are shipped with the product. The test cases that ship with the macro typically do not represent the full test suite used to verify the macro. Typically, a subset is shipped that is sufficient to ensure that the macro has been installed correctly at the integrator's site. The integrator then develops a test suite to verify the functionality of the macro in the full chip.

The bus functional models used to develop and verify the macro can be used by the integrator to create a testbench environment for the SoC chip. See Chapter 11 for more discussion on using bus functional models for system-level testing.

System Integration Files

Depending on the specific macro, there may be additional deliverables that are useful for the integrator.

For large macros, where simulation speed in the system environment may be an issue, it can be useful to include cycle-based simulation and/or emulation models. In general, RTL that complies with the coding guidelines in this document will work with cycle-based simulation and emulation. However, testbenches and bus functional models, unless coded to these same RTL guidelines, may not be usable with these verification tools. It is up to the macro provider to determine which models need to be provided in cycle-based simulation/emulation compatible forms.

For macros that have significant software requirements, such as microcontrollers and processors, it is useful to include a list of compilers, debuggers, and real-time operating systems that support the macro. For other designs, we may want to reference software drivers that are compatible with the design. In most cases, the macro provider will not be providing the software itself, but should provide information on how to obtain the required software from third-party providers.

9.1.2   Hard Macro Deliverables

Table 9-2 lists the deliverables for a hard macro.

The list of deliverables in Table 9-2 assumes that the physical integration is being done by the silicon vendor rather than by the chip designer who is using the macro. This model applies when the silicon vendor is also the macro vendor. In the case where the chip designer is also doing the physical integration of the macro onto the chip, the physical GDSII design files are also part of the deliverables.

Table 9-2   Deliverables for hard macros

Group	Deliverables
Product files	• Installation scripts
Verification files	• None
Documentation files	• User guide/functional specification • Datasheet
System Integration files	• ISA or behavioral model • Bus functional model for macro • Full functional model for macro • Cycle-based simulation/emulation models as appropriate to the particular macro • Timing and synthesis model for macro • Floorplanning model for macro • Recommendation of commercially available software required for hardware/software cosimulation and system integration, as appropriate for the particular macro • Test patterns for manufacturing test, where applicable

The deliverables for hard macros consist primarily of the documentation and models needed by the integrator to design and verify the rest of the system. These models are described in Chapter 8.

For processors, an ISA model provides a high level model that models the behavior of the processor instruction-by-instruction, but without modeling all of the implementation details of the design. This model provides a high speed model for system testing, especially for hardware/software cosimulation. Many microprocessor vendors also provide a tool for estimating code size and overall performance; such a tool can help determine key memory architecture features such as cache, RAM, and ROM size.

For other macros, a behavioral model provides the high speed system-level simulation model. The behavioral model models the functionality of the macro, on a transaction-by-transaction basis, but without all the implementation details. A behavioral model is most useful for large macros, where a full-functional model is too slow for system-level verification.

For large macros, bus functional models provide the fastest simulation speed by modeling only the bus transactions of the macro. Such a model can be used to test that other blocks in the system respond correctly to the bus transactions generated by the macro.

The full functional model for the macro allows the integrator to test the full functionality of the system, and thus is key to system-level verification.

As in the case of soft macros, cycle-based simulation and/or emulation models, especially for the macro testbench, may be useful for the integrator. These models are optional deliverables.

The timing and synthesis models provide the information needed by the integrator to synthesize the soft portion of the chip with the context information from the hard macro. These models provide the basic timing and loading characteristics of the macro's inputs and outputs.

The floorplanning model for macro provides information the integrator needs to develop a floorplan of the entire chip.

Test patterns for manufacturing test must be provided to the silicon manufacturer at least, if not to the end user. For scan-based designs, the ATPG patterns and control information needed to apply the test patterns must be provided. For non-scan designs, the test patterns and the information needed to apply the test patterns is required; usually access is provided through a JTAG boundary-scan ring around the macro.

9.1.3   The Design Archive

Table 9-3 lists the items that must be stored together in the design archive. All of these items are needed when any change, upgrade, or modification is made to the macro. The use of a software revision control system for archiving each version is a crucial step in the design reuse workflow, and will save vast amounts of aggravation and frustration in the future.

Table 9-3   Contents of the design archive

Group	Contents
Product files	• Synthesizable Verilog for the macro and its subblocks • Synthesizable VHDL for the macro and its subblocks • CBA reference library • Verilog /VHDL design examples that instantiate the macro • Synthesis scripts • Installation scripts
Verification files	• Bus functional models/monitors used in testbench • Testbench files
Documentation files	• User guide/functional specification • Technical specification • Datasheet • Test plan • Simulation log files • Simulation coverage reports (VHDLCover, VeriSure, or equivalent) • Synthesis results for multiple technologies • Testability report • Lint report that demonstrates compliance to coding guidelines
System Integration files	• Bus functional models of other system components • Recommendation of commercially available software required for hardware/software cosimulation and system integration, as appropriate for the particular macro • Cycle-based simulator and hardware emulator models

9.2   Contents of the User Guide

The user guide is the key piece of documentation that guides the macro user through the selection, integration, and verification of the macro. It is essential that the user guide provides sufficient information, in sufficient detail, that a potential user can evaluate whether the macro is appropriate for the application. It must also provide all the information needed to integrate the macro into the overall chip design. The user guide should contain, at a minimum, the following information:

- Architecture and functional description
- Claims and assumptions
- Detailed description of I/O
- Exceptions to coding/design guidelines
- Block diagram
- Register map
- Timing diagrams
- Timing specifications and performance
- Power dissipation
- Size/gate count
- Test structures, testability, and test coverage
- Configuration information and parameters
- Recommended clocking and reset strategies
- Recommended software environment, including compilers and drivers
- Recommended system verification strategy
- Recommended test strategy
- Floorplanning guidelines
- Debug strategy, including in-circuit emulation and recommended debug tools
- Version history and known bugs

The user guide is an important element of the design-for-reuse process. Use it to note all information that future consumers of your macro need to know in order to use the macro effectively. The following categories are especially important:

Claims and assumptions

Before purchasing a macro, the user must be able to evaluate its applicability to the end design. To facilitate this evaluation, the user guide must explicitly list all of the key features of the design, including timing performance, size, and power requirements. If the macro implements a standard (for example, the IEEE 1394 interface), then its compliance must be stated, along with any exceptions or areas where the macro is not fully compliant to the published specification. VSIA suggests that, in addition to this information, the macro documentation include a section describing how the user can duplicate the development environment and verify the claims.

For soft IP, the deliverables include a reference library, complete scripts, and a verification environment, so these claims can be easily verified.

For hard IP, the end user does not have access to the GDSII, and so many of the claims are unverifiable. We recommend including actual measured values for timing performance and power in the user guide.

Exceptions to the coding/design guidelines

Any exceptions to the design and coding guidelines outlined in this manual must be noted in the user guide. It is especially important to explain any asynchronous circuits, combinational inputs, and combinational outputs.

Timing specifications and performance

Timing specifications include input setup and hold times for all input and I/O pins and clock-to-output delays for all output pins. Timing specifications for any combinational inputs/outputs must be clearly documented in the user guide. Timing for soft macros must be specified for a representative process.

CHAPTER 10

System Integration with Reusable Macros

This chapter discusses the process of integrating completed macros into the whole chip environment. The topics arc:

- Integration overview
- Integrating soft macros
- Integrating hard macros
- Integrating RAMs and datapath generators
- Physical design

10.1 Integration Overview

Chapter 2 described system design from specification to the point where individual blocks could be designed. The succeeding chapters described how these blocks should be designed in order to make them reusable. We now return to the issue of system design, and discuss how to assemble these blocks into the final chip.

At this point in system design, there are two key tasks remaining: physical design and functional verification. Each of these tasks has a dominant challenge. For physical design it is achieving timing closure; for verification, it is knowing when we are done, when we are confident enough in the functionality of the chip that we can tape out and go to fabrication.

In this chapter, we address the integration of the blocks and the physical design of the chip. In the next chapter, we discuss functional verification.

The process of integrating the blocks and doing the physical design can be broken into the following steps:

- Selecting IP blocks and preparing them for integration
- Integrating all the blocks into the top-level RTL
- Planning the physical design
- Synthesis and initial timing analysis
- Initial physical design and timing analysis, with iteration until timing closure
- Final physical design, timing verification, and power analysis
- Physical verification of the design

10.2 Integrating Macros into an SoC Design

Integrating macros into the top-level SoC design poses several challenges. In this section, we will discuss typical integration problems and strategies for dealing with them.

10.2.1 Problems in Integrating IP

Assembling a set of blocks into a top-level design presents a series of challenges to the design team. Naturally, we did a good job of decomposing the design into well-specified blocks, then selected the IP we needed and designed the new blocks required as specified. Nonetheless, when we get down to assembling these blocks and making them work together, we often find issues.

For blocks that were designed specifically for this chip, we tend to find:

- The low level interfaces do not work; for example, a handshake signal is inverted.
- There was a misunderstanding of the functionality of the block.
- There are functional bugs in the design.

Usually we have access to the block designers and the system architect, so these problems are reasonably easy to fix.

For IP that has been obtained from an external source, either a third party or some other division of the company, there are additional problems that frequently occur:

- Someone on the team needs to become familiar enough with the IP to integrate it into the design.
- The documentation is incomplete, making this understanding harder to obtain.
- The interface of the IP does not match the interface of the system bus.

- The verification models, such as bus functional models, are poorly written and difficult to integrate into the system verification environment.
- Only limited support is available from the IP provider.

We will defer the discussion of the verification issues until the next chapter. For now we will focus on the most serious of the other problems: interfaces that don't match the system.

It is not unusual for a team to purchase a piece of IP that consists of 20k gates or so, and then find that they have to design an additional block of 20k gates just to interface it to the rest of the system. Most digital block interfaces are designed to pass data; that is, they perform data reads and writes to other blocks. The protocol for these transactions may be quite different between different designs, and differ at different levels.

The detailed handshake may differ; one block may required a "ready for data" signal from the target before it does a write, while the target may expect a "request for write" signal before it reports status. At a higher level, blocks may have different kinds of transactions: posted writes, burst reads with or without out of order return data, and interrupted or aborted transactions. Incompatibilities at this level are more difficult to resolve.

The most difficult interface problems usually involve exception handling: interrupts, aborted transactions, and other unusual transactions. Differences at this level may have to be resolved at a high level, perhaps even requiring changes to the architecture of one of the blocks or the entire system.

10.2.2 Strategies for Managing Interfacing Issues

There is no universal solution for these interfacing issues except to adopt a universal interface standard. Some groups are attempting to establish internal standards within their companies, but we are a long way from having anything approaching a uniform standard across the industry. The power, performance, and protocol needs of different designs are just too disparate to make this approach practical.

There are several steps designs teams can take, however, to mitigate the problem:

- Plan the interfaces. We can identify early the kinds external IP to be used and analyze the interface protocols involved. We can then select the specific IP, and define the interfaces for the custom blocks, so that they can all be integrated with a minimum amount of additional interface design. What additional interface design is required can be included in the overall project plan. The main idea here is not to leave these interface issues until the last moment, and then be surprised at the additional work, and schedule slip, involved.

- Keep all interfaces as simple as possible, whether we are designing IP or custom blocks. These interfaces should usually include data read and ready for data signals, so the connecting blocks know the ready status at all times.

- Standardize on a few common buses and block-to-block interfaces. It may not be possible for a company or even a design team to standardize on a single bus, but in many cases it is possible to standardize on a few. One design team has standardized on three standard buses; all IP is developed to support all three buses, as a user-selectable option. All chips are designed using only these three buses. This may result in some sacrifice of timing, area, or power, but the time-to-market advantage more than compensates for this.

- Accumulate IP and experience with the IP. Once a team has gained experience with a piece of IP, has used it successfully in a design, and has learned how to interface it to other blocks, that IP has significantly increased in value. There is a significant advantage to building a library of such IP, and leveraging it to create new designs. Some software reuse books talk of "product line planning", where multiple related products are developed over time to leverage investments in reusable IP.

- Document this expertise. If a piece of IP has deficient documentation, supplement it with the knowledge accumulated using it in a design. One of the most challenging aspects of using someone else's design is learning how it works, and how to use it. Capturing this knowledge in a document can help other integrators of the IP.

10.2.3   Interfacing Hard Macros to the Rest of the Design

In addition to the issues discussed above, hard IP presents some additional challenges for the integrator. For soft macros, power and clock tree routing, as well as scan insertion, are done during chip-level integration. This fact ensures the consistent and compatible power, clock, and test structure design. For hard macros, these are done during macro design, and the interfaces between the hard macro and the rest of the chip must be well thought out before integrating the macro into the chip.

Clock distribution

Typically, the macro has its own internal clock tree. The overall clock distribution for the chip must accommodate the (already fixed) timing of the hard macro clock. In some cases, a clock output from the hard macro is used to synchronize the clocks for the rest of the system.

Power and ground

Typically, the macro also has its own power and ground rings within the macro. The physical design of the rest of the chip must account for this, and provide the appropriate power and ground connections to the macro.

Test Structures

Well designed hard macros have their own embedded testability structures. These may include a JTAG port or a full scan port. The macro may also have embedded structures for facilitating debug. These structures must be integrated into the overall chip design.

10.3 Selecting IP

In addressing the issues raised in the previous sections, one key step is to select IP that can be easily integrated into the overall chip design. Choosing well-designed, well-documented IP can greatly reduce the integration effort.

10.3.1 Hard Macro Selection

The first step in selecting a macro from an external source, or in specifying a macro that is to be developed by an internal source, is to determine the exact requirements for the macro. For microprocessor cores, this means developing an understanding of the instruction set, interfaces, and available peripherals.

Once the requirements for the macro are fully understood, the most critical factors affecting the choice between several competing sources for a hard macro are:

Quality of the documentation
Good documentation is key to determining the appropriateness of a particular macro for a particular application. The basic functionality, interface definitions, timing, and how to integrate and verify the macro should be clearly documented.

Completeness of the design and verification environment
In particular, functional, timing, synthesis, and floorplanning models must be provided.

If the macro is a microprocessor core, the vendor should supply or recommend a third-party supplier for the compilers and debuggers required to make the system design successful.

Robustness of the design
The design must have been proven in silicon.

Physical design limitations
Aspect ratio, blockage and porosity of the macro — the degree to which the macro forces signal routing around rather than through the macro — must be considered. A design that uses many macros that completely block routing may result in very long wires between blocks, producing unacceptable delays.

10.3.2   Soft Macro Selection

The first step in selecting a macro from an external source, or in specifying a macro that is to be developed by an internal source, is to determine the exact requirements for the macro. For a standards-based macro, such as a PCI core or a IEEE 1394 core, this means developing a sufficient understanding of the standard involved.

Once the requirements for the macro are fully understood, the choices can quickly be narrowed to those that meet the functional, timing, area, and power requirements of the design. The most critical factors affecting the choice between several competing sources for a soft macro are:

Quality of the documentation

Good documentation is key to determining the appropriateness of a particular macro for a particular application. The basic functionality, interface definitions, timing, and how to configure and synthesize the macro should be clearly documented.

Robustness of the verification environment

Much of the value, and the development cost, of a macro lies in the verification suite. A rich set of models and monitors for generating stimulus to the macro and checking its behavior can make the overall chip verification much easier. These models and monitors should be compatible with the chip-level verification environment.

Robustness of the design

A robust, well-designed macro still requires some effort to integrate into a chip design. A poorly designed macro can create major problems and schedule delays. Verifying the robustness of a macro in advance of actually using it is difficult. A review of the deliverables for compliance to the design, coding, and verification guidelines in this book is a first step. But for a macro to be considered robust, it must have been proven in silicon.

Ease of use

In addition to the above issues, ease of use includes the ease of interfacing the macro to the rest of the design, as well as the quality and user-friendliness of the installation and synthesis scripts. Some IP providers offer user interface tools, such as Synopsys coreBuilder and coreConsultant and Altera's MegaWizard to make soft cores easier to use.

10.3.3   Soft Macro Installation

The macro, its documentation, and its full design verification environment should be installed and integrated into your design environment much like an internally developed block. In particular, all components of the macro package should be under revision control. Even if you do not have to modify the design, putting the design under revision control helps ensure that it will be archived along with the rest of the design, so that the entire chip development environment can be recreated if necessary.

10.3.4 Soft Macro Configuration

Many soft macros are configurable through parameter settings. Designing with a soft macro begins with setting the parameters and generating the complete RTL for the desired configuration. A key issue here is to make sure that the combination of parameter settings is consistent and correct. Some IP providers supply configuration wizards with their IP to guide the user and prevent illegal configurations of the IP.

10.3.5 Synthesis of Soft Macros

The final step in preparing the IP for integration is to perform an initial synthesis with the target technology library. This initial synthesis can give a good preliminary indication of whether the macro will meet the timing, area, and power goals of the design.

10.4 Integrating Memories

Memories are a special case of the hard macro, and are worth some additional comment.

Large, on-chip memories are typically output from memory compilers. These compilers produce the functional and timing models along with the physical design information required to fabricate the memory. The issues affecting memory design are identical to those affecting hard macro designs, with the following additional issues:

- The integrator typically has a wide choice of RAM configurations, such as single port or multi-port, fast or low-power, synchronous or asynchronous.

- Asynchronous RAMs present a problem because generating a write clock requires a very timing-critical design that is tricky to create and difficult to verify. A fully synchronous RAM is strongly preferred.

- Large RAMs with fixed aspect ratios can present significant blockage problems. Check with your RAM provider to see if the aspect ratio of the RAMs can be modified if necessary.

- BIST is available for many RAM designs, and can greatly reduce test time and eliminates the need to bring RAM I/O to the chip's pins. However, the integrator should be cautious because some BIST techniques do not test for data retention problems.

10.5 Physical Design

The major challenge in the physical implementation of large SoC design is achieving timing closure. This process is inherently iterative; a typical spiral process where each iteration gets us closer to our performance goals. The problem that design teams often encounter is that many iterations are required to achieve their timing objectives, and each iteration can take many days. The result is often major delays to the project.

Many of the design guidelines in this book are intended to minimize the number of iterations in physical design by making timing closure as contained and local a problem as possible. In particular, the rules on partitioning, registering outputs, and fully synchronous design are key to containing the timing closure problem.

In this section we outline a process that can help make the iterations as few and quick as possible.

Figure 10-1 outlines the process of integrating the various blocks into the final version of the chip and getting the chip through physical design. There are several variations on the flow shown here depending on the size of chip, the number of hard and soft blocks, and targeted performance. We describe here a representative flow, and will discuss briefly some of the main variants.

This process consists of four major activities:

- **Preparation of the design** – Planning the physical implementation of the chip, performing block-level and then chip-level synthesis, doing a detailed floorplanning, and initial route of the chip.
- **Placement loop** – Iterating on placing the chip, analyzing the timing results, and modifying placement until timing goals are met.
- **Timing closure** – Adding clocks and detailed routing, doing a more accurate timing analysis, and fixing any remaining timing problems.
- **Physical verification** – Running the final checks on the design prior to tapeout.

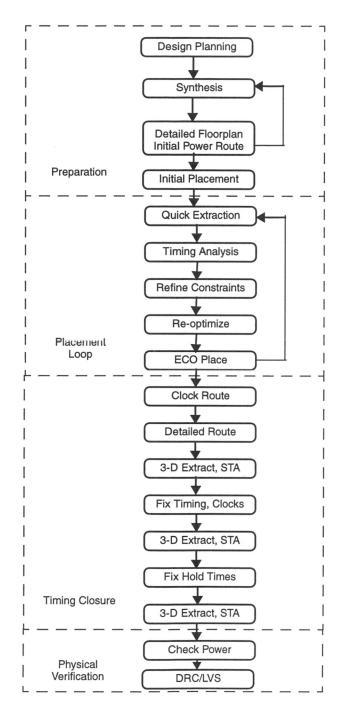

Figure 10-1 Integrating blocks into a chip

10.5.1 Design Planning to Initial Placement

Preparation of the design involves design planning, synthesis, floorplan, and initial routing.

Design Planning

Physical design starts with planning, and this planning can be done quite early in the design process. At the very start of the design, before blocks are designed or IP selected, the team should do an initial estimate of die size and power dissipation. This information is key for determining package type.

Once the team has partitioned the design into blocks, the team can do a preliminary floorplan. This initial floorplan should include a rough placement of blocks and I/O pads, as well as some preliminary planning for the power and clock distribution. This information can be used to provide more accurate wire load models and timing budgets for synthesis.

If the inputs and outputs of each block are registered, then the timing budget is quite straightforward — the block just has to meet the clock frequency target of the design. The wire load model can be determined from the gate count of the block. The floorplanning information primarily helps identify long wires between blocks, or from blocks to I/O pads, which will required extra buffering.

If only the outputs of each block are registered, then the relative placement of the block on the chip affects both the wire load model and the time budget of the block. In Figure 10-2(a), the blocks are close so that the arrival times at the inputs of Block B are nearly the same as the output time of Block A. The wire load model for Block A is probably accurate enough for the outputs of Block A as well as the internal signals. In Figure 10-2(b), the blocks are at opposite corners of the chip; this can mean a significant wire delay between the blocks. The outputs in Block A must be buffered up to drive the capacitance of the long wires, and the timing budget of Block B must be modified to allow for a later arrival time at its inputs.

Once the team has RTL (for the soft blocks) and GDSII (for the hard blocks), the team can use an RTL floorplanner such as Chip Architect to refine the floorplan. In particular, the team can assign physical locations for the I/Os of each block and do top-level routing. This approach can give very accurate estimates of the capacitive loading on the top-level interconnect, making synthesis much more accurate.

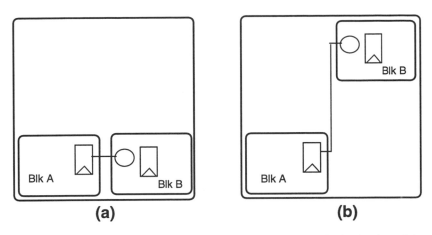

(a)   **(b)**

Figure 10-2   The floorplan affects timing budgets and wire load models

Synthesis

Armed with this preliminary physical design information, the design team can now do a full synthesis of the chip. Using the wire load models and timing budgets from the initial floorplan, we synthesize each block independently.

Once each block is meeting timing, we do a top-level synthesis of the entire chip, using timing models for the hard macros. At the top level, synthesis should be required only to stitch together the top-level netlist and refine the system-level interconnect: resizing buffers driving inter-block signals, fixing hold-time problems, and the like. For critical inter-block paths, some re-budgeting may be required. For this, we can go back to the design planning tool to readjust block placement, or I/O placement for the key blocks, or to re-route some top-level nets. Then, we can generate a new top-level timing budget and wire loads, and re-run block-level synthesis.

The inputs to the top-level synthesis include:

- Timing budgets and wire load models from the design planning stage
- RTL (or a netlist synthesized from RTL) for the synthesizable blocks
- Synthesis models for the hard macros and memories
- Netlists for any modules generated from a datapath generator
- Any libraries required, such as the DesignWare Foundation Library
- Top-level RTL that instantiates the blocks, the I/O pads, and top-level test structures

The synthesis models for the hard macros and memories include the timing and area information required to complete synthesis on the whole chip and to verify timing at the chip level.

The top-level test structures typically include any test controllers, such as a JTAG TAP controller or a custom controller for scan and on-chip BIST (Built-In Self Test) structures.

After the top-level netlist has been generated, scan cells should be inserted in the appropriate blocks for testability. An ATPG (Automatic Test Pattern Generator) tool can then be used to generate scan test vectors for the chip. Scan insertion is typically done by a test synthesis tool. Note that at this point, test synthesis merely replaces standard flops with scan flops. The actual stitching of flops into the scan chain is typically done as part of the chip routing. Thus, the scan interconnect between flops, which is arbitrary, can be optimized for minimum wire length.

Similarly, if JTAG is required, JTAG structures should be added to the netlist. Typically, this step is also performed by a tool.

If clock gating is needed to reduce power, then the power compiler should be used to convert mux-hold flops into gated clocks.

Once all the test structures are in place, a final timing analysis is performed to verify chip timing and, if necessary, an incremental synthesis is performed to achieve the chip timing requirements.

The final netlist, along with timing information, is now ready for detailed floorplanning.

Note: As we go through the block and chip-level budgeting and synthesis, we begin to realize the benefit of some of the design and coding guidelines. In particular, it quickly becomes obvious that false paths and timing exceptions present a real problem. Any exception to the basic timing goals, such as paths that take two cycles, or test signals that do not have to meet the operating frequency, need to be listed in the synthesis and budgeting scripts. This manual process is very prone to error. The authors have seen large chips where there were literally thousands of timing exceptions. In cases like these, the designers consistently miss a significant number of paths, either specifying a path as false when it is not, or the other way around.

Either of these cases can result in synthesis and timing problems. If the path is not false and we mark it as false, then clearly it will not be synthesized to meet timing. On the other hand, if a path is false and is not marked as false, then synthesis will work hard to get it to meet timing, often to the extent of not optimizing other paths that really are critical.

Thus, to meet timing, it is essential that the false path lists be completely correct. For this reason, we strongly recommend that designers avoid false and multicycle paths completely. Worst case, the list of paths should be very short.

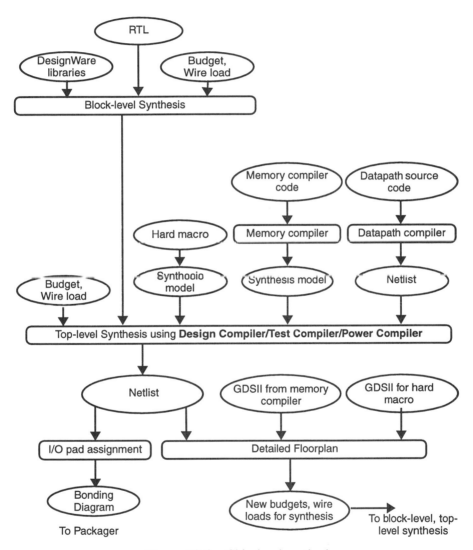

Figure 10-3 Chip-level synthesis

Detailed Floorplan and Initial Power Route

At this point, we can read the final netlist into the floorplanning tool and complete the preparation for placement. We can fix, if we haven't already:

- Block placement
- I/O pad placement
- Placement of the I/O cells for each block

Next, we do an initial route of the power mesh, the distribution of power and ground in the chip. Designers have found that doing the power routing before detailed placement improves the overall design. Power routing takes routing resources on the chip that could otherwise be used for routing signals. Thus, an optimal placement may need to place critical cells away from the blocked routing channels.

Typically power routing involves placing wide power and ground rings around the periphery of the chip, and then cross-hatching the chip with a mesh of power and ground wires. For large chips, the chip may be divided up into sections, with each section having its own power and ground rings.

Often, chips will have different power supplies (and power rings) for I/O and the core logic, especially if they run off of different voltages. For example, in low power designs, the core is often run at as low a voltage as possible (for example, 1.5v) while the I/O must run at standard voltages, such as 3.3v. Also, any analog block, such as a PLL or A/D converter, may need a separate power and ground supply to provide noise isolation.

Initial Placement

Once the synthesized netlist meets timing based on wire load models, the placement engine needs to place the design such that the timing goals of the design can be met. The effective use of timing driven placement engines is the key to achieving this goal.

Timing driven placement has been a goal of tool providers and engineers for many years. Today, the technology is mature enough to make timing closure on large chips dramatically easier than it has been in the past. To use this technology effectively, we need to provide to the placement engine:

- A good technology file that describes the parameters of the silicon technology
- Accurate timing constraints
- An optimization-friendly design

Timing driven placement takes as input the timing constraints and the gate-level netlist (typically in Verilog). It then attempts to place the cells in the design so as to meet the timing constraints. The placement engine uses estimates for routing delays, so that a full route of the design is not required to determine if it meets timing. The accuracy of these estimates is key in achieving timing closure.

The placement tool relies on a technology file to tell it how to estimate the capacitance of metal interconnect. Coupling capacitance between adjacent wires (both beside the wire in question, and above and below it), greatly affect the total capacitance seen by the driving gate, and thus the delay of the gate. The capacitance model used by the placement engine must be pessimistic in order to ensure that estimated routing delays are no worse than those from the actual, final route. One way to do this is to force the tool to assume that each wire has other wires in adjacent routing tracks both beside and above and below the wire. The technology file is where we can specify this data to the placement engine.

In deep submicron designs, wires are taller than they are wide; as a result, fringe capacitance has a significant effect on overall capacitance. This effect must be modeled in the technology file to achieve accurate capacitance estimates.

Once the capacitance per unit length is well modeled, the placement engine must estimate the actual length of each interconnect. It does this by assuming a Steiner route; that is, an optimal route based on orthogonal routing. Congested areas, though, may prevent some routes from being Steiner; they may have to take longer, "scenic" routes (like going from San Francisco to Cleveland by way of New York if all the direct flights are booked). The good placement tools are able to estimate congestion and its effect on routing resources, and factor this into the delay estimate.

Clearly, accurate timing constraints are essential to good timing-driven placement. If a false path is not identified, the placement engine can spend all of its time attempting to meet timing on this false path, and produce sub-optimal placement on actual critical parts of the design. Once again, avoiding false and multicycle paths can greatly help achieve rapid timing closure.

Timing driven placement is much like synthesis; the tool spends much of its time doing static timing analysis on a particular configuration, then using this information to refine the design. Many of the guidelines in this book are aimed at producing designs on which it is easy to perform static timing analysis. Following these guidelines can make synthesis and timing driven placement run much faster and converge with many fewer iterations through the tools.

In particular, a fully synchronous, flop-based design can allow timing driven placement to produce excellent results.

Flat vs. Hierarchical Placement

One critical issue in doing placement is deciding how much hierarchy to maintain during physical design.

Some designs (microprocessor designs, for example), are designed with a strict hierarchy that is maintained throughout physical design. Typically this includes:

* A careful floorplan is developed early, and a location for each major block identified.
* Pin locations for the I/O of each block are assigned.
* Some room between blocks is reserved for top-level routing; all routing between blocks is restricted to this area.
* Top-level routing is performed before place and route of the blocks; as a result, the wire length and capacitive loading for each top-level wire is fixed.
* Based on the information from the above steps, each block is placed and routed independently, and then placed in the top-level design.

Another approach is to maintain hierarchy, but not to reserve top-level routing areas. In this approach:

* A careful floorplan is developed early, and a location for each major block identified.
* Pin locations for the I/O of each block are assigned.
* Based on the information from the above steps, each block is placed (and potentially routed) and then placed in the top-level design.
* Detailed routing (or potentially just top-level routing) is performed. Top-level routing is done through blocks rather than around them.

A third approach is to do a completely flat place and route. In this approach:

* A careful floorplan is developed early, and a location for each major block identified.
* Pin locations for the I/O of each block are assigned.
* Based on the information from the above steps, timing constraints are developed for the design. The floorplan is not used; instead, the entire design is placed as a unit.
* Detailed routing is performed on the chip as a single unit.

The irony in the flat approach is that a detailed floorplan is still needed; it allows us to develop the timing constraints for placement. But the floorplan itself is thrown away.

Real designs may use a combination of the above approaches. Many teams will initially try a hierarchical approach. If the design still has problems meeting timing or has excessive routing congestion, they then will try a flat placement. Based on the results, they then pursue the approach that looks the most promising.

The only strong recommendation we make in this area is that the physical hierarchy should reflect the logical hierarchy. A physical block may consist of several logical blocks, but a single logical block should never be split across several physical blocks. The resulting name changes makes it very difficult to work with the post-layout netlist and to troubleshoot problems.

10.5.2   Placement Loop

One always hopes that after an initial placement, timing has been met and all that is required is to route the chip and tape out. One is almost always disappointed.

There are two major sources of timing problems at this point: the timing constraints, and the design itself.

If the design has false paths that are not listed in the constraints, then we are likely to find that the long paths in the design are paths we do not care about. But we are also likely to find that a number of critical paths were not appropriately placed, and are failing timing. The solution to this problem is to update the constraints and re-run placement.

If the timing is close but not quite passing, then it may be useful to refine the timing budgets. This can be done manually by changing the constraints or automatically by using a timing budgeting tool, such as PrimeTime. Then we re-run placement.

If the timing is still not met, then we may have to modify the design itself, changing the RTL to add pipeline stages or the like. In this case, we have to repeat the floor-planning, synthesis, and initial placement.

Under any of the above scenarios, as well as a host of others, it becomes necessary to iterate through placement. The goal is to make this iteration as short as possible, so that we can converge quickly to a placement that meets timing. If our routing delay estimates are accurate, then we can then achieve full timing closure quickly.

The actual loop through placement, analysis, and re-optimization is described below.

Quick Extraction

After placement is complete, the placement tool generates a report of the estimated capacitances in the routing. This report is relatively quick to generate, but not as accurate as a full 3D extraction from tools such as Arcadia. The accuracy depends largely on the way the technology file is written; that is, how the capacitances are modeled.

Timing Analysis

A timing analysis tools such as PrimeTime or Pearl can read these capacitances, along with the netlist and timing constraints, and output a timing report. This timing report lists all the paths that are violating the timing constraints (as well as a host of other reports, as required).

Refine Constraints

We then analyze the timing reports to determine if the violating paths are real and if so, what to do about them. If the violations are false paths, we update the timing constraints.

Re-optimize

If the timing violations are real, the most of them will probably be from excessive capacitance loading gate outputs. The solution here is to increase drive strengths, add buffers, or even restructure logic.

The best timing-driven placement tools have the capability of doing much of this automatically as part of timing-driven placement. They can resize buffers and add/or buffers to improve timing.

If the available placement tools do not re-optimize, or if significant restructuring of logic is required, then we have to use the in-place optimization capabilities of the synthesis tools. In place optimization preserves as much of the placement as possible while making the structural changes needed to meet timing.

ECO Place

If we had to go outside the placement tools to do our optimization, then we need to get our changes back into the placement. The ECO placement capabilities of the placement tool allows us to give it a revised netlist and (approximate) physical locations for the new devices. The tool then updates the placement, including placing the new parts in legal locations, and we are ready to re-analyze the results.

The goal of ECO placement is to maintain as much of the existing placement as possible. In this way, we can be reasonably confident that we are fixing timing problems without creating new ones. There is a limit, however, to how many cells can be changed at once and still use the incremental placement. Usually this limit is a few percent of the cells in the design. If we need to make more changes than this, we need to do a complete new placement, possibly resulting in a whole new set of timing problems. For this reason, it is essential that our initial timing-driven placement be of high quality, otherwise timing can end up diverging instead of converging. A design that is easy to optimize (fully synchronous, etc.) can make a huge difference in achieving timing closure.

This basic placement iterative loop is the key step in achieving rapid timing closure. The overall time for this loop, even for very large designs, can usually be kept to less than a day. Even if we have to do multiple iterations, we can produce a placement with a high probability of meeting timing in a reasonable amount of time.

10.5.3 Timing Closure

After placement meets timing, we have several key tasks to complete the design.

Clock Route

Before doing a full route of the design, we route the clock(s), also known as clock tree synthesis. Since these are the most critical nets in the design, and need to be balanced to minimize clock skew, they are routed first. One common problem with routing clock trees is that they typically require a very large number of buffers. As mentioned above, inserting large numbers of buffers can perturb the design enough that we cannot use ECO place and route. This would be a major problem for clock tree synthesis, since we are optimizing the clock for a specific placement of flip-flops.

For this reason, some designers reserve a buffer site next to each flop. This site can be used for the clock tree buffer. If the site is not needed it takes up some small incremental area, but this is well worth it if it speeds convergence of clock tree synthesis.

Detailed Route

After the clock is routed and meeting skew, we do a full detailed route of the design. This is the first time we have a complete physical design. We can now do a much more accurate assessment of the timing and power.

During detailed route, we need to ensure that we comply with the process' rules for antennas. During chip fabrication there is a time during which metal one has been added to the chip, but the other metal layers have not. At this time, the metal one stub can act like an antenna, picking up a static charge and damaging the chip. Each process has a set of rules for how long the stub can be for each metal layer. By adding these rules to the cell library, we can get the router to comply with them during route. Otherwise, it is necessary to go back after the route and fix any antenna violations, a time consuming process.

Extraction and Timing Analysis

We now use a full 3-D extraction engine to calculate the actual capacitance of each segment of metal interconnect in the design. These tools are full field solvers that give very accurate results. With this data, we can now do a full static timing analysis and determine the timing of the design.

Fixing Timing and Clocks

If the timing estimates used in placement were accurate, there should be few timing violations at this point. We would typically expect a couple of long paths that need repair. We also would expect some hold time violations. Both of these can result from the fact that we used estimates both for metal delays and for clock skew. There may also be some remaining clock tuning required to meet our skew requirements.

We fix the clock and the long paths first; if there are literally just a couple of fixes required, we may be able to do these interactively in the place and route tool. For larger numbers of fixes, we may have to go back and readjust our timing constraints, re-optimize, and go back through place and route.

After these fixes have been implemented in the physical design, we again do a full extraction and timing analysis. We iterate as required until the clock meets our requirements.

Fixing Hold Time Violations

Once the clock tree is finalized and is meeting timing, we need to fix any remaining hold time problems. Hold time problems result from a combination of fast data paths from register to register and clock skew. They are typically fixed by inserting buffers in the fast data paths.

Virtually all the hold time problems should be fixed during the placement loop. Hold time violations, like long path problems, are fixed by the in-place optimization process. A few new hold time problems may appear as the clock is tuned; these we fix at this point in the process.

Final Extraction and Timing Analysis

After all known timing problems have been fixed, we do one final (hopefully!) extraction and timing analysis. At this point we typically have a review of the final timing report, verifying that our false and multicycle paths specified earlier are really false.

10.5.4 Verifying the Physical Design

The last major step in the physical design process is verifying that the physical design is correct and in compliance with the design rules for the target silicon process.

Checking Power

First we do a check of the power distribution system. We can estimate the voltage drop across the power meshes using tools such as RailMill. Our initial power mesh design was intended to be conservative, so we should see no surprises here.

We can also use tools such as PowerMill to get a final estimation of the power dissipation of the design.

DRC and LVS

Finally we run DRC (Design Rule Checking) and LVS (Layout vs. Schematic). DRC verifies that the design does not violate any physical design rules.

For full custom designs, this step can involve many iterations as subtle problems with the placement of cells are discovered and fixed. But in the standard model of reuse presented in this book, full custom designs should only be imported into SoC designs after they have been physically designed and verified. No full custom DRC violations should occur at the chip level.

For standard cell designs, there should be very few DRC violations. Typical problems that do occur are usually caused by problems in the library or by interface problems between the standard cell sections and any hard blocks that have been imported. These problems are usually quite straightforward to fix.

LVS compares the design as physically implemented to the gate-level netlist. It extracts a post-layout netlist back from the physical design by mapping polygons back into gates. It then compares this post-layout netlist to the pre-layout netlist. Again, for standard cell designs, there tend to be few LVS errors in the final design. The ones that do appear tend to be library problems and are usually straightforward to fix.

Of course, we need to make sure that the final netlist, with added buffers and resized gates, and clock fixes, still is functionally equivalent to the original netlist. Formal verification should be used to check this equivalence.

Once these steps are completed, the chip is ready for fabrication.

10.5.5 Summary

The physical design of very large chips is an extremely challenging and complex task. The algorithms used by the tools are very complex, and the databases huge. It is very easy to spend many months trying to reach timing closure for a large chip.

There is much the designer can do to reduce the risk of runaway schedules in physical design. The key is to make timing closure and physical design a series of local, relatively small problems. The process described above performs most of the real effort in timing closure during placement. Once placement is successful, the rest of the design process is straightforward and should require few iterations. The runtimes for extraction can be very long, and DRC and LVS can take several days. However, by ensuring a high probability of needing only one or two runs of each, this long runtime is tolerable.

The highly iterative loop is in timing driven placement. By carefully choosing a set of simplifying assumptions, mainly in how we estimate routing delay, this loop can be made relatively fast (hours instead of days), so that we can tolerate these iterations.

Above all else, the most important key to rapid timing closure is the quality of the design itself. A fully synchronous design, with few or no timing exceptions, where the levels of logic between registers is well understood and consistent with the timing goals, can make it through physical design with few schedule surprises.

CHAPTER 11   *System-Level Verification Issues*

This chapter discusses system-level verification, focusing on the issues and opportunities that arise when macros are integrated into a complete System on a Chip. The topics are:

- The importance of verification
- Test plan
- Application-based verification
- Fast prototype testing
- Gate-level verification
- Verification tools
- Specialized hardware for system verification

11.1 The Importance of Verification

Verifying functionality and timing at the system level is probably the most difficult and important aspect of SoC design. It is the last opportunity to find conceptual, functional, and implementation errors before the design is committed to silicon. For many teams, verification takes 50 to 80 percent of the overall design effort.

For SoC design, verification must be an integral part of the design process from the start, along with synthesis, system software, bringup, and debug strategies. It cannot be an afterthought to the design process.

System verification begins during system specification. The system functional specification describes the basic test plan, including the criteria for completion (what tests must run before taping out). As the system-level behavioral model is developed, a testbench and test suite are developed to verify the model. Similarly, system software is developed and tested using the behavioral model rather than waiting for real hardware. As a result, a rich set of test suites and test software, including actual application code, should be available by the time the RTL and functional models for the entire chip are assembled and the chip is ready for verification.

Successful (and rapid) system-level verification depends on the following factors:

- Quality of the verification plan
- Quality and abstraction level of the models and testbenches used
- Quality and performance of the verification tools
- Robustness of the individual predesigned blocks

11.2 The Verification Strategy

The system-level verification strategy for an SoC design uses a divide-and-conquer approach based on the system hierarchy. This strategy consists of the following steps:

- Verify that the leaf nodes — the lowest-level individual blocks — of the design hierarchy are functionally correct as stand-alone units.
- Verify that the interfaces between blocks are functionally correct, first in terms of the transaction types and then in terms of data content.
- Run a set of increasingly complex applications on the full chip.
- Prototype the full chip and run a full set of application software for final verification.
- Decide when it is appropriate to release the chip to production.

Block Level Verification

For large SoC designs, it is essential that each block be fully verified before it is integrated into the chip design. In this sense, block-level verification is a prerequisite and precursor to chip-level verification.

Block-level verification is described in detail in Chapter 7. It uses code coverage tools and a rigorous methodology to verify the RTL version of macro as thoroughly as possible. A physical prototype is then built to provide silicon verification of functional correctness.

This verification methodology should, in general, be used for any block to be used in the chip design, even if that block is not intended for reuse. Verifying blocks fully before integration greatly reduces the overall verification effort, since bugs are much easier to find at the block level rather than chip level.

The only exception to this rule is that the design team may well decide not to produce prototypes of single-use blocks before they are integrated into the chip. This approach seems a reasonable risk/benefit tradeoff, but the risk involved should be recognized.

Any block in the SoC design that has not gone through this process, including silicon verification, is not considered fully verified as a standalone block. If the chip contains any such partially verified blocks, the first version of the chip must be considered a prototype. It is virtually assured of having bugs that require a redesign of the chip before release to production.

Prototyping the chip, however, is part of the overall chip verification plan, so it is reasonable to have some number of new, single-use blocks that have been robustly verified, but that have not been prototyped.

11.3 Interface Verification

Knowing that the individual blocks have been robustly verified, chip-level verification consists primarily of verifying the interfaces and interaction between the blocks. Thus we start chip verification with interface verification.

Inter-block interfaces usually have a regular structure, with address and data buses connecting the blocks and some form of control — perhaps a request/grant protocol or a request/busy protocol. The connections between blocks can be either point-to-point or on-chip buses.

Because of the regular structure of these interfaces, it is usually possible to talk about *transactions* between blocks. The idea is that there are only a few permitted sequences of control and data signals; these sequences are called transactions and only the data (and data-like fields, such as address) change from transaction to transaction.

11.3.1 Transaction Verification

Interface testing begins by listing all of the transaction types that can occur at each interface, and systematically testing each one. If the system design restricts transactions to a relatively small set of types, it is fairly easy to generate all possible transaction types and sequences of transaction types and to verify the correct operation of the interfaces to these transactions. Once this is done, all that remains is to test the behavior of the blocks to different data values in the transactions. Thus, a simple, regular communication architecture between blocks can greatly reduce the system verification effort.

In the past, this transaction checking has been done very informally by instantiating all the blocks in the top-level RTL, and then using a testbench to create activity within the blocks and thus transactions between blocks. If the overall behavior of the system is correct, perhaps as observed at the chip's primary I/O or in the memory contents, then the chip — and thus the interfaces — were considered to be working correctly.

There are several changes that can be made to improve the rigor of transaction checking. First of all, as shown in Figure 11-1(b), you can add a bus monitor to check the transactions directly. This monitor can be coded behaviorally and thus provide very good simulation performance. For a chip such as that shown in Figure 11-1(a), with point-to-point interconnections, it is possible to build some simple transaction checking into the interface module of each block. Testbench automation tools can be useful tools for creating effective transaction checkers very quickly.

This monitor approach improves observability during transaction testing, but it is also possible to improve controllability. If we use simple, transaction-generating bus functional models instead of a full functional models for the system blocks, we can generate precisely the transactions we wish to test, in precisely the order we want. This approach can greatly reduce the difficulty of developing transaction verification tests and can reduce simulation runtime as well.

11.3.2   Data or Behavioral Verification

Once the transactions have been verified, it is necessary to verify that the block behaves correctly for all values of data and all sequences of data that it will receive in actual operation. In most chips, generating the complete set of these data is impossible because of the difficultly in controlling the data received by any one block.

The approach described above helps here as well. We use the bus functional models for all blocks except the block under test, for which we use the full RTL. We can then generate the desired data sequences and transaction from the BFMs. We can construct test cases either from our knowledge of the system or by random generation.

Automatic checking of the block's behavior under these sequences of transactions is nontrivial and depends on how easy it is to characterize the correct behavior of the block. For complex blocks, the semantics of a testbench generation tool may be the only way to describe the block's behavior such that its outputs can be checked automatically.

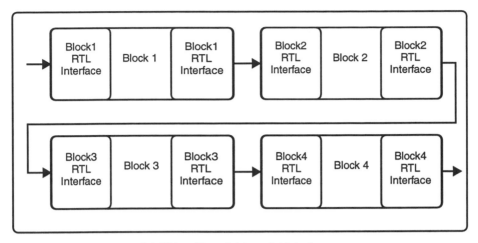

(a) Chip with point-to-point interfaces

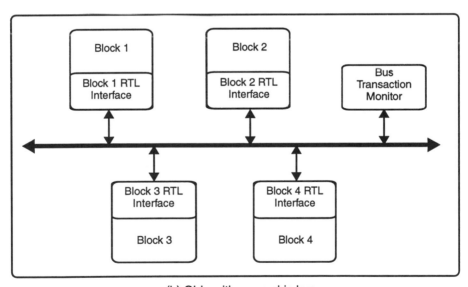

(b) Chip with an on-chip bus

Figure 11-1 System verification using interface testing

This test method often reveals that the block responds correctly to data sequences that the designer expected the block to receive, but that there are some (legal or illegal) sequences that can occur in the actual system to which the block does not respond correctly. This must usually be considered a bug, requiring redesign of the block.

Another method for dealing with the problem of unanticipated or illegal inputs is to design a checker into the block interface itself. This checker can suppress inputs that are not legal and prevent the block from getting into incorrect states. This approach has been used effectively in high-reliability system designs.

11.3.3 Standardized Interfaces

Interface verification and transaction checking can be greatly facilitated if the interfaces are standardized. Clearly it is easier to get a bus functional model or bus monitor out of a library than to create one from scratch.

This is one of several reasons why design teams are trying to standardize the primary interfaces to the chip and the on-chip buses. Once these standards are established, bus functional models and bus monitors can be developed and reused on many chip designs.

11.4 Functional Verification

Once the basic functionality of the system has been verified by the transaction testing, system verification consists of exercising the entire design, using a full functional model for most, if not all, of the blocks. The ultimate goal of this aspect of verification is to try to test the system as it will actually be used. That is, we come as close as we can to running actual applications on the system.

Verification based on running real application code is essential for achieving a high quality design. However, this form of verification presents some major challenges. Conventional simulation, even at the RTL level, is simply not fast enough to execute the millions of vectors required to run even the smallest fragments of application code, much less to boot an operating system or test a cellular phone.

There are two basic approaches to addressing this problem:

* Increase the level of abstraction so that software simulators running on workstations run faster.
* Use specialized hardware for performing verification, such as emulation or rapid-prototyping systems.

This section addresses the first approach: how to use abstraction and other mechanisms to speed conventional simulation techniques. Subsequent sections address the second approach.

The types of abstraction techniques we can use depend on the nature of the design, so it is useful to use a specific design as an example. Fortunately, most large chips are converging to an architecture that looks something like the chip design shown in Figure 11-2, the canonical SoC design described in Chapter 2.

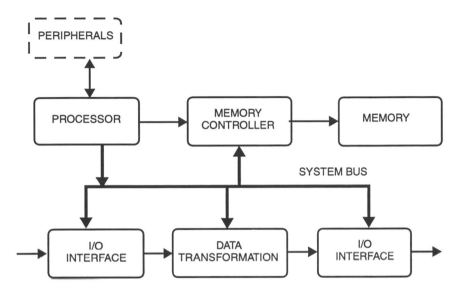

Figure 11-2 Canonical SoC Design

Figure 11-3 shows a possible testbench environment for verifying the canonical design. The key features of this verification environment are:

- The full RTL model is used as the simulation model for most of the functional blocks.
- Behavioral or ISA (Instruction Set Architecture) models may be used for memory and the microprocessor.
- Bus functional models and monitors are used to generate and check transactions with the communication blocks.
- It is possible to generate real application code for the processor and run it on the simulation model.

With this test environment, we can run a set of increasingly complex application tests on the system. Initially, full functional models for the RAM and microprocessor are used to run some basic tests to prove that the system performs the most basic functions. The slow simulation speeds of this arrangement mean that we can do little more than check that the system is alive and find the most basic system bugs. Errors are detected manually (by looking at waveform displays), by means of the bus monitor, and by the sequence monitor on the communication port. At this level of abstraction, we are probably simulating at a rate of tens of system clocks per second.

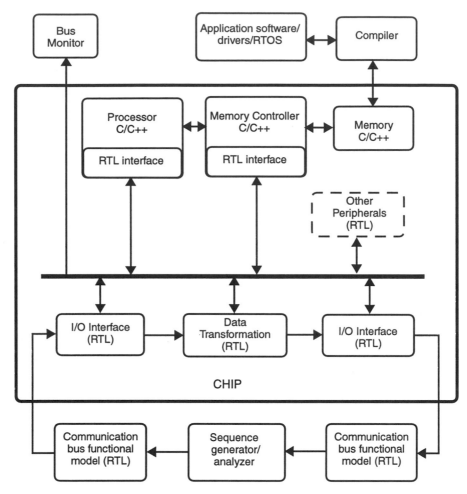

Figure 11-3 System verification environment

Behavioral models are now substituted for the memory and microprocessor. These models can be high-level C/C++ models that accurately model the instruction set of the processor, but abstract out all implementation detail. These models are often called ISA (Instruction Set Architecture) models. Another approach is to code a very high-level, behavioral model in Verilog or VHDL, abstracting out much of the cycle-by-cycle details, but retaining the basic functionality of the processor. If enough timing detail is retained so that the bus transactions at the I/O port of the processor are accurate on a clock-cycle by clock-cycle basis, the model is often referred to as a cycle-accurate model.

Using these behavioral models for the memory and processor, real code is compiled and loaded into the memory model and the processor model executes this code. At the same time, representative data transactions are generated at the communication interfaces of the chip, usually by bus functional models. For instance, if the data transformation block is an MPEG core, then we can feed in a digital video stream.

Using C/C++ models for both the processor and memory dramatically improves simulation speed over full RTL simulation. In designs like our canonical example, most cycles are spent entirely in the processor, executing instructions, or in accessing memory. With these abstractions, execution speeds in the thousands of device cycles per second can be achieved. Operating on top of this environment, hardware/software cosimulation packages allow the engineer to run a software debugger, the ISA software, and an RTL simulator simultaneously.

Most system-level hardware and software bugs can be detected and fixed at this stage. To complete software debug, it may be necessary to develop an even more abstract set of models to improve simulation speed further. In our example, we could substitute a C++ model for the RTL model of the data transformation block, and achieve very high simulation speeds.

To complete hardware debug, however, we need to lower our abstraction level back to RTL. The lack of detail in our ISA/behavioral models undoubtedly masks some bugs. At this point, we can run some real code on the RTL system model and perhaps some random code as well for testing unforeseen sequences. But simulation speed prohibits significant amount of real application code from being run at the RTL level.

During this debug phase, as we run application code on a high-level model and targeted tests on the RTL model, the bug rate follows a predictable curve. Typically, the bug rate increases during the first part of this testing, reaches a peak, and then starts declining. At some point on the downward slope, simulation-based testing is providing diminished returns, and an alternate method must be found to detect the remaining bugs.

11.5 Application-Based Verification

For most design teams, a key goal is to have first silicon be fully functional. This goal has motivated the functional verification plan and simulation strategies. To date, most teams have been fairly successful. According to some estimates, about 90% of ASIC designs work right the first time, although only about 50% work right the first time in the system. This higher failure rate probably results from the fact that most ASIC design teams do not do system-level simulation.

With the increasing gate count and complexity of SoC designs, it is not clear that the industry can maintain this success rate. Assume that, in a 100k gate design with today's verification technology, there is a 10% chance of a serious bug. Then for a 1M gate design, consisting of ten such modules comparably verified, the probability of no serious bugs is:

$$P_{bug-free} = .9^{10} = .35$$

Design reuse can also play an important role. If we assume that a 1M gate design consists of ten 100k blocks, with two designed from scratch (90% chance of being bug-free) and eight reused (for the purpose of discussion, 98% chance of being bug-free), then for the overall chip:

$$P_{bug-free} = .9^2 * .98^8 = .69$$

But to achieve a 90% probability of first-silicon success, we need to combine design reuse with a verification methodology that will either get individual blocks to a 99% or allow us to verify the entire chip to the 90% level.

Running significant amounts of real application code is the only way to reach this level of confidence in an SoC design. For most designs, this level of testing requires running at or near real time speeds. The only available technologies for achieving this kind of performance involve some form of rapid prototyping.

The available options for rapid prototyping include:

- FPGA or LPGA prototyping
- Emulation-based testing
- Real silicon prototyping

11.5.1 FPGA and LPGA Prototyping

For small designs, it is practical to build an FPGA or Laser Programmable Gate Array (LPGA, such as the one provided by Chip Express) prototype of the chip. FPGAs have the advantage of being reprogrammable, allowing rapid turnaround of bug fixes. LPGA prototypes can achieve higher gate counts and faster clock speeds, but are expensive to turn. Multiple iterations of an LPGA design can be very costly, but can be done quickly, usually within a day or two.

Both FPGAs and LPGAs lag state-of-the-art ASIC technologies in gate count and clock speed by significant amounts. They are much more appropriate for prototyping individual blocks or macros than for prototyping SoC designs.

A number of engineering teams have used multiple FPGAs to build a prototype of a single large chip. This approach has at least one major problem: the interconnect is difficult to design and almost impossible to modify quickly when a bug fix requires repartitioning of the design between devices.

Rapid prototyping systems from Aptix address this problem by using custom, programmable routing chips to connect the FPGAs. This routing can be performed under software control, providing a very flexible fast prototyping system.

11.5.2 Emulation Based Testing

Emulation technology such as that provided by Mentor Graphics and QuickTurn grew out of attempts to provide a better alternative to using a collection of FPGAs for rapid prototyping of large chips. They provide programmable interconnect, fixed board designs, relatively large gate counts, and special memory and processor support. Recent developments in moving from FPGAs to processor-based architectures have helped to resolve partitioning and interconnect problems.

Emulation can provide excellent performance for large-chip verification if the entire design can be placed in the emulation engine itself. If any significant part of the circuit or testbench is located on the host, there is significant degradation of performance.

For our canonical design, we need to provide emulation-friendly models for the RAM, microprocessor, BFMs, monitor, and sequence generator/checker. Developing these models late in the design process can be so time consuming as to negate the benefit of emulation. It is much better to consider the requirements of emulation from the beginning of the project and to work with the memory and hard macro providers to provide these models. Similarly, the requirements of emulation must be considered in the design of the BFMs and monitors.

If executed correctly, emulation can provide simulation performance of one to two orders of magnitude less than real time, and many orders of magnitude faster than simulation.

11.5.3 Silicon Prototyping

If an SoC design is too large for FPGA/LPGA prototyping and emulation is not practical, then building a real silicon prototype may be the best option. Instead of extending the verification phase, it may be faster and easier to build an actual chip and debug it in the system.

To some extent this approach is just acknowledging the fact that any chip fabricated without running significant amounts of real code must be considered a prototype. That is, there is a high probability that engineering changes will be required before release to production.

The critical issue in silicon prototyping is deciding when one should build the prototype. The following is a reasonable set of criteria:

- The bug rate from simulation testing should have peaked and be on its way down.
- The time to determine that a bug exists should be much greater than the time to fix it.
- The cost of fabricating and testing the chip is on the same order as the cost of finding the next n bugs, where n is the anticipated number of critical bugs remaining.
- Enough functionality has been verified that the likely bugs in the prototype should not be severe enough to prevent extensive testing of other features. The scenario we want to avoid is building a prototype only to find a critical bug that prevents any useful debug of the prototype.

There are a number of design features that can help facilitate debug of this initial prototype:

- Good debug structures for controlling and observing the system, especially system buses
- The ability to selectively reset individual blocks in the design
- The ability to selectively disable various blocks to prevent bugs in these blocks from affecting operation of the rest of the system

11.6 Gate-Level Verification

The final gate-level netlist must be verified for both correct functionality and for timing. A variety of techniques and tools can be used for this task.

11.6.1 Sign-Off Simulation

In the past, gate-level simulation has been the final step before signing off an ASIC design. ASIC vendors have required gate-level simulation and parallel test vectors as part of signoff, using the parallel vectors as part of manufacturing test. They have done this even if a full scan methodology was employed.

Today, for 100k gate and larger designs, signoff simulation is typically done running Verilog simulation with back-annotated delays on hardware accelerators from IKOS. Running full-timing, gate-level simulations in software simulators is simply not feasible at these gate counts. Even with hardware accelerators, speeds are rarely faster than a few hundred device cycles per second.

RTL sign-off, where no gate-level simulation is performed, is becoming increasingly common. However, most ASIC vendors still require that all manufacture-test vectors submitted with a design be simulated on a sign-off quality simulator with fully back-annotated delay information and all hazard checking enabled. Furthermore, they require that these simulations be repeated under best case, nominal case, and worst case conditions. This has the potential to be a resource intensive task.

This requirement is rapidly becoming problematic for the following reasons:

- Thorough, full timing simulation of a million-gate ASIC is not possible without very expensive hardware accelerators, and even then it is very slow.
- Parallel vectors typically have very low fault coverage (on the order of 60 percent) unless a large and expensive effort is made to extend them. As a result, they can be used only to verify the gross functionality of the chip.
- Parallel vectors do not exercise all the critical timing paths, for the same reason they don't achieve high fault coverage. As a result, they do not provide a sufficient verification that the chip meets timing.

As a result of these issues, the industry is moving to a different paradigm. The under-lying problems traditionally addressed by gate-level simulation are:

- Verification that synthesis has generated a correct netlist, and that subsequent operations such as scan and clock insertion have not changed circuit functionality
- Verification that the chip, when fabricated, will meet timing
- A manufacturing test that verifies that the chip is free of manufacturing defects

These problems are now too large for a single solution, such as gate-level simulation. Instead, the current methodology uses separate approaches to address each issue:

- Formal verification is used to verify correspondence between the RTL and final netlist.
- Static timing analysis is used to verify timing.
- Some gate-level simulation, either unit-delay or full timing, is used to complement formal verification and static timing analysis.
- Full scan plus BIST provides a complete manufacturing test for functionality. Special test structures, provided by the silicon vendor, are used to verify that the fabricated chip meets timing and other analog specifications.

11.6.2 Formal Verification

Formal verification uses mathematical techniques to prove the equivalence of two representations of the circuit. Typically, it is used to compare the gate-level netlist to the RTL for a design. Because it uses a static, mathematical method of comparison, formal verification requires no functional vectors. Thus, it can compare two circuits much more quickly than can be done with simulation, and with much greater accuracy. Formal verification is available from a variety of vendors; one such tool is Synopsys Formality.

Formality compares two design by reading them into memory and then applying formal mathematical algorithms on their data structures. The designs can be successfully compared as long as they have the same synchronous functionality and correlating state holding devices (registers or latches). The two circuits are considered equivalent if the functionality is the same at all output pins and at each register and latch.

Formal verification can be used to check equivalence between the original RTL and:

- The synthesized netlist
- The netlist after test logic is inserted. For scan, this is quite straightforward; for on-chip JTAG structure, some setup is required, but the equivalence can still be formally verified.
- The netlist after clock tree insertion and layout. This requires comparing the hierarchical RTL to the flattened netlist.
- Hand edits. Occasionally engineers will make a last-minute hand edit to the netlist to modify performance, testability, or function.

One key benefit of formal verification is that it allows the RTL to remain the golden reference for the design, regardless of modifications made to the final netlist. Even if the functionality of the circuit is changed by a last minute by editing the netlist, the same modification can be retrofitted into the RTL and the equivalence of the modified RTL and netlist can be verified.

For large designs, formal verification between the gate-level design and the RTL can be too slow, especially for multiple iterations. In such cases, it is better to use formal verification once between the RTL and the gate-level netlist, then use that gate-level netlist as the golden reference for future iterations. For example, you can use formal verification to compare gate-level netlists before and after clock tree insertion. Formal verification algorithms work more efficiently when comparing gates to gates than when comparing gates to RTL.

11.6.3 Gate-Level Simulation with Unit-Delay Timing

Unit-delay simulation involves performing gate-level simulation with unit delay for each gate. It is much faster than full-timing simulation, but much slower than RTL simulation.

Unit-delay simulations can be used to verify that:

- The chip initializes properly (reset verification).
- The gate implementation functionally matches the RTL description (functional correctness).

Gate-level simulation complements formal verification. Dynamic simulations are rarely an exhaustive test of equivalence, but simulation is necessary to validate that an implementation's behavior is consistent with the simulated behavior of the RTL source. Gate-level simulation is particularly important for verifying initialization because gate-level simulation handles propagation of unknown (X) or uninitialized states more accurately than RTL simulation.

Because it can be time-consuming and resource-intensive, it is usually good to begin unit-delay simulation as soon as you complete a netlist for your chip, even though the chip may not meet timing.

11.6.4 Gate-Level Simulation with Full Timing

Full-timing simulation on large chips is very slow, and should be used only where absolutely necessary. This technique is particularly useful for validating asynchronous logic, embedded asynchronous RAM interfaces, and single-cycle timing exceptions. In a synchronous design, these problem areas should not exist, or should be isolated so they are easily tested.

These tests should be run with the back-annotated timing information from the place and route tools, and run with hazards enabled. They should be run with worst case timing to check for long paths, and with best-case timing to check for minimum path delay problems.

11.7 Specialized Hardware for System Verification

Design teams have long recognized the limitations of software simulators running on workstations. Simulation has never provided enough verification bandwidth to do really robust system simulation. Over the last fifteen years there have been numerous efforts to address the needs of system simulation through specialized hardware systems for verification.

Early efforts focused on hardware accelerators. Zycad introduced the first widely-available commercial accelerators in the early 1980's; in the early 1990's, Ikos introduced competitive systems based on somewhat similar architectures. The Zycad systems provided very fast fault simulation; at the time fault, simulation of large chips was not really practical with software simulators. These systems were also used for gate-level system simulation. Ikos systems focus exclusively on system-level simulation.

These accelerators map the standard, event-driven software simulation algorithm onto specialized hardware. The software data structures used to represent information about gates, netlists, and delays are mapped directly into high-speed memories. The algorithm itself is executed by a dedicated processor that has the simulation algorithm hardwired into it. A typical system consists of anywhere from 4 to over a hundred of these processors and their associated memory. These systems are faster than workstations because each processor can access all the needed data structures at the same time and operate on them simultaneously. Additional performance results from the parallel execution on multiple processors.

The introduction of FPGAs in the 1980's made possible another kind of verification system: emulation. These systems partition the gate-level netlist into small chunks and map them onto FPGAs; they use additional FPGAs to provide interconnect routing. These systems can execute many orders of magnitude faster than hardware accelerators. Large circuits that run tens of cycles per second on software simulators might run hundreds or a few thousand of cycles per second on a hardware accelerator. These same circuits run at hundreds of thousands of cycles per second on emulation systems.

Emulation systems achieve their high performance because they are essentially building a hardware prototype of the circuit in FPGAs.

Emulation systems, however, have a number of shortcomings:

- They operate on gate-level netlists. Synthesis is typically used to generate this netlist from the RTL. Any part of the circuit that is coded in non-synthesizable code, especially testbenches, must run on the host workstation. This considerably slows emulation. A circuit with a substantial part executed on the workstation may run as much as two orders of magnitude slower than one with the entire circuit in the emulator.

- The partitioning of the circuit among numerous FPGAs, and dealing with the associated routing problems, presents a real problem. Poor utilization and routing inefficiencies result in the need for very large numbers of FPGAs to emulate a reasonably sized chip. The resulting large systems are very expensive and have so many mechanical components (chips, boards, and cables) that they tend to experience reliability problems.

- The use of FPGAs tends to make controlling and observing individual nodes in the circuit difficult. Typically, the circuit has to be (at least partially) recompiled to allow additional nodes to be traces. This makes debugging in the emulation environment difficult.

The first problem remains an issue today, but important progress has been made on the second and third problems. New systems, such as those from Mentor Graphics (the Accelerated Verification System) and from QuickTurn have moved from a pure FPGA-based system to a custom chip/processor-based architecture. Where previous systems had arrays of FPGAs performing emulation, the new systems have arrays of special purpose processors. These processor-based systems usually use some form of time-slicing: the processor emulates some gates on one cycle, additional gates on the next cycle. Also, the interconnect between processors is time-sliced, so that a single physical wire can act as several virtual wires. This processor-based approach significantly improves the routing and density problems seen in earlier emulation systems.

The processors used on these new systems also tend to have special capabilities for storing stimulus as well as traces of nodes during emulation. This capability helps make debug in the emulation environment much easier.

These new systems hold much promise for addressing the problems of high-speed system verification. The success of these systems will depend on the capabilities of the software that goes with them: compilers, debuggers, and hardware/software cosimulation support. These systems will continue to compete against much less expensive approaches: simulation using higher levels of abstraction and rapid prototyping.

The rest of this chapter discusses emulation in more detail, using the Accelerated Verification System from Mentor as an example.

11.7.1   Accelerated Verification Overview

Figure 11-4 shows the major components of Mentor Graphics' Accelerated Verification System process. The components are:

Models

RTL blocks and soft IP are synthesized and mapped onto the emulation system hardware. Memory blocks are compiled and emulated on dedicated memory emulation hardware.

Physical environment

Hard macros (IP cores) that have bonded-out chips, can be mounted on special board and interfaced directly to the rest of the emulation system. Similarly, hardware testbenches, such as signal generators, can be connected directly to the emulation system.

In-circuit verification

The emulation system can be interfaced directly to a board or system to provide in-circuit emulation. Thus, an application board can be developed and debugged using an emulation model of the chip.

System environment

A software debug environment (XRay debugger) and a hardware/software co-simulation environment (Seamless CVE) provide the software support necessary for running and debugging real system software on the design.

Testbenches

Behavioral RTL testbenches can be run on the host and communicate with the emulation system. Note that running any significant amount of code on the host will slow down emulation considerably.

Stimulus

Synthesizable testbenches can be mapped directly onto the emulation system and run at full emulation speeds. Test vectors can be stored on special memories in the emulation system, so that they too can be run at full speed.

These components combine to provide all the capabilities that designers need to verify large SoC designs including:

- RTL acceleration
- Software-driven verification at all levels in the design cycle
- In-circuit verification to ensure the design works in context of the system
- Intellectual property support

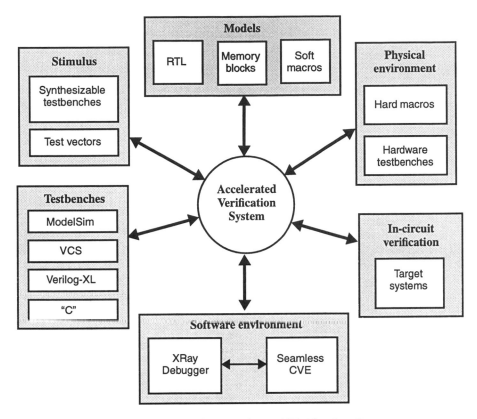

Figure 11-4 Mentor Graphics Accelerated Verification System process

11.7.2 RTL Acceleration

Designers continue to use software simulators like ModelSim, VSS, or Verilog-XL to debug their designs, but a threshold is reached where simulator performance becomes a major bottleneck for functional verification at the RTL level, especially for large SoC designs. This threshold will vary based on the design team and the verification environment. As the RTL functional simulations reach duration of more than 6-8 hours, it will become more efficient to compile the design and run it in an emulator. As an example, an RTL design that may only take several minutes to compile on a simulator, but runs for eight hours, may compile in 30 minutes on the emulator and run in a matter of seconds.

Thus, at some point in the design cycle, system simulation and debug may be more appropriately done on the emulator than on the simulator. For this debug strategy to be effective, however, we need an RTL symbolic debug environment that provides users with complete design visibility, real time variable access, and support for enumerated types and state variable assignments.

11.7.3 Software Driven Verification

As the software content in SoC designs increases and design cycles shrink, hardware/software co-development and software-driven verification become increasingly important. Software-driven verification plays two key roles in an SoC verification strategy:

- Verification of the hardware using real software
- Verification of the software using (an emulation model of) real hardware, well before the actual chip is built

Traditionally, using the software to verify the hardware has been confined to very late in the design cycle using breadboards, or early prototype runs of silicon. With reusable hardware and software blocks, it is possible to assemble an initial version of the RTL and system software very quickly. With the new emulation systems, it is possible to test this software on an emulation model of the hardware running at near-real-time speeds. Incremental improvements to both the hardware and software can then be made and tested, robustly and quickly.

In particular, the high performance of emulation systems allows the design team to:

- Develop and debug the low-level hardware device drivers on the virtual prototype with hardware execution speeds that can approach near real-time
- Boot the operating system, initialize the printer driver, or place a phone call at the RTL phase of the design cycle

11.7.4 Traditional In-Circuit Verification

As the design team reaches the end of the design cycle, the last few bugs tend to be the most challenging to find. In-circuit testing of the design can be key tool at this stage of verification because the ultimate verification testbench is the real working system. One large manufacturer of routers routinely runs its next design for weeks on its actual network, allowing the router to deal with real traffic, with all of the asynchronous events that are impossible to model accurately.

In the case of systems that operate with the real asynchronous world, with random events that might occur only on a daily or weekly basis, complete information capture is essential. The emulation system provides a built-in logic analyzer that records every signal in the design during every emulation run, using a powerful triggering mechanism. This debug environment allows designers to identify and correct problems without having to repeat multiple emulation runs.

11.7.5 Support for Intellectual Property

Mentor Graphics Accelerated Verification System offers very secure encryption mechanisms and advanced macro compile capabilities that allow IP developers to have complete control over what parts of the IP modules are visible to the end user.

11.7.6 Design Guidelines for Accelerated Verification

Most of the guidelines for Accelerated Verification are identical to guidelines for design reuse listed in Chapter 5. These include:

Guideline – Use a simple clocking scheme, with as few clock domains as possible. Emulation works best with a fully synchronous, single-clock design.

Guideline – Use registers (flip-flops), not latches.

Guideline – Do not use combinational feedback loops, such as a set-reset latch in cross-coupled gates.

Guideline – Do not instantiate gates, pass transistors, delay lines, pulse generators, or any element that depends on absolute timing.

Guideline – Avoid multi-cycle paths.

Guideline – Avoid asynchronous memory. Use the modeling techniques described in Chapter 5 to model the asynchronous memory as a synchronous memory.

The following guidelines are requirements specific to emulation:

Guideline – Hierarchical, modular designs are generally easier to map to the emulation hardware than flat designs. The modularity helps reduce routing between processors.

Guideline – Large register arrays should be modeled as memories, to take advantage of the special memory modeling hardware in the emulation system.

11.7.7 Testbenches for Emulation

To realize the benefits of emulation, virtually all of the circuit and testbench for the design must run on the emulator. This means that the testbench should be synthesizable.

One approach would be to make the testbench synthesizable from the beginning, and to use the same testbench for both RTL verification and for emulation. We believe that this approach is flawed.

The behavioral testbenches that can be created with current testbench automation tools are significantly more powerful than any synthesizable testbench. The capabilities for stimulus creation and automated response checking are essential for RTL test and debug, and cannot easily be replicated in the synthesizable subset of HDLs.

Instead, we recommend that a new, synthesizable, and relatively simple testbench be used for emulation. Once a bug is found, the circuit (and its current state) can be moved back to RTL simulation for debug.

If we take our canonical design, the following approach seems reasonable. In Figure 11-5, the software for the processor is compiled and loaded into memory in the emulator. This allows the processor and peripherals to run at full emulation speed.

The stimulus for the data transformation block is also loaded into memory on the emulator. In this case, since it is an MPEG2 decoder, we can store a bit stream that represents encoded video data. A simple state machine (marked "SM") transfers data from the stimulus memory to the I/O interface. Similarly, the serial data from the output of the MPEG2 decoder is sent to a response capture memory in the emulator. Another simple state machine handles the handshake for the data transfer.

Although this approach requires a second testbench to be built, including two state machines, this is significantly less incremental effort than requiring the RTL testbench to be synthesizable.

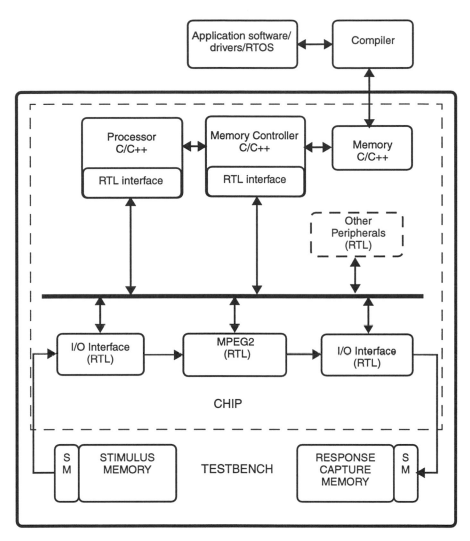

Figure 11-5 Emulation testbench

CHAPTER 12   *Data and Project Management*

This chapter discusses tools and methodologies for managing the design database for macro design and for system design. The topics are:

- Data management
- Project management

12.1 Data Management

Data management issues include revision control, bug tracking, regression testing, managing multiple sites, and archiving the design project.

12.1.1 Revision Control Systems

A strong revision control system is essential for any design project. A good revision control system allows the design team to:

- Keep all source code (including scripts and documentation) in one centralized repository that is regularly backed up and archived
- Keep all previous versions of each file
- Identify, quickly, changes between different revisions of files
- Take a snapshot of the current state of the design and label it

RCS, SCCS, and Clearcase are examples of tools with which revision control systems can be built. Additional scripts and processes are typically used to create a complete revision control system.

The most common paradigm is for each designer to be able to check out the entire design structure and recreate it locally, either by copying files or creating pointers to them. The designer then works and tests locally before checking the design files back into the central repository.

There are two different models for controlling this check-in process: the always-broken and always-working models.

The Always-Broken Model

In the *always-broken* model, each designer works and tests locally and then all the designers check in their work at the same time. The team then runs regression tests on the whole design, fixing bugs as they appear.

There are two problems with this model. First, when regressions tests fail, it is not clear whose code broke the design. If there are complex inter-dependencies between the modules, debugging regression failures can be difficult and time consuming.

The second problem with this model is that there tends to be a long integration period during which the design is essentially broken. No new design work can be done during this integration and debug phase because designers cannot check out a known-working copy of latest version of the design.

The Always-Working Model

The *always-working* model overcomes the major problems presented by the always-broken model. For the initial integration of the design, when separate modules are first tested together, the always-working model is the same as the always-broken model. Everyone checks in the initial version of the blocks and a significant debug effort ensues. In some designs, it may be possible to integrate a subset of the whole design, and then add additional blocks once the first subset is working. This approach greatly reduces the debug effort.

Once an initial baseline for the design is established, the always-working model uses the following check-in discipline:

- Only one designer can have a given block checked out for editing.
- When a block is being checked in, the entire central repository is locked, blocking other designers from checking modules in.

- The designer then runs a full regression test with the existing design plus the modified block.

- Once the regression tests pass, the designer checks in the block and removes the lock.

This model ensures that the entire design in the central repository always passes regression testing; that is, it is always working. It also greatly reduces the debug effort because only one new module at a time is tested.

We recommend the always-working model of revision control.

12.1.2 Bug Tracking

An effective bug tracking system is essential for rapid design of complex blocks and systems. A central database that collects all known bugs and desired enhancements lets the whole team know the state of the design and prevents designers from debugging known problems multiple times. It also ensures that known problems are not forgotten, and that any design that is shipped with known bugs can include documentation for the bugs.

Another key use for bug tracking is bug rate tracking. In most projects, the bug rate follows a well-defined curve, reaching a peak value early in the integration phase and then declining as testing becomes more robust. The current bug rate and the position on this curve help define the most effective testing and debug strategy for any phase of the project, and help determine when the chip is ready to tape out.

Formal bug tracking usually begins when integration begins; that is, as soon as the work of two or more designers is combined into a larger block. For a single engineer working on a single design, informal bug tracking is usually more effective. However, some form of bug tracking is required at all stages of design.

12.1.3 Regression Testing

Automated regression testing provides a mechanism for quickly verifying whether changes to the design have broken a previously-working feature. A good regression testing system automates the addition of new tests, report generation, and distribution of simulation over multiple workstations. It should also highlight differences in output files between passing and failing tests, to help direct debug efforts.

12.1.4 Managing Multiple Sites

Many large projects involve design teams located at multiple sites, sometimes scattered across the globe. Effective data management across these sites can facilitate cooperation between the teams.

Multiple site data management starts with a high-speed link between sites; this is essential for sharing data. The revision control central repository must be available to all sites, as well as bug tracking information. Regression test reports must be available to all sites.

The key to managing a multi-site project is effective communication between the individual engineers working on the project. Email, voicemail, and telephones have been the traditional tools for this. Technology is now readily available for desktop video conferencing with shared displays and virtual whiteboards. All of these techniques are needed to provide close links between team members.

One management technique that helps make these technology-based solutions more effective is to get the entire team in one place for an initial planning and teambuilding session. Once team members get to know the people at other sites, the daily electronic communication becomes much more effective.

12.1.5 Archiving

At the end of any design project, it is necessary to archive the entire design database, so that it can be re-created in the future, either for bug fixes or for enhancements to the product. All aspects of the design must be archived in one central place: documentation, source code, all scripts, testbenches, and test suites. All the tools used in the design must also be archived in the revision control system used for the design. If these tools are used for multiple projects, obviously one copy is enough, and the tool archives can be kept separate from the design archive.

The above observation may seem obvious, but let me interject a personal note. Several years ago, I was hired to do the next generation design of an existing large system. The first thing I did was to try to find the people who had worked on the previous generation design and to find the design archive.

Well, the designers had all moved on to other companies. The system architect was still with the company but busy with another project, and he wasn't all that familiar with the detailed design anyway. The design files were scattered across a wide variety of machines, some of which were obsolete machines cobbled together from spare parts and whose disks were not backed up! Worse than that, I found several copies of the design tree, with inconsistent data. It was impossible to collect even a majority of design files and know with confidence that they were the latest versions.

In the middle of the previous design effort, the team had changed silicon vendors and tools. The HDL for the design was *almost* accurate, but some (unspecified) changes were made directly to the netlist. This scenario is the manager's nightmare. It took months to recover the design archive to the point where the new design effort could begin; in fact, close to half the design effort consisted of recreating the knowledge and data that should have been archived at the end of the design.

12.2 Project Management

There are many excellent books on project management [1,2,3], and we will not attempt to cover the subject in any depth. However, there are a several issues that are worth addressing.

12.2.1 Development Process

An ISO 9000-like development process, where processes are documented and repeatable, can help considerably in producing consistently high-quality, reusable designs. Such a process should specify:

- The *product development lifecycle,* outlining the specific phases of the design process and the criteria for transitioning from one phase to another
- What *design reviews* are required at the different stages of the design, and how the design reviews will be conducted
- What the *sign-off process* is to complete the design
- What *metrics* are to be tracked to determine the completeness and robustness

Two key documents are used to communicate with the rest of the community during the course of macro design. These documents are the *project plan* and the *functional specification.* These are both living documents that undergo constant modification during the project.

12.2.2 Functional Specification

A key characteristic of a reusable design is a pedigree of documentation that enables subsequent users to effectively use it. The requirements for a functional specification are outlined in Chapter 4. This specification forms the basis for this pedigree of documentation, and includes:

- Block diagrams
- Functional specification
- Description of parameters and their use

- Interface signal descriptions
- Timing diagrams and requirements
- Verification strategy
- Synthesis constraints

In addition to the above basic functional information, it is quite useful to keep the functional specification as a living document, which is updated by each user throughout its life. For each use of the block, the following information would be invaluable to subsequent generations of users:

- Project it was used on
- Personnel on the project
- Verification reports (what was tested)
- Technology used
- Actual timing and area results
- Revision history for any modifications

12.2.3 Project Plan

The project plan describes the project from a management perspective and documents the goals, schedule, cost, and core team for the project. Table 12-1 describes the contents of a typical project plan.

Table 12-1   Contents of a project plan

Part	Function
Goals	Describes the business reasons for developing the macro and its key features and benefits, including the technical goals that will determine the success or failure of the project.
Schedule	Describes the development timeline, including external dependencies and risks. The schedule should contain sufficient contingency time to recover from unforeseen delays, and this contingency should be listed explicitly.
Cost	Describes the financial resources required to complete the project: headcount, tools, NREs, prototype build costs.
Core Team	Describes the human resources required to complete the project: who will be on the team, who will be the team leader.

References

1. Floyd, Thomas et al. *Winning the New Product Development Battle*. IEEE, 1994.

2. McConnell, Steve. *Software Project Survival Guide*. Microsoft Press, 1997.

3. Demarco, Tom and Lister, Timothy. *Peopleware: Productive Projects and Teams*. Dorset House, 1999.

CHAPTER 13

Implementing a Reuse Process

This chapter addresses requirements for establishing reuse processes within a company. These requirements include tools, process inventories, macro libraries, and pilot projects. Topics in this chapter include:

- Key steps in implementing a reuse process
- Managing the transition to reuse
- Organization issues
- Dealing with legacy designs

13.1 Key Steps in Implementing a Reuse Process

The following activities are key steps in implementing a design reuse process:

1. Develop a reuse plan.

   The first step in developing a reuse process is to develop a plan for establishing a reuse process. In particular, it is useful to determine the resources required to establish such a process.

2. Implement reuse training.

   Successful implementation of design reuse requires that design for reuse be an integral part of technical and management training within the company.

3. Inventory tools and processes.

   The next step in developing a design reuse process is to assess the design tools and methodologies already in place. A robust high-level design methodology that uses up-to-date synthesis and simulation tools is a prerequisite for developing a reuse methodology. Good project management practices and documented processes as outlined in the previous chapter are also required.

4. Build up libraries.

   Design reuse can begin with small designs. Build or purchase libraries of relatively simple components and use them in current design projects. Track the effectiveness of using these components and examine any problems that arise from their use.

5. Develop pilot projects.

   Develop pilot projects both for developing reusable designs and for reusing existing designs. This could involve existing internally-developed designs or a macro purchased from a third party.

   These pilot projects are the best way to start assessing the challenges and opportunities in design reuse. It is essential to track and measure the success of design reuse in terms of the additional cost of developing reusable designs and the savings involved in reusing existing designs.

6. Develop a reuse attitude.

   Design reuse is a new paradigm in design methodology. It requires additional investment in block development and produces significant savings in subsequent reuse of the block in multiple designs. This paradigm shift requires a change in attitude on the part of designers and management. Shortcuts in the name of "time-to-market" are no longer acceptable; the long-term cost to the organization is simply too high.

   Design reuse is the single most important issue in SoC designs. Unless they consist almost entirely of memory, million-gate designs cannot be designed from scratch and hope to make their time-to-market and quality requirements. Reuse of previously designed and verified blocks is the only way to build robust million-gate chips in a reasonable amount of time.

   The most important step in developing a design reuse process is to convince the management and engineering team to adopt *the reuse attitude*: that the investment in design reuse is the key to taking advantage of the remarkable silicon technology currently available.

The following sections describe these steps in more detail.

13.2 Managing the Transition to Reuse

Managing the transition to reuse-based design involves identifying the technical and organizational barriers to reuse and taking incremental steps to effect the required changes.

13.2.1 Barriers to Reuse

Many engineering managers are very reluctant to make the investment required for effective, systematic reuse. Design for reuse is expensive. Our best estimate is that it takes 2-3 times the effort to develop a block for reuse than it does to design the same block for a single use. No rational manager is going to delay a critical chip project in order to make some blocks reusable on future designs.

On the other hand, the benefit of design reuse is large. Our best estimate is that integrating a reusable block into a chip design is 10 to 100 times less effort than designing the block from scratch. But this benefit is only realized after the investment in design for reuse has been made.

In addition, transitioning a whole organization to reuse-based design requires a significant investment in retooling design teams, organizational structures, and management practices. So transitioning to design reuse is a non-trivial problem. The argument for reuse-based design is compelling: we simply won't be able to build tomorrow's chips without it. But there is an investment required, both in time and in engineering resources. The benefit is large, but delayed. This is why the books on software reuse all say that reuse is not a technical problem, but a management and cultural one.

Most experts agree that process change, to be effective, must be incremental. To transition to a reuse paradigm, we must find the incremental steps that are gradual enough to ensure success. But the adoption must be rapid enough to allow design productivity to keep pace with Moore's Law. The intent of the next few sections is to give some insight into this very difficult problem.

13.2.2 Key Elements in Reuse-Based Design

There are four key elements to a reuse-based SoC design methodology:

- **Design for Reuse** – The methodology, tools, and services to enable the creation of reusable designs, as well as the ability to import third-party IP effectively.
- **IP Repository** – The central library of reusable IP and the tools, infrastructure, and services to support it.

- **SoC Design** – The tools and methodology required to develop large chips incorporating reusable IP.
- **Reuse Support Structure** – The organizational structure, incentives, people, management and cultural norms required to make reuse-based design work effectively.

Design for Reuse

The design for reuse methodology is the cornerstone for a reuse-based chip design methodology. The design practices described in this book can form the basis for this methodology, but many of the detailed processes need to be customized to the particular design environment. The fundamental goal of this methodology is to ensure that the IP in the repository is easy to integrate into chip designs.

The reuse methodology must be supported by the appropriate tools. In addition to the usual design tools such as simulators, synthesis tools, and so on, there need to be tools to facilitate reuse and check for compliance to the standards defined in the methodology. Tools such as a methodology-specific version of linting tools, code coverage tools, and automated checklists are some examples of reuse support tools.

These tools and processes are also useful in qualifying third-party IP. Third-party IP providers are a key source of standards-based IP, but it is essential to validate the quality of this IP before using it in chip design projects.

In addition to the methodologies and tools, many organizations are looking at providing reuse services to design teams. Experts in the methodology can be assigned to development teams to help them develop reusable designs. These experts can also provide training in design-for-reuse to the development engineers.

Repository of Reusable IP

The second key element in a reuse-based design environment is the IP itself: the collection of high-value, easily-integrated IP stored in an assessable repository. The design-for-reuse methodology exists primarily to provide a source of high-quality IP for the repository.

A set of infrastructure tools provide engineers with access to the IP in the repository, enabling them to browse the contents of the library, view datasheets and specifications, download the appropriate models, and report back any problems with the IP.

Associated with the IP repository is a set of services for acquiring IP and ensuring the quality of IP. This would include dealing with third-party IP providers and qualifying their IP before adding it to the repository. Legacy IP services provide the expertise and bandwidth to take existing, internally developed blocks and make them reusable.

SoC with Reuse

The whole purpose for both the design-for-reuse processes and the repository is to facilitate the development of large chips. Thus, there must be an SoC development process that can make effective use of the IP in the repository. This process must allow rapid integration of soft and hard IP. Among other things, the design team must have access to high-quality cell libraries (for synthesizing the soft IP), and use physical design rules that are consistent with those of the hard IP being integrated.

Realistically, though, no chip design methodology can compensate for poor IP. Well-designed IP is a cornerstone of reuse, and well-designed IP can be easily integrated into almost any modern flow. Poor IP — IP with functional bugs, or missing key deliverables — is always a struggle to integrate into a chip design.

Reuse Support Structure

Finally, the company must have the processes, people, infrastructure, organization, management, and passion for quality required to make a reuse-based methodology successful.

Above all else, the engineers, their managers, and senior management must, as a team, agree that the benefits of a reuse-based chip design methodology justify the cost. The key benefit of reuse is increased productivity, leading to faster time-to-market. But design reuse always requires some tradeoff in terms of dies size and/or performance. You can always make a specific block for a specific application smaller and faster than the same function that has been make reusable, and applicable to many different designs. Teams that are used to handcrafting transistors to get the last picosecond or the last square millimeter out of the design will have to make some tough decisions, and potentially go through a tough cultural transition.

13.2.3 Key Steps

A basic plan for implementing a reuse-based chip design methodology consists of the following steps:

1. **Develop** the basic reuse methodology, at least among a specific design team.
2. **Demonstrate** the effectiveness of the methodology in improving designer productivity.
3. **Proliferate** the methodology throughout the organization.
4. **Refine** the methodology by continually measuring its effectiveness and making improvements.

In practice, this process consists of the following activities:

- Assessment and planning
- Training
- Buying/developing new tools
- Implementing a set of pilot projects
- Building the repository
- Proliferation of the methodology

Assessment and Planning

The goal of the assessment and planning is to determine what modifications are required to the existing development methodology and to the organizational structure to support a reuse methodology. This requires a clear assessment of current methodologies and organizational structure, and an initial vision of the required methodology and structure. The team can then plan how to implement the required modifications and measure their effectiveness.

The assessment and planning process should also extend to the final products being designed. Product line planning — planning what related designs will be developed, and how successive designs can leverage IP from previous designs — is one of the keys to successful reuse. This planning can help determine which IP will be added to the repository in what order, and from what internal or third-party sources.

Some of the issues that must be examined as part of this assessment and planning process include:

- Engineering practices – Are designed teams making effective use of RTL-based design methodologies and tools? What design reuse is currently practiced, including ad-hoc reuse and incorporation of third-party IP?
- Project management practices – Are project management processes documented, followed, and measured?
- Cultural issues – Will "not invented here" factors adversely affect a transition to reuse-based design? Which design groups are most supportive of reuse, and how can their support be leveraged to accelerate adoption of reuse practices?
- Product line assessment – Can the current and future product lines be designed to achieve high amounts of reuse?

Planning the Reuse Project

As a result of the assessment project, the overall design reuse project plan can be refined and updated. Based on the assessment, a detailed plan should be developed to address the following issues, as required:

- How to bring all teams to state-of-the-art RTL design
- Organizational changes required to support reuse and how to staff
- Documenting the reuse methodology
- Defining the tools needed to support the methodology
- Sequence of pilot projects and target IP for demonstrating reuse
- Plan for proliferating reuse and integrating it into a product line plan

Training

In many organizations, on-going technical training is viewed as essential to keeping engineers up-to-date on design tools and methodologies, as well as on domain-specific design issues. For other groups, investment in training is not a standard practice. Often these groups are found during the assessment phase to be somewhat lagging the current state-of-the-art design techniques and methodologies.

As a result of the assessment phase, the assessment team may identify either specific design teams or specific subject areas where training is required to get the engineering team(s) up to the appropriate level of high-level design. Since design reuse is built upon high-level design practices, this is the first level of training that must be done as part of implementing a reuse-based design methodology.

In addition, the assessment team should identify the engineering teams that will participate in the reuse pilot projects. These engineers should receive specific reuse methodology training before participating in the pilot projects. The goal of this training is to establish a baseline of engineering practices required to execute the projects.

During the proliferation phase of the reuse initiative, training will once again become important. The pilot projects are key to demonstrating the value of reuse. In the same way, training in reuse methodology, along with actual practice in designing for reuse and use of tools that verify compliance with reuse standards, is key to establishing effective design-for-reuse practices throughout the organization.

As reuse practices proliferate through the organization, and the organizations move on to the refinement stage, continual training is key to reinforcing reuse practices and communicating the latest techniques and tools to the practicing engineers.

Tools

Design reuse is fundamentally a methodology issue; that is, it is an approach to improving design practices using, predominantly, the existing tool set. There are, however, some reuse-specific tools that can greatly facilitate reuse.

First, some comments on existing design tools are in order. Today, chip designers really need to be proficient in architectural tools (C++, COSSAP, SPW, and the like), simulation, synthesis, datapath tools, behavioral synthesis, static timing verification, formal verification, power analysis, test insertion and ATPG, and many more tools. There are significant advantages to having a single engineering team able to deal with all these tools; the team can only make well-informed design decisions if the information from all these tools is well understood. But it is virtually impossible for an engineer to be really expert in all these tools. For this reason, developing an infrastructure for automating the use of these tools is one element in developing a state-of-the-art reuse methodology.

That said, there are some additional tools that can greatly facilitate reuse. These include:

- **Infrastructure tools** – Effective tools for data and project management are key for establishing the kind of design discipline required to produce genuinely reusable designs. These tools include revision control and bug tracking, as well as automated checklists and statistic-gathering tools. An effective repository management system that supports easy access to the library of IP also is key to supporting design reuse.

- **Reuse-specific tools** – There are several reuse-specific tools either available now or in development that could help support reuse-based design methodologies. A lint-like tool to enforce reuse coding guidelines is particularly useful. Even with the best intentions, human error will generate inadvertent violations if they are not automatically checked. In addition, tools are needed to help automate the packaging and delivery of IP, in order to eliminate the need for users to modify code or scripts to adapt the IP to their specific applications. Synopsys' coreConsultant and Altera's IP Wizard demonstrate the advantages of such tools.

Pilot Projects

The most important element in establishing a reuse-based methodology is the execution of a set of pilot projects for developing and demonstrating the reuse methodology and its benefits. A pilot project involves developing a block of reusable IP and using it in a chip design. There two general types of reusable IP development:

- **Redesign for Reuse** projects involve taking the most valuable existing IP and making it reusable. Because of the additional cost of designing for reuse, it is important to take high value IP that can be used in many applications and design projects. Such a project will show immediate benefits to the company by reducing chip development costs on many different projects. Redesigning an existing piece of IP also highlights the differences between current design practices and the requirements of design for reuse.

- **Design for Reuse** projects involve identifying high-value IP that is needed for several future projects, but which has not yet been designed. These projects allow the team to develop IP with reuse in mind, rather than re-engineering reuse into existing IP. These projects also allow the team to quantify the cost of design for reuse vs. redesign for reuse.

Both redesign for reuse and design for reuse projects should include follow-up projects where the IP is used in a chip design. These follow-up projects are key for understanding the advantages and problems that result from doing design with reuse, and help refine the design-for-reuse methodology before it is proliferated through the organization.

Chip design with reuse involves taking IP developed during the design-for-reuse or redesign-for-reuse pilot projects and using them to implement a chip design. This chip pilot project is the key definition of success of the overall pilot projects. The goals of the project are to:

- Measure the productivity and quality gain achieved through reuse
- Demonstrate the value of reuse in developing chips quickly
- Refine the chip design process employing reuse
- Determine additional tools or processes necessary to improve the design-for-reuse process
- Determine additional tools or processes necessary to improve the process of designing chips with reusable blocks.

At the end of this pilot project, the team will have demonstrated the effort required for design for reuse and the value of reuse in accelerating chip design projects. The team will have the data to support its conclusions, and a well-defined, reuse-based methodology for designing blocks and chips.

Building the repository

The next step in implementing a reuse-based design methodology is to add IP to the repository. The value of reuse only becomes compelling when the IP repository contains a significant collection of valuable, reusable blocks.

The first blocks to be added to the repository are typically high-value, domain independent parts such as processors (including DSP) and their peripherals. These can be followed by lower-value, standards-based parts such as PCI, USB, and other interfaces.

Domain independent parts are likely to be used the most broadly, and in the most chip design projects, and so can most readily justify the cost of design for reuse. Many of the standards-based IP can be obtained from third-party IP providers, and thus can be added to the repository fairly easily. However, it should be noted that the quality of third party IP does vary, and care should be taken to select IP that meets the standards of quality and reusability established by the repository management team.

Once a reasonable set of domain-independent parts have been added, it makes sense to add the most valuable domain-specific IP to the repository. These could include multimedia blocks like MPEG, or data communication blocks like ATM or Ethernet.

Proliferation

Once chip design teams become aware that there are useful IP blocks in the repository, proliferation of reuse throughout the organization can take place. Additional training in design for reuse and chip design with reuse can help design teams acquire the skills to support and use this methodology. Additional resources and engineers with reuse-specific skills may still be required to help chip design teams take the blocks they develop and turn them into reusable designs.

There are several problems that are likely to appear as a reuse methodology is proliferated through a large organization. Some of these are technical. In particular, it is important to have a consist design, verification, and integration flows between the different design teams. This consistent set of flows greatly facilitates the exchange of IP between groups.

However, the really major issues in proliferating reuse are organizational. We address these in the next section.

13.3 Organizational Issues in Reuse

If we look at the reuse initiatives at different companies, we find that there are three models being used for managing reuse and the development of IP:

- **As-Is reuse** – Blocks are designed as part of chip-development projects; that is, they are designed for a single use. Once the chip project is concluded, the major blocks are put into the IP repository as-is. Users are on their own in terms of integrating these blocks into future designs. A central CAD group manages the repository, but does not provide technical support for the IP.

- **Rework-based reuse** – Again, blocks are designed as part of chip-development projects. Once the chip project is concluded, the major blocks are given to a separate team that re-engineers them to make them reusable. This separate reuse team provides technical support for the IP, and is usually part of the CAD team that manages the IP repository.
- **IP-based reuse** – Here, key IP is developed explicitly for reuse by a dedicated engineering team. This team is usually part of a product business unit, and not connected to central CAD. The support arm of the business unit provides technical support to users.

All of these models have advantages and disadvantages, although all share a common and serious problems.

The advantage of as-is reuse, is that it has no engineering overhead. No additional engineering cost is required to make the design available to other groups. Teams that use this approach take the position that "users are going to have to modify the design anyway, so why bother with all this design-for-reuse stuff."

The problem with this approach is that it achieves very little productivity gain. Data from software reuse [1] and preliminary data from hardware reuse indicate that reuse where you have to modify the design provides only a 2–3x improvement over no reuse at all. On the other hand, the same data suggests that reuse without modification can achieve gains of greater than 10x.

The advantage of rework-based reuse is that it produces fully reusable designs, and the incremental time and effort are done after the chip design is complete. Thus, it does not slow down chip development.

The problems with this approach is that, for some blocks, this rework may be as great an effort, or even greater, than designing the block from scratch for reuse. If the block was not architected for reuse, if future users will need features not provided, or if the design and coding is not reuse-friendly, then substantial work may be required. And since the rework is not done by the original designer, additional effort is required just to understand the original design.

The advantage of IP-based reuse is that the design is done once, it is designed for reuse from the beginning, and it can consistently produce the most reusable designs.

The disadvantage of this approach is that the IP is not developed by an actual user, so the design may not meet the needs of the SoC teams that integrate the block into chip designs. The IP may be elegant, but too late to meet critical market windows.

13.3.1   A Combined Solution

A combination of the above approaches makes the most sense. For blocks that are unlikely to be reused more than once or twice, as-is reuse is the most economically sound approach. The block should be designed and coded to be compliant with the reuse guidelines, and should have a reasonable specification and testbench. These efforts will not slow down the block design, and in many cases may accelerate it. But no reuse packaging is justified for so few projected reuses.

For blocks that are likely to be reused many times, but which have relatively fixed architectures, rework-based design works well. Blocks that execute a well-defined function, and which will not require parameterization, are good candidates. The rework team can focus on packaging these blocks for reuse.

For all other blocks, especially high-value blocks that will be used many times, the IP-based reuse approach is best. Processors and highly configurable I/O blocks like PCI and USB fall into this category. Explicitly designing for reuse will always produce the most reusable designs, and the designs that will provide the greatest productivity boost to chip design teams.

13.3.2   A Common Problem

The common and serious problem that all these approaches share is: who owns and supports the IP. Some case histories can help indicate the seriousness of this problem. (The following case histories are real examples; the names of the companies have been withheld for obvious reasons.)

In one major semiconductor company, a design team is producing a next-generation chip. The previous generation used a number of hard macros from other divisions. These macros were provided only in hard form, but they all need to be ported to a new technology and modified for small changes in functionality. The other divisions are busy on their own next-generation chips, and have no interest in supporting our design team in modifying the blocks. No RTL or scripts are available to our team. So the team is forced to port the macros to the new process at the polygon level, and to make the functional modifications at the polygon level as well. Instead of achieving a 10x productivity improvement from reuse, they realize 2x at most.

In another major semiconductor company, a team has developed a next-generation DSP intended for widespread use in many designs in many divisions of the company. Unfortunately, the team focused exclusively on making the fastest, lowest power DSP on the planet, and paid no attention to ease of use for the integrators. They shipped only a transistor netlist to the chip design teams — no simulation models, no instruction set simulator, and no testbench or bus functional models. Software debug had to be performed with a switch-level simulation of the hardware!

These cases highlight the disasters that can happen if IP is not well supported and if IP developers are not sensitive and responsive to the needs of the IP integrators. The key to organizing for reuse success is to establish a structure that ensures a close and effectively link between IP developers and IP integrators within the company.

13.3.3 A Reuse Economy

Most companies work like small economies: managers and engineering teams have financial incentives to develop chips with specific features for a specific market window. Today, these incentives actively discourage design for reuse; any additional effort spent making a block reusable is seen as an impediment to getting today's chip out as soon as possible. Similarly, many IP development teams are rewarded for the technical merits of the IP, in terms of speed and power, but not in terms of ease-of-integration.

To foster reuse, the company must set up financial incentives that will motivate the design teams to design for reuse. If the design teams are expected to support the IP they develop, there must be strong financial (and other) rewards for doing so. In essence, a miniature economy must be set up, so that the design teams that benefit from reuse reward the groups that are developing reusable IP. Toshiba, for example, has announced plans to let divisions to allow its various divisions to buy and sell IP among themselves through an inter-departmental program [2]. This kind of financial model may well be a key to fostering reuse, and we expect it to be adopted in other large companies.

Such an economy might look something like Figure 13-1.

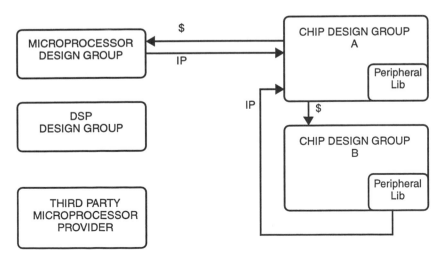

Figure 13-1   A reuse economy

Chip design group A is developing an SoC design. It decides to use a microprocessor from an internal group. It pays (through some internal transfer of budgets) the Microprocessor Design Group for the IP. Group A expects in return a quality, easy to integrate design, and good technical support. If Group A is not happy with the quality of IP or technical support it receives from the internal supplier, it is free to purchase a microprocessor from a third party IP provider.

After an initial round of financing from the company, the Microprocessor Design Group receives its budget only from (happy) customers. If internal customers consistently find the internal IP unacceptable, the internal IP development teams go out of business. These teams should now be very motivated to produce quality, easy to integrate IP.

In our example, it turns out that Chip Design Group B has already developed some peripherals or other blocks that could be useful in Group A's design. These blocks have been designed for reuse and are in Group B's local IP repository. Group A can again purchase the IP from Group B, helping Group B offset the cost of making the IP reusable. This added revenue also provides an incentive for Group B to make their local IP highly reusable.

Such a reuse economy solves many of the problems existing today in promoting reuse. The customer-vendor relationship ensures that the link between developers and integrators of IP is close. This tight link is the key to ensuring the high quality, reusable designs that can dramatically improve chip design productivity.

13.3.4 Summary

The preceding sections show the significant organization and technical changes required to implement a full reuse process. The investment required is also significant. This amount of change can be intimidating, and may discourage design teams from adopting reuse. However, there are many small, incremental changes that engineering teams can make to start implementing reuse. For example, the following changes incur little cost, yet can yield dramatic benefits:

- Register outputs to make timing problems local, not global.
- Verify from the bottom up to make verification problems local, not global.
- Plan before you do; good specifications allow design at the local level with confidence that it will integrate into the global design correctly.
- Hold IP providers, internal and external, accountable for the quality and ease of use of their IP.

13.4 Redesign for Reuse: Dealing with Legacy Designs

Another key issue that can impede the adoption of reuse is the difficulties in reusing existing, or legacy designs. Legacy designs — those designs we wish to reuse but were not designed for reuse — present major challenges to the design team. Often these designs are gate-level netlists with little or no documentation. The detailed approach to a specific design depends on the state of design. However, there are a few general guidelines that are useful.

13.4.1 Recapturing Intent

The most difficult part of dealing with a legacy design is recapturing the design intent. With a good functional specification and a good test suite, it is possible to fix, modify, or redesign a block relatively quickly. The specification and test suite fully define the intent of the design and give objective criteria for when the design is functioning correctly.

If the specification and test suite are not available, then the first step in reusing the design must be to recreate them. Otherwise, it is not possible to modify the design in any way, and some modification is nearly always required to port the design to a new process or to a new application.

The problem with recreating the specification and test suite, of course, is that these activities represent well over half of the initial design effort. Almost none of the benefits of reuse are realized.

Thus, if the specification and test suite exist and are of high quality, then reuse is easy, in the sense that even if a complete redesign is required, it will take a fraction of the time and cost of the original development. If the specification and test suite do not exist, then reuse of the design is essentially equivalent to a complete redesign.

13.4.2 Using the Design As-Is

In spite of the observations in the above section, some unfortunate design teams are required to try to reuse existing designs, usually in the form of netlists, for which documentation and testbenches are mostly nonexistent. In such cases, most teams attempt to use the design as-is. That is, they attempt to port the design to a new process without changing the functionality of the circuit in any way.

Formal verification is particularly useful in this scenario because it can prove whether or not modifications to the circuit affect behavior. Thus, synthesis can be used to remap and reoptimize the design for a new technology, and formal verification can be used to verify the correctness of the results.

13.4.3   Retiming

For some designs, the above approach does not provide good enough results. In these cases, behavioral retiming may be an effective solution. Behavioral retiming can automatically change the pipelining structure of the design to solve timing problems. Again, formal methods are used to prove that the resulting functionality is correct.

13.4.4   Tools for Using Legacy Designs

A large investment was probably made in legacy designs that are still very valuable macros. For example, a design team might want to reuse a macro developed for QuickSim II. ModelSim-Pro allows the team to simulate a VHDL and/or Verilog design that contains instantiations of QuickSim II macros.

If the design team wants to use a VHDL legacy design within a Verilog design (or vice versa), the ModelSim single-kernel architecture allows reuse of that macro within the context of the entire design.

13.4.5   Summary

Reusing legacy designs should definitely be the last aspect of design reuse implemented as part of establishing a design reuse methodology. Developing the processes for designing for reuse and for reusing well-designed blocks provides dramatically more benefit than attempting to reuse designs that were not designed with reuse in mind.

References

1. Poulin, Jefferey. *Measuring Software Reuse: Principles, Practices, and Economic Models.* Addison-Wesley, 1997

2. Cataldo, Anthony, "Toshiba Plans Internal Licensing Program" EE Times, September 2, 1998, http://www.transeda.com/resources_area/100_issue_5.pdf

Glossary

Arcadia – An Synopsys tool for extracting parasitics (resistance and capacitance) from a physical chip design. Used for accurate timing analysis of the final physical design.

ATPG – Automatic Test Pattern Generation.

BFM – Bus Functional Model.

BONeS – A Cadence tool for modeling and simulating network designs.

BIST – Built-In Self Test; usually a local generator and signature analysis block for implementing on-chip test on a design block.

COSSAP – A Synopsys system-level design tool featuring a stream-driven simulator.

Escalade – A company offering a variety of reuse-oriented tools, including capabilities for checking compliance to coding and design guidelines. (See http://www.escalade.com)

FSM – Finite State Machine.

HDL – Hardware Description Language, principally Verilog and VHDL.

ISA (ISS) – Instruction Set Architecture (Instruction Set Simulator); used interchangeably for an instruction set executable model of a processor.

LEDA – A French EDA company that provides Proton, a lint-like tool for checking compliance to design and coding guidelines. (See http://www.leda.fr)

MatLab – A mathematics package for numeric computation and visualization, from MathWorks. Often used for algorithm development and signal processing design. (See http://www.mathworks.com/products/matlab/)

NuThena Foresight – A system level modeling and simulation tool. (See http://www.nuthena.com)

RTL – Register Transfer Level.

SDL – Specification and Description Language; a language for high-level design, especially of communication systems.

SDT – A tool implementing SDL. (See http://www.kvatro.no/telecom/sdt/sdt.htm)

SoC – System-on-a-Chip.

SPW – A Cadence system-level design tool, originally developed for signal processing algorithm capture and simulation.

Steiner Route – In chip physical design, refers to a minimal or optimal route using orthogonal (vertical and horizontal) routing.

Specman Elite – A testbench automation tool from Verisity, Ltd.

SWIFT – Software Interface Technology, used by Synopsys modeling tools.

Vera – A testbench automation tool from Synopsys.

Verilint – A linting tool for checking Verilog code compliance to design and coding guidelines. (See http://www.interhdl.com/verilint.html)

VFM – Verilog Foundry Model, a Synopsys tool.

VHDLlint – A linting tool for checking VHDL code compliance to design and coding guidelines. (See http://www.interhdl.com/vhdllint.html)

VMC – Verilog Model Compiler, a Synopsys tool.

VSIA – Virtual Socket Interface Alliance. (See http://www.vsi.org)

VSPEC – An extension to VHDL to provide formal specification capabilities. (See http://www.ececs.uc.edu/~kbse/projects/vspec/)

Bibliography

Books on software reuse:

1. *Measuring Software Reuse*, Jeffrey S. Poulin, Addison-Wesley, 1997.
2. *Practical Software Reuse*, Donald J. Reifer, Wiley, 1997.

Formal specification and verification:

1. http://www.ececs.uc.edu/~pbaraona/vspec/, the VSPEC homepage.
2. *Formal Specification and Verification of Digital Systems*, George Milne, McGraw-Hill, 1994.
3. *Formal Hardware Verification*, Thomas Kropf (ed.), Springer, 1997.

Management processes:

1. http://www.sun.com/sparc/articles/EETIMES.html, a description of the UltraSPARC project, mentioning construct by correction.
2. *Winning the New Product Development Battle*, Floyd, Levy, Wolfman, IEEE.

Books and articles on manufacturing test:

1. "Testability on Tap," Colin Maunder et al, IEEE Spectrum, February 1992, pp. 34–37.
2. "Aiding Testability also aids Testing," Richard Quinell, EDN, August 12, 1990, pp. 67–74.
3. "ASIC Testing Upgraded," Marc Levitt, IEEE Spectrum, May 1992, pp. 26–29.
4. Synopsys *Test Compiler User's Guide*, v3.3a, 1995.
5. Synopsys *Test Compiler Reference Manual*, v3.2, 1994.

6. Synopsys *Certified Test Vector Formats Reference Manual.*

7. *Digital Systems Testing and Testable Design*, M. Abromovici et al, Computer Science Press, 1990.

8. *The Boundary Scan Handbook*, Kenneth Parker, Kluwer Academic Publishers, 1992.

9. *The Theory and Practice of Boundary Scan*, R. G. "Ben" Bennetts, IEEE Computer Society Press.

10. *Testability Concepts for Digital ICs*, Franz Beenker et al, Philips Corp, 1994.

11. "A Comparison of Defect Models for Fault Location with IDDQ Measurements," Robert Aitken, *IEEE Design & Test*, June 1995, pp. 778–787.

Books and articles on synthesis:

1. "Flattening and Structuring: A Look at Optimization Strategies," Synopsys Application Note Version 3.4a, April 1996, pp. 2-1 to 2-16.

2. *VHDL Compiler Reference Manual*, Synopsys Documentation Version 3.4a, April 1996, Appendix C.

3. *DesignTime Reference Manual*, Synopsys Documentation Version 3.4a, April 1996.

4. "Commands, Attributes, and Variables," Synopsys Documentation Version 3.4a, April 1996.

Index

memory
  BIST 49
  coding guidelines 123
  design issues 134
  test methodology 49
microprocessor
  system-level modeling 235
  test strategy 49
Module Compiler 65, 138
multibit signals 75
multicycle paths 120
multiplexers 108

N

naming conventions 74
nonblocking assignments (Verilog) 105
NuThena 20

P

packages (VHDL) 88
parameter
  assigning values 88
  mapping 82
  naming convention 74
partitioning
  asynchronous logic 118
  chip-level 122
  combinational logic 115
  critical path logic 116
  macro into subblocks 54, 60
path coverage 167
phase locked loop 34
physical design
  hard macro 181
  of SOC with macros 214
PI-Bus 43
pin placement 178
place-and-route 133
point-to-point exceptions 120
porosity 177
port
  grouping 81
  mapping 82
  naming convention 75
  ordering 81
power analysis 66, 69
Power Compiler 66, 69
power distribution 178
product development lifecycle 257
productization
  hard macro 181
  soft macro 69
project plan 257

prototype 71, 150, 152

Q
QuickPower 66, 69

R
RAM generators 140, 213
random tests 149
rapid prototyping 152
registers
  for output signals 114
  inferring 97
regression tests 254, 255
report_timing 132
reserved words 81
reset
  asynchronous 35
  coding guidelines 91
  conditional 96
  hard macro 176
  internal generation 96
  naming convention 75
  strategy 35
  synchronous 35
  synthesis 131
resource sharing 118
revision control
  always-broken model 254
  always-working model 254
  implementing 254
  requirement 69, 142, 204
routing channels 177

S
scan insertion 54, 59, 68
SDT 20
sensitivity list 103
sequential blocks 105
set_driving_cell 131
set_load 131
signal
  naming convention 76
  registering outputs 114
signal assignments (VHDL) 107
silicon prototype 239
simulation
  code profiling 125
  event-based 149
  gate-level 71, 169
  interpreted 149
simulator
  compatibility 87
  macro portability 71